# Language, Ideology, and Japanese History Textbooks

The Japanese history textbook debate is one that keeps making the news, particularly with reference to claims that Japan has never 'apologized properly' for its actions between 1931 and 1945, and that it is one of the few liberal, democratic countries in which textbooks are controlled and authorized by the central government. There are frequent protests, both from within Japan and from overseas, that a biased, nationalistic history is taught in Japanese schools.

This is the first time that all the authorized history textbooks currently in use in Japanese high schools have been analysed using a critical discourse approach that is anchored firmly in a theory of 'language in society', thereby elucidating the meanings and associated ideologies created by the language of textbooks. Barnard examines the meaning-making potential of language, questions why certain choices are made, and links these choices to the ideological construction of meaning within Japanese history textbooks. Perhaps controversially, this ideological construction is then linked to debates within Japanese society regarding war responsibility and the textbook authorization system.

Among the historical incidents dealt with in the book are the Manchurian Incident, the Rape of Nanking and the Japanese attack on Pearl Harbor. This book will appeal to anyone interested in how language constructs ideology, as well as prove essential to specialists in Japanese studies, sociology, and social and cultural history.

**Christopher Barnard** is Associate Professor in the Department of Anglo-American Language and Culture, Teikyo University, Tokyo.

# Language, Ideology, and Japanese History Textbooks

Christopher Barnard

LONDON AND NEW YORK

First published 2003
by RoutledgeCurzon
11 New Fetter Lane, London EC4P 4EE

Simultaneously published in the USA and Canada
by RoutledgeCurzon
29 West 35th Street, New York, NY 10001

*RoutledgeCurzon is an imprint of the Taylor & Francis Group*

© 2003 Christopher Barnard

Typeset in Times by
Florence Production Ltd, Stoodleigh, Devon
Printed and bound in Great Britain by
MPG Books Ltd, Bodmin

All rights reserved. No part of this book may be reprinted
or reproduced or utilized in any form or by any electronic,
mechanical, or other means, now known or hereafter invented,
including photocopying and recording, or in any information
storage or retrieval system, without permission in writing
from the publishers.

*British Library Cataloguing in Publication Data*
A catalogue record for this book is available from the British
Library

*Library of Congress Cataloging in Publication Data*
A catalog record for this book has been requested

ISBN 0–415–29797–4

# Contents

*Preface*   vii
*Acknowledgements*   xi

**1 Introduction**   1

*The history problem in Japan 1*
*Post-war education and textbook authorization 10*
*Society, education, and the curriculum 17*
*The linguistic analysis of ideology 20*
*Functional grammar: a social view of language 22*
*Functional grammar and Japanese 35*
*A preliminary analysis 37*
*Data and selection procedures 46*
*Overview of the rest of the book 49*
*Potential objections 51*

**2 The Rape of Nanking: processes and participants**   55

*Historical background 56*
*Analysis and discussion 57*
*The nature of closed texts 72*
*A partial answer to some objections 74*
*A note concerning Prince Asaka 76*
*Summary and conclusion 78*

**3 The attacks by Germany and Japan: the ideology of irresponsibility**   81

*Historical background 82*
*The ABCD line 84*

*The German and Japanese attacks: a comparison 95*
*Statistical analysis 114*
*Summary and conclusion 117*

## 4 The surrenders of Germany and Japan: the ideology of face-protection — 121

*Historical background 122*
*The surrender and the threat to face 126*
*Face theory 128*
*Applying face theory to the surrender 131*
*Statistical analysis 149*
*Summary and conclusion 151*

## 5 Conclusion: locating the findings in a wider context — 153

*Reasons for the ideologies 158*
*Conclusion 168*

*Works cited* — 173
*Index* — 181

# Preface

This book has its origins in my work on Japanese high school history textbooks (e.g. Barnard 1998a, 1998b, 2000a, 2000b, 2001, forthcoming). As far as I know, this is the only research which approaches the 'Japanese history textbook problem' from a linguistic point of view, rather than from the point of view of a sociologist, anthropologist, historian, specialist in education, or in Japanese Studies. My interest is specifically in critical discourse analysis. Critical discourse approaches to language frequently seek to answer questions related to how language creates meanings, the range of meanings that a language can create, why particular choices from the language system are made on particular occasions, and what other choices could have been made, what other meanings would have been created if different language had been used, how language influences society, and, in turn, how society is influenced by language. It is with such questions in mind that I will address the language data that form the subject of this study.

It is convenient, here, to explain the general organization of this book. Chapter 1 deals with the political and social background to the history textbook problem in Japan, including the compulsory textbook authorization system of the Ministry of Education. In this chapter, the meaning of the word 'ideology' is defined and the connection between language and ideology is discussed with some illustrative examples. A major part of this chapter is devoted to introducing systemic-functional grammar, the particular model of grammar that is used in this book as a tool for critical discourse analysis.

Chapter 2, Chapter 3, and Chapter 4 deal, respectively, with the following historical events: the Rape of Nanking, the Japanese attacks which started the Pacific War, and the Japanese surrender in 1945. In each chapter, a somewhat different approach is taken to the linguistic analysis of the data. The general conclusions are that the language of the textbooks very consistently downplays the responsibility of the Japanese state for aggressive actions during the period in question and that the textbooks consistently seek to protect the dignity, authority, and status of the Japanese state at the time of the Japanese surrender in 1945. I argue that these can be seen as ideologies of irresponsibility and face-protection.

In Chapter 5, the final chapter, I examine the possible reasons for the existence of the ideologies expressed in the language of the textbooks. Some of the reasons suggested include the high level of continuity between the wartime Japanese state and that of today, the fact that there are outstanding unresolved questions from the war (including the question of reparations), the taboo regarding Emperor Hirohito's role in the war, the reluctance of the present Ministry of Education to clarify the responsibility of its predecessor for teaching mytho-history and propaganda to pupils in order to further the aims of the imperial state, and the civil nature (or rather lack of civil nature) of the modern Japanese state. Several of the points brought up in the first chapter will be returned to in Chapter 5, in this case with the benefit of hindsight which the analysis of the language of the textbooks provides.

Obviously, the language data that will be analysed and discussed is Japanese. Nevertheless, I feel that readers who do not know Japanese will have no difficulty appreciating the nature of the data and understanding the arguments made. To this end, it has been my aim to avoid letting the Japanese language data become a weight, burdening down the text.

The following conventions have been adopted. Japanese personal names are given in the Japanese order, family name followed by given name. The romanization I have used is very similar to Hepburn romanization, but instead of using a macron over $o$ and $u$, I have doubled the vowel letter. I have only marked the syllabic nasal ($n'$) in cases of possible ambiguity. I have used a slash to represent the Japanese punctuation mark of 'nakaguro'. In block quotes from the textbooks, I have given first the Japanese text, followed by my translation. When I include Japanese in the running text, I first give the English translation, often followed by the Japanese in parentheses and in italics. It goes without saying that this is illogical, since the Japanese has priority over the English and it is the actual Japanese that I am discussing. However, for many readers, who I assume do not know Japanese, this seems to be the most comfortable solution. The alternative is to keep stumbling over italicized Japanese and having to check the English translation enclosed within parentheses. In neither the romanizations nor the translations have I reproduced the use of bold lettering that exists in the original texts. In a few cases I have, for the sake of clarity, fleshed out the translations. In a few other cases I have inserted an explanatory comment. In both such cases, I have placed the added material in square brackets, and in the latter case the comment is followed by my initials, 'CB'. The translations will sometimes seem unnatural. I hope that readers will be tolerant. To tread the fine line between giving readers a reasonable idea of the structure of the original Japanese, on the one hand, and, on the other hand, presenting a translation that is not positively off-putting is not easy. In all cases, it should be clear whether translations from Japanese to English are by me or not.

When discussing, in the main running text, the language of the textbooks, usually given in block quotes, Japanese verbs and the English translations will not always accord; thus, for example, a Japanese verb in the *-te* form (the gerund) will usually be translated by an English verb in the past tense, since this is how it is so translated in the relevant block quote. This seems more sensible than getting involved with the dictionary (citation) forms of Japanese verbs.

Although the numerical data that are presented in this book have been checked by me many times, I cannot positively say that someone else counting these same data will arrive at exactly the same numbers. When counting linguistic forms, there are always ambiguous cases which nevertheless have to be assigned to specific categories; in such cases my policy has been to make decisions which do *not* favour my argument. Also, it is possible that I have overlooked retrospective references in later sections of the textbooks to certain historical events which I discuss. There might be a very few cases in which I have overlooked a footnote or marginal note. Nevertheless, bearing all this in mind, I am confident that, whatever inaccuracies there might be in the data, these do not affect the argument and conclusions in any significant way.

Linguistics, like any other specialized field, has its own terminology. Some of this we have learnt in some form or another at school, and some of it is common sense. Nevertheless, there is an extensive and complex set of technical language. The area of linguistics I myself work in, namely systemic-functional linguistics and critical discourse analysis, tends to have its own terminology, which is not even very comprehensible to linguists working in other fields. I have used no more specialized technical terminology than I think is necessary.

Finally, readers are entitled to ask what particular background or qualifications I have for writing this book. When I read any book in any field of Japanese studies, Japanese history, or Japanese linguistics,

I always find myself asking the question: How much does this writer know about Japan? How well can she speak the Japanese language? In my opinion, many writers are less than straightforward about this. Because of this, and because the 'self-introduction' is a common and necessary ritual in Japanese society, and one which I have become used to, I will give my 'self-introduction', as far as it is relevant to this book. I have lived in Japan for 32 years, and for most of that time have been studying or using the Japanese language on a more or less daily basis. I hold an MA in linguistics, with a specialization in Japanese linguistics, and a doctor of education degree, in which the doctoral dissertation was a very early version of this book. I have been working on the Japanese history textbook problem for eight years. Since I am not a native speaker of Japanese, I have over the years asked many hundreds of questions to Japanese informants regarding my interpretations and their interpretations of the language of the history textbooks. As well as my work directly related to this book, I have also worked in the field of English–Japanese translation studies and Japanese–English/English–Japanese lexicography for many years.

# Acknowledgements

I would like to thank Dr Martin Willis, who has generously helped me with my statistical work over the years. Dr Kazuhiro Teruya very generously let me see a pre-publication copy of his 'Metafunctional Profile of the Grammar of Japanese' and Dr Elizabeth Thomson kindly let me see an early version of her doctoral thesis, and sent me the final version of 'Exploring the Textual Metafunction in Japanese: A Case Study of Selected Written Texts'. Dr Katalin Ferber has always been helpful in filling me in on the political and economic background of the Shoowa period, and pointing me to some important references. To these scholars, my sincere thanks. I thank the following for permission to use copyrighted materials: John Benjamins Publishing Company for an article in *Functions of Language* (Barnard 2000a), *Revista Canaria de Estudios Ingleses* (for Barnard 2000b), and Taylor & Francis – http://www.tandf.co.uk – for an article in *British Journal of Sociology of Education* (Barnard 2001).

# 1 Introduction

**The history problem in Japan**

'The war', from a European or North American perspective generally refers to the Second World War, lasting from 1939 to 1945 or, in the case of the war against Japan, the Pacific War phase of the Second World War, from 1941 to 1945. However, Japan was at war for a much longer period of time, and the war against the Western Allies (the United States, Britain, the Netherlands, Australia, etc.) was but a small part of what, in Japan, is sometimes referred to as the Fifteen Years War. This is conventionally dated from the time of the Mukden Incident of 18 September 1931 (which then became part of the wider Manchurian Incident), in which elements within the Japanese army, (perhaps acting independently of the Japanese government (Hata 1983: 309–311), or perhaps acting with either its tacit or reluctant consent (Bix 2000: 231, 232; Ienaga 1978: 58–65)), stationed in the Japanese leasehold of Kwantung and, by treaty arrangement, in other parts of North-East China, faked a sabotage attempt on the Japanese-owned South Manchurian Railway. This gave the army a pretext to take over all of Manchuria. The establishment of the Japanese-controlled puppet state of Manchuria, and the subsequent expansion and escalation of the war against China (described by the Japanese government and press at the time as being a series of 'incidents') soon followed.

The war against the Western Allies is, of course, dated from 8 December 1941 (Japan time), when Japanese forces attacked Britain in Malaya and the United States at Pearl Harbor. The Asia-Pacific War (used in this book to refer to the war against both China and the Western Allies) came to a conclusion with Japan's surrender to the Allies on 2 September 1945.

Whereas in Germany there is a reasonably clear national consensus on the kind of war it was that Germany fought, this is less so in Japan

(Buruma 1994: 9, 10), where war responsibility was not as rigorously pursued as in the case of Germany (Fujiwara 1999: 241). There is a small, but vocal and influential, segment of Japanese society, led by politicians, journalists, certain publishing and media groups, academics, and patriotic organizations who hold views that generally go under the label of 'revisionist' (T. Yoshida 2000: 71) regarding what kind of war it was that Japan fought from 1931 to 1945, or from 1941 to 1945. The events of the war are themselves subject to fierce debate – and no event more so than the Rape of Nanking, concerning which there is a vast scholarly and popular literature. Did the Rape of Nanking really occur, or is it a complete fabrication, or at least an exaggeration, both by the Chinese after the war and the Allies at the Tokyo war crimes trials (i.e. the International Military Tribunal for the Far East)?

In recent years the debate regarding the war and Japan's role in it has intensified, with the revisionists becoming more and more vocal (see Fujiwara 1999: 240–249; McCormack 2000), and with their views being given increasing prominence by the press and broadcast media. Key topics of debate include whether or not the war Japan fought was one of aggressive territorial expansion, or whether it was, on the other hand, a war that was unselfishly fought by Japan in order to liberate fellow Asians from Western imperialism and white colonialism. Did Japan have no choice but to fight this war for its national self-preservation since economic sanctions were being implemented against it by, most importantly, the United States? Does Japan owe its present prosperity to those who laid down their lives for their country?

As readers may have noticed, these questions themselves have already confused different aspects of the Asia-Pacific War, since, for example, even if Japan had been fighting a war of colonial liberation, this could only date from, at the earliest, the time of Japan's more or less forcible entry into the southern part of Vietnam, then part of Vichy-controlled French Indochina, in 1941. This lack of distinction between the different phases of the war that Japan fought from 1931 to 1945 was, and is, a common feature of the debate. The revisionist case becomes easier to argue if there is a blurring of the distinction between the China phase of the war (clearly a war of aggression) and the war against the Western Allies (arguably a war of colonial liberation, provided the nature of Japanese rule in the conquered territories and the atrocities against the peoples of Asia and the Pacific are overlooked).

In 1995, Okuno Seisuke, a member of the House of Representatives (the lower house of parliament) and a former Minister of Education, made the comment that, 'It is America and Britain that carried out a war of aggression. It is America and Britain that we fought, not Asia' (*Asahi Shimbun*, 17 March 1995). The Pacific War lasted a mere three years and eight months, and American and British (including Empire and Commonwealth) deaths totalled approximately 300,000. Asian deaths amounted to millions. Okuno's position is not tenable. In fact, it is nothing more than an example of forgetting about the Chinese phase of the Asia-Pacific War, as well as forgetting about Japanese actions against the inhabitants of South-East Asia and the Pacific during the Pacific War itself.

Okuno's statement is but one example of the common tendency of important politicians to state opinions about the righteousness of the war that Japan fought and thereby cause a storm of protest, both in Japan and, most particularly, in China and South Korea. Such politicians are often, but by no means always, made to retract their statements, and if they hold a cabinet post or some such important position are forced to resign or are dismissed from their posts (McCormack 1996: 227–229; T. Yoshida, 2000: 109). In 1995, the *Asahi Shimbun*, one of Japan's leading national newspapers, gave a summary of, then recent, questionable statements made by certain politicians (*Asahi Shimbun*, 1 January 1995). For example, in May 1994, the Minister of Justice, Nagano Shigeto, said that the Nanking Incident (i.e. the Rape of Nanking) was a fabrication, and later amended this by saying it was an exaggeration. Hashimoto Ryuutaroo, then Minister of Trade and Industry, and later Prime Minister of Japan, is quoted as saying:

> Limiting ourselves only to the Second World War [i.e. the Pacific War phase of the Second World War, CB], it is true that one aspect of it was that of Japan fighting the United States, fighting Britain, and fighting the Netherlands, and it is a fact that Japan waged war, but when it comes to whether it was a war of aggression, I still have my doubts about this. ... For Japan at that time, it is a fact that, while not intending to fight with the people of those areas, it made many parts of the Pacific into battlefields. [... *Tooji no Nihon toshite, sono chiiki no katagata o aite toshite tatakatte iru tsumori wa nai mama ni, Taiheiyoo no kaku chiiki o senjoo to shita jijitsu ga aru.*]

As well as the confusion or lack of discrimination between the different phases of the war that Japan fought, another common position of the revisionists, as shown by Hashimoto's words quoted above, is to adopt what may be called the 'accidental involvement theory of Asian suffering': Japan was fighting against the Western imperialists, but unfortunately some Asians were killed in this war.

This accidental involvement theory does not bear up to even casual examination. To take just one specific case, Dear and Foot (1995: 179) report a possible death toll of 12,000 Allied prisoners-of-war on the Burma–Thailand Railway, built by the Japanese in order to move troops and supplies from Thailand to the Burma front. The death toll of labourers conscripted from within Thailand and the surrounding areas is estimated to be about 90,000. Other authors give similar figures (e.g. Daws 1994: 221; Hicks 1994: 132). Nevertheless, for anyone arguing that Japan's war was primarily a war of colonial liberation, the accidental involvement theory, provided it is not examined in any detail, conveniently clouds the issue.

The confusion, or indeed ignorance, of the different phases of the war that Japan fought is not limited to Japan. As mentioned above, the view in the Western mind is that *the* war that Japan fought was from 1941 to 1945. The war that started in 1931 disappears from history and historiography, as pointed out by Dower (1999: 27):

> Asian contributions to defeating the Emperor's soldiers and sailors were displaced in an all-consuming focus on the American victory in the 'Pacific War.' By this same process of vaporization, the crimes that had been committed against Asian people through colonization as well as war were all the more easily put out of mind.

But as we will see, the crimes that were committed against Asian people is an issue that has come back to haunt Japan in the last ten or fifteen years.

In 1995, on the fiftieth anniversary of the end of the war, in an attempt to bring some kind of closure to the war, the House of Representatives (i.e. the lower house of parliament) passed what had originally been intended to be an apology, or at least an expression of remorse, for Japanese actions during the war. After much bitter debate and political machinations, this eventually became a watered-down 'Resolution to Renew the Determination for Peace on the Basis of Lessons Learned from History', which pleased no one, least of all those who were seeking a clear statement of Japanese responsibility for wartime actions and some kind of apology. In part, this resolution contained the following paragraph (translation by the secretariat of the House of Representatives):

> Solemnly reflecting upon many instances of colonial rule and acts of aggression in the modern history of the world, and recognizing that Japan carried out those acts in the past, inflicting pain and suffering upon the peoples of other countries, especially in Asia, the Members of this House express a sense of deep remorse.

This was widely seen as nothing more than an attempt to obfuscate the specific acts and especially violent nature of Japanese aggression, and the attendant atrocities, by lumping them together with a generalized aggression and colonial rule. A further controversy regarding the resolution concerned to what extent the word 'remorse' (*hansei no nen*) implied an apology, and whether 'remorse' was a suitable translation of the Japanese expression. It was argued by some that the English translation was 'adjusted' so that it would be more acceptable internationally, while the original Japanese would be more acceptable to certain groups within Japan.

At about the same time, a spate of resolutions were passed by prefectural assemblies (a prefecture in Japan being a unit of regional government comparable to an English county or French département). However, in many cases, far from being a recognition of the aggressive nature of Japan's military actions, or being a clear apology, these resolutions were, on the contrary, often a reaffirmation of the righteousness of the war. As of 23 March 1995, 17 prefectural assemblies in Japan had passed such resolutions. The contents of these resolutions were varied, but they are summed up by Miura (1995) as generally having the following points in common:

a) The fallen laid down their lives for the safety of their country and to protect their loved ones and their birthplaces.
b) The fallen laid the foundations for today's peace and prosperity.
c) The resolutions incorporated an expression of condolences by the assembly for the hardship caused to many people in Asian countries by the turmoil of war.

According to Miura (1995), these resolutions represent a view of history that is far from reality. For example, the first point above gives the impression that Japan was being actually invaded by a foreign army and the Japanese soldiers rose up to fight against this invasion. The second point seeks to invest the war with some deep significance and moral righteousness, but this, even if it were true or could be causally proved, would imply that Japan owes its present prosperity and peace to the deaths of three million Japanese and perhaps twenty million other Asians. Finally, the third point is expressed in such a way as to suggest that Asians became indirectly and accidentally involved in the 'turmoil' of war (presumably without Japanese soldiers committing any aggressive actions against them), and suffered the consequences of it – an example of the accidental involvement theory mentioned above.

Another characteristic of such resolutions was the way they illogically linked the modern Japanese 'peace-state' (which in the post-war constitution renounced the right of belligerency of the state) to the expression of thanks and condolences to the Japanese soldiers who died in the war in order to give the impression, without actually saying so in so many words, that these soldiers laid down their lives in order to bring peace to the world. Part of the resolution of Ehime prefecture (*Asahi Shimbun*, 1 Oct. 1994) read as follows: 'The assembly expresses thanks and condolences to those who fell in the war and pledges to build everlasting peace'.

Underlying the discourse of Japan's actions in the war and questions of responsibility for these actions, but unstated by all but the brave and rash, is the role of the former Emperor, Hirohito. Not to try him as a war criminal, or even summon him as a witness, at the Tokyo war crimes trials, meant that his role could never be investigated or clarified, and that even today to publicly suggest, more than ten years after his death, that he must bear at least some responsibility for the war is to put one's life at risk from certain fanatical sections of Japanese society.

The continuing position of Hirohito as head of state up to 1947 and then, according to article 1 of the post-war constitution, as the symbol of the people and the unity of the nation up to the time of his death in 1989, meant that the post-war Japanese state had a high level of continuity with that of the pre-war and wartime state. The Japanese state did not collapse at the time of the Japanese defeat, as the German state did with its defeat; Japanese bureaucrats, government officials, and politicians went back to work the next day, and in very many cases continued in their jobs under, and after, the Allied occupation. The Allied occupation authorities did not replace the Japanese bureaucracy, but worked through it, issuing suggestions, directives, and orders. The last Imperial Diet (the Diet under the old constitution) dissolved itself in 1946. This continuity of the Japanese state is a point frequently made by writers about Japan (e.g. Buruma 1994: 61–62; McCormack 1996: 189; McCormack 2000: 63; van Wolferen 1989: 259, 268). It is often argued that one natural result of this is that Japan has never morally come to grips with its responsibility for its past. McCormack (1996: 231) writes that:

> ... from war to postwar, the Japanese state maintained an essential continuity of sovereign [sic], bureaucracy, and (with few exceptions) political leadership; its courts have never recognized any criminality of state or of individual war actions.

It has been argued (e.g. Bergamini 1971; Bix 2000) that Hirohito played a very active and involved role in the war, and the decision not to hold him accountable was a pragmatic one taken by General Douglas MacArthur, the Supreme Commander of the Occupation Forces, in order to effect an orderly occupation and rebuilding of Japan. But by not holding Hirohito responsible for the acts of his government and of his armed forces, a moral lid was placed on the examination of guilt and war responsibility within Japan.

The purges of the occupation authorities were half-hearted, and it was not long before the same governmental and bureaucratic elites were in power again; Japan was soon to have a prime minister who had been a government minister during the war and had been indicted, but never tried, as a Class A war criminal. His brother also later became prime minister. Because Japan never experienced a truly wrenching dislocation from its past as, say, Germany did, it meant that there was no ideological refocusing. Skeletons were not brought out of cupboards and since Hirohito's role in the war, and the question of his responsibility, could not be discussed, the Japanese themselves never had to come to grips with their past and their own responsibility as Japanese:

> Eventually Hirohito became the prime symbol of his people's repression of their wartime past. For as long as they did not pursue his central role in the war, they did not have to question their own.
> 
> (Bix 2000: 17)

The fact that there are unresolved problems from the war years is something of which every reasonably well-informed Japanese is keenly aware. The number of lawsuits brought against both the Japanese government and individual companies by former sex slaves of the Japanese army (the so-called 'comfort women'), conscripted labourers, victims of atrocities, former prisoners-of-war, and so on, has increased over the last dozen years or so (McCormack 2000: 53), and in some cases either out-of-court settlements, partial victories, or victories have been won (*The Japan Times*, 27 April 2002; see 'Forced laborers win suit: Mitsui Mining ordered to pay ¥165 million'). Such cases are continually making headline news in Japan. As I was writing this section, I woke up to find on the front page of my newspaper (*Asahi Shimbun*, 28 Aug. 2002): 'The Unit 731 Lawsuit: Recognition of the Existence of Biological Warfare, But Tokyo District Court Rejects Plaintiffs Demands'.

This was a lawsuit brought by the surviving Chinese kin of victims of a biological warfare unit of the Japanese army. These kin were demanding compensation and apologies from the Japanese government. Although the court rejected these demands, it nevertheless established a landmark by being the first Japanese court to acknowledge that Unit 731 carried out biological warfare. The plaintiffs plan to appeal.

Then, as I am rewriting and revising this section, a month later, I have just come across in my evening newspaper (*Asahi Shimbun*, 26 Sept. 2002): 'Hearings in US Congress on Former American Prisoners-of-War. Voices seeking compensation from Japan for wartime forced labour'.

And then, believe it or not, as I am revising this once more, almost exactly a month later, there is an article on the wages which still remain unpaid to the Koreans who either served in, or were attached to, the Japanese army during the war (*Asahi Shimbun*, 28 Oct. 2002). I am giving these 'real time' reports to stress how the issue of Japan's wartime responsibility is a continuing and pressing concern. It is something which simply will not go away.

The statute of limitations on claims against Japan and Japanese companies and the hitherto prevailing view that Japan was absolved of responsibility for such acts by the terms of post-war treaties (Hein and Selden 2000: 25) is being increasingly challenged under new interpretations of Japanese and international law (McCormack 1996: 245, 246, 273, 274).

Within Japan, the general public is very much aware of these controversies, and many large book shops will have shelf space of perhaps a metre in length devoted to 'the history textbook problem' and then another metre or so on 'Nanking'.

The history problem and the associated history textbook problem is a subject frequently take up by the media outside Japan (e.g. Kunii *et al.* 1996), and there is certainly a widespread international perception that Japan has not come clean about the war. *The Economist* (2 Sept. 2000) writes that:

Even now Japan stands in puzzling contrast to Germany in its reluctance to acknowledge guilt for its monstrous wartime actions – first in China and then throughout the Pacific theatre during the merciless campaigns of 1931–1945.

Given this brief sketch of the history problem in Japan, the question arises how this might be carried over to history textbooks themselves. If we regard history textbooks as being products of a society, it follows that ideological struggles within that society are likely to be reflected in such textbooks.

In a sense, history is a school subject that is set apart from other subjects. There are two reasons for this. First, teaching the succeeding generations history is an important part of the process by which the officially recognized narratives of the nation are passed on down the ages to succeeding generations, and by which these generations define themselves with reference to the nation state; learning one's history is part of the process by which citizens learn to position their country and the values that their country espouses within the wider international society. Learning the story of our country and seeking to understand the actions of our ancestors is an important part of growing up and becoming a new and responsible citizen of the state. This reason, while not an intrinsic part of the subject of history per se, for many people would nevertheless seem to be rather a natural one. The second reason why history as a school subject is set apart is an extension of the first reason – and is more controversial. History is not only seen as a matter of learning the narratives of the nation, but it is often taken for granted that one of the aims of the school subject of history is to inculcate in pupils patriotism and pride in the nation state (Loewen 1995: 14, 272–273). This is often the issue at stake for the revisionists in Japan, as pointed out by T. Yoshida (2000: 107):

> In all their activities and writings, what is most at stake for revisionists is not the memory of the Chinese who were killed by Japanese soldiers, but the issue of 'Japan' and 'Japaneseness.' The revisionists have engaged in their activities to promote an idea of 'a Japanese national history for the Japanese people.'

Given this situation, it is likely that the language of the history textbooks currently used in Japan reflects the controversies concerning interpretations of the war, and the disputes concerning the accuracy or veracity of such events as the Rape of Nanking.

## Post-war education and textbook authorization

In Japan, all textbooks used in all schools up to the end of high school have to pass the official screening or authorization procedures of the Japanese Ministry of Education. The state lays down strict curricular guidelines and, by means of the textbook authorization system, maintains control over the content and language of textbooks. This has been the case in Japan for a hundred years, with direct state control of textbooks dating from 1903 (Beauchamp and Vardaman 1994: 5; Yamazumi 1989: 235).

After the end of the War, during the brief period (1945 to 1952) of the Allied, basically American, occupation of Japan, attempts were made to democratize Japanese education. What may be called the founding document for this was the Fundamental Law of Education of March 1947 (translated in Beauchamp and Vardaman 1994: 109–111). In this attempt to democratize education, the American model was followed. One important aspect of this was the decentralization of education by transferring power from the Ministry of Education to local authorities. To this end, the Board of Education Law was passed in July 1948.

But, as pointed out by many authors, the educational freedoms of the immediate post-war period were quickly whittled away (e.g. Horio 1988: 138–152; McVeigh 1998: 148, 149; Seddon 1987; Yamazumi 1989). The usual reason given for this was the need by the American government to develop Japan as a bulwark against what was perceived as the growing Communist threat in the Cold War period. Thus, it was not long before the occupation authorities were protecting the status quo, which of course had its roots in the pre-war period.

New laws were passed that effectively superseded those dating from the immediate post-war period; or existing laws were circumvented by administrative means. For example, the Board of Education Law, which had provided for the election of members of the local boards of education, was replaced in 1956 by a law mandating the appointment of these members by prefectural governors or local mayors (Nozaki and Inokuchi 2000: 100–101). This had the effect of reintegrating what had been, for a short time, locally controlled and administered education into the centralized hierarchy of the Ministry of Education (McVeigh 1998: 148).

Seddon (1987: 219) argues that one of the aims of those in power, the politicians and bureaucrats, was to use education as a form of social control, just as it had been used before and during the war:

The US occupying forces began the process of establishing the structures which would protect the status quo. The Japanese ruling class has continued this process, reversing 'undesirable' reforms and creating an intricate network of structures including the textbook authorization system, which tame the populace and reduce the possibility of class antagonism.

Seddon, at the time of writing in 1987, argued that there had been four major post-war trends in Japanese education: (a) the recentralization of educational control; (b) efficiency oriented school and teacher management; (c) emphasis on cultivation of patriotism and duty as Japanese; (d) subordination of education to economic policy. Much of the discussion of post-war Japanese education in one way or another involves these four trends.

The abolishment of election to the boards of education is but one example of the recentralization of education. The introduction of the internship programme for new teachers (*shoninsha kenshuu*) from 1989 (Okano and Tsuchiya 1999: 221–226) was one of the latest examples of an efficiency oriented project, although many claimed it was also a means of controlling the left-leaning Japan Teachers' Union and training nationalistic teachers (222, 223). The subordination of education to economic policy has been frequently discussed (e.g. Horio 1988: 215, 216; McVeigh 2002: 82; Okano and Tsuchiya 1999: 39, 40), with the general point being made that in the post-war period the state has always seen one of the primary goals, perhaps the primary goal, of education as that of supplying literate, well-trained, pliable workers to the fields of commerce and industry, on which Japan's economic success depends.

The campaign to officially inculcate patriotism and duty in pupils has been a long one, with some of the strongest resistance coming from the Japan Teachers' Union. But this struggle has always been one in which the political and bureaucratic establishment continued to win incremental victories over the years. To take one contentious and central issue, over a period of more than a decade there was gradual and mounting pressure, in the form of steadily escalating 'advice' and 'guidance', from the Ministry of Education that Japan's unofficial national anthem and unofficial national flag, both of which enjoyed no legal status, should form a part of school ceremonies. This campaign finally culminated in the passing of a law in 1999 designating *Kimigayo* (a song glorifying the Emperor's reign) and the *Hinomaru* (Rising Sun) flag as the official national anthem and flag. This law was strongly opposed by those to whom the flag and anthem were redolent of the pre-surrender period. The issue became so controversial and divisive that one school principal in Hiroshima, where feelings regarding the issue were likely to be most intense given that city's great suffering during the war, committed suicide.

During this period, the concept of 'internationalization' was both officially and unofficially trumpeted throughout the land. This had the effect of seemingly downplaying the nationalistic agenda, since internationalization was presented in the form that, to become true citizens of the modern world, Japanese young people must learn to appreciate and value other people's customs and beliefs, and they can only do this if they value their own. Thus, under the guise of 'internationalization', which certainly, on the surface, seems a good thing, a nationalist agenda stressing 'Japaneseness' was introduced (Gerow 2000: 85, 86; McVeigh 2002: 149). One of the arguments advanced for passing the national anthem and flag legislation, and mandating their use in schools, was that the Japanese people should respect and appreciate the flags and anthems of other countries, but they could hardly be expected to do this if they did not respect their own national symbols – a case of nationalism through internationalization.

As far back as January 1970, the Paris-based Organization for Economic Cooperation and Development issued its Report on Japanese Education. Prior to this, a team of experts on education had visited Japan, at the official invitation of the Japanese, in order to give advice on the future development of education in Japan. Points raised in that report have a direct bearing on this discussion. An extract from that report (quoted in Beauchamp and Vardaman 1994: 203, 204) follows:

> The Ministry of Education however, has great formal control over the contents of Japanese education – perhaps in this respect one of the most centralized in the world. It has:
>
> i) the power to determine the courses of study in each subject, a power which is exercised in the form of such detailed prescriptions that the teacher's freedom to vary the curriculum is restricted.
> ii) licensing power over all textbooks to be used.
>
> This power has inherent in it the danger of possible uniformity in the political values offered in connection with such subjects as history. Also, centralization and required uniformity largely prevent the wide variety and experimentation in content and teaching

methods so greatly needed to improve education if it is to meet the needs of modern society. Thus what commences as an effort to control the value content of education also has serious negative effects on the purely educational side.

It is true to say that the situation has not changed since then. Within Japan, there has been protest against the textbook authorization system, most particularly with reference to history textbooks. Horio (1988: 175) calls it nothing less than a form of censorship, and contrary to the Japanese constitution. He writes that the Ministry of Education 'has been quite meddlesome with regard to the language used for example in describing Japan's modernization, the Imperial Constitution of 1889, the Imperial Rescript on Education, Japan's repeated warmaking and the daily lives of the masses of ordinary people'.

As we will see, the ministry has a strong and directly coercive power, which it does not hesitate to use in order to maintain its control of textbooks. But, as the following article (*The Daily Yomiuri*, 20 July 1994) shows, this is usually not necessary since publishers (and presumably almost all authors) know very well what the ground rules are, and have little choice but to toe the line:

> In an apparently self-imposed bid to gain government authorization, five publishing companies have submitted drafts for primary-school social studies textbooks that include all 42 figures cited as examples by the Education Ministry as being 'significant historic persons,' it was learned Tuesday. ...
>
> Although the ministry says the prominent figures were given just as examples, most publishing companies have included all 42 in their drafts submitted for authorization last spring.
>
> 'The omission of any cited figure will most certainly cause the ministry to issue a recommendation for a second consideration on including that figure,' a company official said. Another official said that omitting any of the 'examples' could result in failing the ministry's screening for publication. ...
>
> Editors at three of the five publishing companies told The Yomiuri Shimbun they would not have included several of the historic figures cited by the ministry ... in their textbooks if the ministry had truly cited them as just 'examples.'

The point about this is that even if it is not true that the Ministry would have failed the textbooks that did not include the suggested figures, the fact that it is *seen* to be true by a majority of the publishers has a strong coercive effect.

As pointed out in the OECD report quoted above, the authorization process leads to a lack of pedagogic experimentation in textbook publication. Horio (1988: 174) reports that a physics textbook by Tomonaga Shin'ichiroo, a Nobel Prize winner, failed the screening process of the Japanese Ministry of Education because the knowledge was not presented in the approved, predetermined, and exact style, which, by definition, must be a characteristic of a textbook. According to Horio, Tomonaga was trying to encourage children to think in a different and non-traditional way about physics, but the Ministry of Education was not prepared to countenance such an approach.

One of the most persistent and vocal critics of the textbook authorization system has been Ienaga Saburoo, who challenged the system by bringing a series of lawsuits extending over a period of more than three decades (Nozaki and Inokuchi 2000: 96–126). His struggle has been so protracted that his name has become familiar even to non-specialists outside Japan. In the course of these lawsuits, details of the textbook screening process became known because the ministry was forced by the court to gradually release documents, despite its claim to confidentiality, explaining why it had censored Ienaga's textbooks, the reasons for rejection, the process of authorization, and the names of the examiners (109–111). As Nozaki and Inokuchi write (Nozaki and Inokuchi 2000: 111) 'the ministry's own documents revealed an arbitrary process, one rife with abuses of power'.

In one lawsuit filed by Ienaga against the state in 1984, among the points at issue were the disagreements between the ministry and Ienaga regarding the extent of killing of Japanese civilians (including women and children) by the soldiers of the Japanese army during the battle of Okinawa, the necessity of including the mention of rape at the time of the Nanking atrocities, Korean resistance to Japanese invasion in the period 1894–1895 (the Sino-Japanese War), and the nature of imperial power during two events in Japanese history (Nozaki and Inokuchi 2000: 115–117).

Ienaga's lawsuits are extraordinary with regard to his persistence (and that of the Ministry of Education). The Ministry of Education has, over the years, refused to concede that decisions regarding the content of history textbooks and historical interpretation are something vested in the Japanese people themselves; it is the ministry that is the arbiter of history in Japan. Ienaga's lawsuits make this clear. But the pattern is a common one, as shown by a recent article in the *Asahi Shimbun* (30 May 2002a). The headlines are as follows:

**Yokohama Textbook Suit**

Complete Defeat for Plaintiff

According to Tokyo High Court 'Not a case of exceeding discretionary powers'

In the first lawsuit brought in the Yokohama District Court, one of the issues of contention was whether a comment made by a textbook examiner about part of a textbook which referred to the dispatch of minesweepers of the Japanese Maritime Self-Defense Force (i.e. the Japanese navy) during the Gulf War was a personal comment or an official comment. The plaintiff, Professor Takashima Nobuyoshi, won a partial victory and the state was ordered to pay him 200,000 yen (approximately US$1,700). However, this judgement was overturned in the Tokyo High Court. The plaintiff's further claim that the textbook authorization system itself was unconstitutional in that it violated freedom of expression, education, and speech was also rejected. Professor Takashima plans to appeal.

In what seems to be in conformity with the usual practice in such cases, readers of the newspaper are told the presiding judge's name and the plaintiff's name, but the names of all the people in the Ministry of Education, including the individual examiner himself, who were responsible for this decision are omitted. Either the ministry did not reveal the names, or the newspaper knew the names and decided not to release them, both of which situations seem unacceptable since this means that there is now a situation in Japan in which unnamed bureaucrats can make decisions to tenaciously pursue, over many years, such lawsuits (at taxpayers' expense).

As pointed out in a related and adjacent article (*Asahi Shimbun*, 30 May 2002b) the actual authorization procedure has consistently put authors and publishers at a disadvantage vis-à-vis the ministry. From 1948, the opinions of the examiner were given orally. From 1990 there was a reform of this system, with publishers being given a list of the parts of the textbook that were deemed problematic, but the nature of the actual problem was explained orally. From 2000, the ministry's opinions were given in writing. However, there is still dissatisfaction with this new system since the opinions are given in stereotyped, standardized language, and the publishers have to ask the examiners to explain themselves in detail. Furthermore, the fact that the examiner is simply conveying the opinions of the examining committee itself, not his or her own opinion, creates a lack of transparency and makes for misunderstandings.

Dissatisfaction with the authorization process and the content of textbooks is not limited to textbook writers, teachers, or publishers. Sometimes young people can have an eye-opening experience that makes them realize with a shock that the type of history education they are receiving is seriously deficient. Letters from young people, often written after a visit overseas, criticizing the deficiencies of history education not infrequently appear in the letters column of daily newspapers. In my small collection of such letters, there are examples of a high school pupil being shocked by photographs of Japanese atrocities in China seen during a visit to a bookshop in Hong Kong, and of another pupil having a similar reaction during a visit to a waxworks museum and to a war memorial in Singapore. One of these letters makes the point that textbooks stress the hardships and disasters that the Japanese suffered during the war (firebombing, the atomic bombs, the evacuation of children from cities, the terrible civilian losses during the battle of Okinawa, etc.), but do not put enough emphasis on the sufferings inflicted on other Asian people by the Japanese.

The history textbook debate and the system of textbook authorization has, in the last few years, been brought to the fore by the activities of the *Atarashii Rekishi-kyookasho o Tsukuru Kai* (the Japanese Institute for New History Education), hereafter referred to as the *Tsukuru-kai*, its short name in Japanese.

The *Tsukuru-kai* (Kobayashi 1998: 8, 9) claims that post-war history education does not inculcate in pupils pride in being Japanese, and that textbooks teach a masochistic view of modern Japanese history in which Japan has to needlessly apologize for past deeds. Furthermore, according to the *Tsukuru-kai*, since the end of the Cold War this tendency has become stronger, to such an extent that textbooks even include, as fact, propaganda from former enemy countries (namely the United States). This is an indirect reference to what the revisionists call the 'Tokyo trials view of history', which is to say the victors' view of the history of the years leading up to the war, and the war itself, which, it is claimed, was forcibly foisted on the Japanese people by the occupation authorities in the form of the findings of the Tokyo trials, which then became the official view of history, and one which places unjust culpability on the Japanese state and the Japanese people for actions during this period – while totally ignoring the war crimes committed by the victors. The aim of the *Tsukuru-kai* is to teach a history in which children develop pride and responsibility as Japanese and thereby learn to contribute to the peace and prosperity of the world (see Gerow 2000, 74–86; Kobayashi 1998: 8, 9). (This can be seen as another example of nationalism through internationalization, which I have previously mentioned.)

The criticism of the above, both in Japan and abroad, was that the *Tsukuru-kai* aims to present a nationalistic history, similar to that taught before and during the war (see Morris-Suzuki 2000: 133–139).

The *Tsukuru-kai*, in 2001, put on the open market a version of its junior high school history textbook (Kanji *et al.* 2001), an action which was, itself, unusual and seen as a breaking of the informal rules regarding textbook publication and distribution. This book was heavily criticized for, among other things, not dealing frankly with the Nanking Massacre and the issue of the sex slaves, and for presenting a nationalistic and Emperor-centred view of history.

There were official protests from China and South Korea (*Asahi Shimbun*, 8 May 2001) and specific requests for corrections made by the Chinese Foreign Ministry regarding (*Asahi Shimbun*, 18 May 2001) for example, the painting of an idealized picture of the economic growth of Manchuria to the exclusion of mention of the Japanese forcible seizure of land and germ warfare experiments carried out on Chinese citizens by the notorious Unit 731 of the Japanese army, and the casting of doubt on the extent and veracity of the Rape of Nanking by means of exaggerating the importance of a very limited number of minority opinions which argue that a major massacre did not occur, and the final historical verdict has not yet been rendered on Nanking.

The Korean government listed 35 points which it said required correction. Its comments were directed towards books from eight publishing companies, but 25 of these required corrections were directed to the *Tsukuru-kai*'s book. Among the charges against five publishing companies (including *Tsukuru-kai*) was that no mention was made of the sex slaves issue.

In conclusion, it must be said that the textbook was adopted by a very small number of schools, given as less than one per cent (*Asahi Shimbun*, 16 Aug. 2001).

## Society, education, and the curriculum

In order to approach the issues taken up in this book from a reasonably broad perspective, and to show that although what I have to say about Japanese history textbooks is, in its particulars, limited to Japan, it is, however, of far wider relevance, in this section the role of the school in society, the content and the form of the curriculum, and the relationship between schools, society, and ideology will be briefly discussed.

Writers on textbooks and the curriculum have found that the content of the curriculum is not something that is arrived at objectively. It is certainly not a question of there being some objectively recognizable knowledge component of the curriculum which unproblematically finds its way into textbooks. Rather, from everything that can potentially be in a school curriculum a selection has to be made. Apple (1982: 19) suggests that we should investigate 'Why and how ... particular aspects of a collective culture [are] represented in schools as objective factual knowledge'. Whitty (1985: 19, 20) argues that by examining the curriculum carefully we can often find that the selection of knowledge and the way this knowledge is presented supports the status quo. Whitty (1985: 19) claims that 'pupils were likely to accept as an immutable "fact" what was but one ideological version of the world'.

FitzGerald (1980) shows that in the United States the political economy of textbook publishing itself, and the relationship of this to changes in society, including social movements and political pressures, means that what is judged to be worth including in these textbooks, and how it is to be presented, has varied through time. Loewen (1995: 255–270) in his examination of American history textbooks, finds that the political economy, the political climate, pressure groups, regional interests, and racial considerations all influence what is included in these textbooks, what is omitted, and how material is presented. He argues that the underlying ideology of these textbooks is one of 'progress'. This ideology of progress comes to drive the historical narrative forward and continually is used to explain, and frequently avoid explaining, causation. This ideology of progress is so basic to the textbooks that even facts and interpretations that are contrary to this ideology are made to fit in with it – even when, far from there being progress, there is an actual worsening of the state of affairs (Loewen: 265–269).

This idea of progress is one of the means by which pride in the nation and national unity is instilled in pupils, and this, in fact, becomes one of the main aims of history education. When the study of history is subverted by what may be called mythic versions of history, historiography is subordinated to other causes. According to Loewen, mythic versions of history tend to serve the interests of certain sections or groups within the society.

Anyon (1979) examined the content of 17 United States history textbooks, focusing on economic and labour history from the American Civil War to the Second World War. Her findings reveal that textbooks contain ideologies, the presence of which is advantageous to particular groups within society. For example, she writes that the socialist movement at the turn of the century is either not mentioned, or downplayed or disparaged; and labour history is almost totally ignored, together with class conflict and social struggle, while the story of successful capitalists is used as an object lesson for workers: if you work hard and save money, you too can become rich.

This discussion naturally raises the question of whether there are ways to identify and elucidate ideology expressed in the language of the textbooks that form the subject of this study. Most of the examination of history textbooks has been carried out from the point of view of historians, sociologists, curriculum theorists, and specialists in education. In this book the approach will be linguistically based.

Goldhagen (1996) criticizes the historiography of the Holocaust from a linguistic point of view:

> The first task in restoring the perpetrators to the center of our understanding of the Holocaust is to restore to them their identities, grammatically by using not the passive but the active voice in order to ensure that they, the actors, are not absent from their own deeds (as in, 'five hundred Jews were killed in city X on date Y'),* and by eschewing convenient, yet often inappropriate and obfuscating labels, like 'Nazis' and 'SS men,' and calling them what they were, 'Germans.'
>
> (p. 6)
>
> * The literature's neglect of perpetrators takes more subtle form than a mere failure to focus on them. Through conscious, half-conscious, and unconscious linguistic usage the perpetrators often, and for some authors, typically, disappear from the page and from the deeds. The use of the passive voice removes the actors from the scene of carnage, from their own acts. It betrays the authors' understanding of the events and forms the public's comprehension of them, an understanding robbed of human agency.
>
> (p. 475)

In this book, my aim is to go quite a bit further along the 'linguistic road' than Goldhagen suggests.

## The linguistic analysis of ideology

Much of the history textbook debate in Japan is about whether, say, the Rape of Nanking or the issue of the sex slaves of the Japanese army, are actually mentioned or not mentioned in the textbooks, or numbers are or are not given for the Chinese dead at Nanking, and whether the numbers are the rather high figures of the Chinese government, or those of the Tokyo trials, or of post-war Japanese researchers. Much of the analysis and discussion of the textbooks is primarily content based, as shown by the Chinese and South Korean criticisms outlined above. While certainly not disparaging such content type analyses of the textbooks, it is my position that a linguistically based analysis will be more revealing about the ideology of these textbooks.

So far, I have been using the word 'ideology' without defining and delimiting it. J. B. Thompson (1990: 56) writes that '*to study ideology is to study the ways in which meaning serves to establish and sustain relations of domination*' [emphasis in original]. This definition, which brings into the picture the question of meaning and, more specifically, the question of how meanings are produced within society, influence that society, and are in turn influenced by it, is a convenient one for the critical discourse analyst precisely because its focus is on a sociological view of language.

The work of Fowler *et al.* (1979) was an early example of the use of linguistics to elucidate ideologies in texts ('texts' in this book having the meaning of any connected stretch of spoken or written language). Fairclough (1989), Hodge and Kress (1993), and Kress (1989) have also been influential in establishing what may be called a linguistics of ideology. Researchers working in the field of language and ideology have examined a range of different discourse types and different genres. In Chilton (1985), the language of the nuclear arms debate, especially as it is dealt with in the media, is analysed. The language of advertising has been examined by Cook (1992). Knowles and Malmkjær (1995) and Stephens (1992) investigate children's literature and the ideologies in such writing. Clark (1992) and Mills (1995) have examined how antiwoman ideologies are expressed in language. Barnard (2000c, 2002) shows how news stories can undergo ideological adjustment in the process of translation and editing.

In particular, critical discourse analysts (by which term I also include critical linguists) working in this tradition have been interested in pointing out ideologies that form part of seemingly neutral, disinterested, and objective discourses. Thus, Mills (1995: 12) writes that 'It is the prime focus of critical linguistics to unmask those ideologies which seem to be hidden within language-use which poses itself as natural'. Fairclough (1992: 9) refers to these seemingly neutral discourses as naturalized discourses. They are naturalized because they come to be regarded as the natural, commonly accepted, unchallenged common sense. It can even become difficult to write or speak in any other way but in the language of the particular naturalized discourse. Thus, going back to Loewen's example of 'progress', it becomes almost impossible to write about American history without progress being the dominant ideology driving the narrative forward and being the causal explanation of historical events, social movements, legal decisions, and so on.

Simpson (1993: 5), in discussing the meaning of the term ideology from the viewpoint of the critical linguist, writes that:

> From a critical linguistic perspective, the term normally describes the ways in which what we say and think interacts with society. An ideology therefore derives from the taken-for-granted assumptions, beliefs and value-systems which are shared collectively by social groups. And when the ideology is the ideology of a particularly powerful social group, it is said to be *dominant.*
>
> [emphasis in original]

An ideology obtains its strength and pervasiveness from the very fact that it is dominant, for it is precisely when we are living in the midst of a dominant ideology that it is difficult to become aware of this. We can easily see others' ideologies, but ours are not noticeable or identifiable because they have become naturalized, and are thus powerful.

Again, this takes us back to the points made by, for example, FitzGerald and Anyon above; when the dominant ideology is the ideology of a powerful group within society, it almost inevitably serves the interests of that group. When Japanese schoolchildren before and during the war were taught not history, but a racially based mythohistory centring on the divine descent of the imperial family and foundation myths of the Japanese people, together with anti-scientific views on the unique nature of the Japanese race and the sacred nature of their land (Brownlee 1997; Wray 1983), the people who were deriving benefit from this were certainly not the ordinary Japanese people themselves. Obviously not, since many of them died for a lie. Benefit was certainly derived by the Emperor, the imperial family, the various shrines and official and semi-official bodies connected with the nationally promoted Shinto religion, the aristocratic elite, those politicians and bureaucrats who owed their positions to the propagation of these myths, right-wing military factions who exploited this mytho-history to their own ends, and so on.

Broadly speaking, the linguists working in the field of critical discourse analysis discussed above, all to some extent make use of the theory and analytical techniques of systemic-functional grammar (hereafter, for the sake of brevity, referred to as 'functional grammar'). My analysis of the language of the textbooks will be very directly and closely related to this model of language. It is my aim to apply functional grammar as a tool for the critical discourse analysis (J. R. Martin 2000a) of a specific corpus, namely all history textbooks currently (the year 2002) approved for use in Japanese high schools. Critical discourse analysts working in the functional grammar field have been increasingly turning their attention to the school curriculum in recent years (e.g. J. R. Martin 1993; J. R. Martin and Veel 1998; Veel 1997). The language of school history has been the special interest of some researchers (Barnard 1998b, 2000a, 2000b, 2001; Coffin, 1997; Eggins, Wignell and J. R. Martin 1993), and it is within this area that this present work is located.

The aim in this book is to argue and demonstrate that the language of the high school history textbooks which form the subject for this study present a naturalized discourse that seems to be the common-sense, and perhaps only, way of talking about the historical events in question, but when we examine this discourse rather more carefully, it can be shown to express an ideology (or set of related ideologies) that serves various group interests within Japan.

## Functional grammar: a social view of language

Precisely because functional grammar is a theory of language use in society, it is a powerful analytical tool for looking at the specific choices of language use, and then linking these choices to social and cultural, and eventually ideological, factors. Using this model of grammar, it is also possible to argue outwards from this ideology to the political and social structures which enable this ideology to exist and to be reproduced.

Fairly detailed treatments of functional grammar can be found in Halliday (1994) and Eggins (1994). Halliday is seen as the leading functional grammarian, to such an extent that functional grammar is sometimes referred to as 'Hallidayan grammar'. Eggins is, in many places, a useful explanation or summary of Halliday. T. Bloor and

M. Bloor (1995) and G. Thompson (1996) give shorter introductory treatments. However, in order to follow the analysis of the language and the argumentation presented in this book, previous knowledge of functional grammar is not necessary.

Since Noam Chomsky seems to be the best-known living linguist, it is useful to point out the main way in which a functional approach to language is different from approaches in the Chomskyan tradition and, in so doing, highlight what a functional approach to language involves. Chomsky views the study of language as being a branch of psychology. This contrasts sharply with the Hallidayan approach, which is not a psychological, but a sociological model of language. Thus Halliday anchors almost everything he has to say about language firmly in society. It is this sociologically oriented view of language that makes functional grammar attractive to those interested in language in society, including the relationship between language, society, and ideology.

Functional grammarians see language as a type of meaning-making behaviour within society, and it is part of the job of the functional grammarian to explain the relationship between language use generally, as well as any specific instance of language use, and the social and cultural context in which this use occurs. From this view of language, there arise a number of consequences. First, it means that the importance of naturally occurring texts, rather than often artificially selected sentences and even smaller fragments of language, is explicitly recognized and the focus is turned on how these stretches of language realize overall meaning within the context in which they are used. Second, at the very core of the functional approach is the view that what is important and interesting about language is not primarily the codification of its rules, but its potential as a resource for making meaning, and as a resource for making different meanings by choosing – that is to say, a semiotic resource.

When we view language as a semiotic resource, this leads to an emphasis on paradigmatic linguistic relations, rather than syntagmatic ones. This point requires some explanation and clarification. We can think of words in any text as being in a paradigmatic relationship with other words. Thus, behind any text there is another range of potential texts that could have been produced. Thus, if I say, 'I'd like a beer', there are behind the words 'a beer' many unsaid possibilities, such as 'some beer' (which certainly is not the same as 'a beer'), 'some water/ a glass of water', 'tea/some tea/a cup of tea', and all sorts of other beverages, all in their appropriate countable and uncountable forms, or in their appropriate containers (cup, glass, carton, etc.). Also, in a similar way, behind 'I'd like' there is, for example, 'I want', which we might assume that in this particular case I rejected out of consideration of manners, the need to adopt an unassuming attitude, and so on. To take another example, if I wake up in the morning and in a voice full of surprise cry out, 'Oh, it's a beautiful day!', I am also admitting that the possibility of it not being a beautiful day existed; I am implicitly bringing the possibility of it being an unpleasant day into the range of possibilities which could exist in that particular situation. It is this 'vertical' axis of language that is termed paradigmatic. This contrasts with the syntagmatic, or horizontal axis, of language. A teacher of English as a foreign language might say to his or her students, 'Remember, we say "I think"; but in the case of "he" or "she" we must say "He or she thinks", because we have to add an "s" to the verb'. This is a syntagmatic statement about language, which is to say a statement about language on its horizontal axis.

This brings us to the third point. Once we see language as a meaning-making resource from which paradigmatic choices can be made, this raises the question of the range of meanings that language can produce with reference to any specific happening or existing in the world. For example, why is one particular form used in a certain context, or how similar, or different, are two related forms? What other choices could have been made in this situation? Or, how are vagueness or ambiguity created in language?

The fourth point concerns the meaning emphasis, over the grammar emphasis, of functional grammar. Since functional grammar privileges meaning over grammar, it follows that it focuses in all the goings-on that a text is about: the who did what to whom, and how, why and where.

Once we start to build a model of the meaning-making potential of language, we find that the traditional distinction between words and grammar disappears. This brings us to the fifth and last point, which is that functional grammar makes no theoretical distinction between grammar and words, since there is no point at which we can say words (or lexis) stop and grammar begins. Words and grammar are seen as being on a continuum, and can be given the non-technical name 'wording'. When we say something like, 'I do not understand the wording in this part of the paragraph', we are not consciously talking about grammar or lexis, and making a distinction between them. We are simply saying that we do not understand the meaning created by the way all the words in that part of the paragraph have been put together (including things like endings of verbs, singular and plural forms, etc.).

In functional grammar, the term 'wording' is technically referred to as 'lexicogrammar', but often shortened to simply 'grammar', which is the term that will be used throughout this book.

Bearing in mind the above very general theoretical overview of functional grammar, it is easy to see why such a model of grammar would be of interest to those who wish to analyse language in society, and the relationship between language and society:

a) Functional grammar is a sociological model of language with emphasis on language behaviour in society.
b) It is a grammar of extended texts, rather than a grammar of shorter segments of language.
c) It is a grammar that focuses on the range of meanings that can be made by making choices from within the language system.
d) A consideration of the choices that exist within the system of language leads us to question why particular choices have been made in any one situation, and what other choices could have been made instead.
e) It is a grammar not of a particular language, but of language as lived human experience.
f) Related to the previous point, is the fact that functional grammar tends to make sense to people, in that it accords with how they view and react to the world around them.

The discussion so far would suggest that in functional grammar we have a theory of language and a means of linguistic analysis that is capable of identifying ideology as it manifests itself in language. Throughout this book, it will be argued and demonstrated that what may be seen as a neutral use of language and the common-sense way of looking at the history is actually ideologically determined. J. B. Thompson's comment (1990: 7), quoted above that ideology is '*meaning in the service of power*' [emphasis in original] would suggest that a linguistic analysis is one way of identifying the meanings that serve to sustain power, and thereby elucidate the nature of any particular ideology, or set of related ideologies.

## *The metafunctional hypothesis*

Central to functional linguistics is the view that language is structured to make three very broad types of meaning (termed metafunctions) simultaneously (Eggins 1994; Halliday 1994). These meanings are expressed by the ideational, interpersonal, and textual metafunctions of language. The ideational metafunction expresses the happenings, the goings-on, and the existings in the world, and our thoughts about, and internal psychological reactions to, these happenings, goings-on, and existings. The interpersonal metafunction is concerned with how language enables us to communicatively interact with others, such as when we ask and answer questions, express our feelings, or interpret or confirm those of others. The textual metafunction is concerned with how language is used in order to organize language itself, by, for example, linking instances of language use to other instances of language use.

This can be illustrated in rather a simplistic way. If I wish to describe someone swimming across a river, my interest will probably be on the person swimming, the place he is swimming, the fact that he is crossing the river (not going up it or down it), and how he is doing it. I could express what I saw by saying, 'John is swimming across the river with difficulty'. This is how I might relate the events in the world to you, my listener. My focus in this case is on the who, what, where, how, etc. of the happening; in other words the ideational metafunction.

But if I say to you, 'Is that John swimming across the river?', I am using language to establish a relationship with you – one in which I ask you something and expect you to supply the information. You could reply, 'It is John, but he isn't swimming. He's almost drowning'. In this example, I am using language to establish an interpersonal negotiation with you, and you are also using language in order to enter into a negotiation with me. As a functional linguist, I might well want to look at this question, and your answer, in terms of the interpersonal metafunction. My interest could be on how I use language to establish a relationship with you, and the type of information you supply me with, and how.

Let us imagine that you were to reply in a more creative and striking way, by saying, 'John it is, but swimming he isn't. He's almost drowning.' This is very different from the more standard and normal answer given in the previous paragraph. We would certainly expect a grammar that emphasizes meaning-making within real-life contexts to be able to make this difference between the rather normal response and the 'creative' response, explicit. In this latter case, you have picked up the 'John' part and the 'swimming' part of my question, and answered in such a way as to give prominence to these two words, but in the case of 'John' confirming that it is him, while in the case of 'swimming' stressing that this is exactly what is not happening. Both your possible replies (the standard one and the creative one) link one instance of language use (i.e. my original question) to another instance of language use (i.e. your answer), in the first case in a normal and rather predictable way, but in the second case in a special and creative way. The relations between different stretches of language, often between different sentences, and such questions as how emphasis is created, are handled in terms of the textual metafunction. The textual metafunction will, within the model of grammar, make the differences between these replies, and their connection to the original question, explicit, and seek to explain why a particular reply was used in a particular case.

The picture sketched out above is complicated by the fact that the ideational metafunction is divided into two components: the experiential component and the logical component. The first of these, the experiential component, is concerned with how the meaning content of language is represented in terms of who did what to whom; the logical component is concerned with the meaning relations between the different experiential elements. To put this differently, the experiential component is concerned with what is said (or written), and the logical component is concerned with how all the things that are said are joined together to form noun phrases, clauses, or sentences consisting of several clauses.

Since, as mentioned above, language is seen as making three kinds of meanings simultaneously, it thus follows that in any text we can examine any, or all, of the metafunctions. Which ones we examine will be determined by our own interests, the purpose of our research, and such considerations as time and space. Students new to functional grammar will ask such questions as 'Is this an example of an interpersonal sentence?'. Such a way of thinking is to be avoided. A more suitable question is something like, 'For the purposes of this study, would it be useful to analyse this text from the point of view of the interpersonal metafunction?'.

In this book, the analysis will be more or less limited to the ideational metafunction. This is not to say that this is the only way to approach the language of the textbooks. Since the relationship between the writer and the reader can be viewed as being dialogic in nature, the language of the textbooks could be examined in terms of the interpersonal metafunction. With respect to the history textbook data, the manner in which textbook writers build up an air of unassailable authority, which places readers in a position from which it becomes difficult for them to question or dispute the authority of the textbooks, can be viewed as one type of communicative interaction. If I wanted to consider how the flow of an argument is constructed, or how new information is brought in to the historical narrative, or how the textbooks can make information prominent or less prominent by using different resources of the grammar (as in, 'Swimming he isn't' vs 'He isn't swimming'), my interest would be on the textual metafunction.

The main reason for focusing on the ideational metafunction (with its experiential and logical components) is in order to make this a study of manageable length, and also because it is by analysis of the ideational metafunction that the naturalized ideology of the textbooks is most clearly and readily identified.

The metafunctional hypothesis further states that experiential meaning is expressed in the system of transitivity (which is a technical term used in functional grammar, with a different meaning from 'transitive' and 'intransitive' in traditional grammar) and logical meaning is expressed in terms of the structure of noun phrases, and in terms of embedding, subordination, and coordination (Halliday 1994: 179, 180, 193–196; G. Thompson 1996: 194–211).

## *The system of transitivity*

Since functional grammar is a grammar that emphasizes meaning, rather than what is typically viewed as comprising grammar (namely grammar along the syntagmatic axis), it must make sense of all that goes on and exists in the world, and of our sensing, perceiving, and reacting to these goings-on and existential phenomena. It is through the system of transitivity and, in particular, through the process types of this system, that functional grammar imposes a conceptual order on the real world. All the existing, happening, creating, doing, behaving, sensing, meaning, being, and becoming in the world are divided into a limited and manageable number of process types.

But in order to get a total picture of the world, it is not sufficient to examine only the process types (the goings-on and existings). We must also examine the participants in the process (the who or what involved in the going-on, existing, etc.) and the circumstances associated with the process (the when, where, how, who with, where from, etc. of the going-on, existing, etc.).

The functional grammar of English divides all processes into just six types, which are explained below:

1) Material processes

    Example: John hit Mary.

    In this sentence, there are two participants ('John' and 'Mary') and a process ('hit'). If we look at these a little bit more closely, we see that one of the participants is a doer (called an Actor, namely, 'John'), and the other participant is the party to whom the doing is directed or extends (called a Goal, namely, 'Mary'), and there is a visible, concrete action or doing (called a process and, specifically in this case, a Material process). We can thus describe this sentence by the transitivity configuration of Actor + Goal + Material process. This is not the only possible transitivity configuration in the case of Material processes, since the Goal is not always obligatory, as the following sentence shows: 'I travelled all night'. In this case 'I' is the Actor and 'travelled' is a Material process, but 'all night' is clearly not a participant since no action of doing extends to it; it is in fact a Circumstance, which tells us how long the travelling continued for and, thus, is termed a Circumstance of time duration.

2) Behavioural processes

   Example: She danced beautifully.

When we look at this sentence, it does seem less 'material' than the example in 1) above and, in fact, the process is closer to a kind of behaving. We thus call the process a Behavioural process. Behavioural processes very often occur with only one participant (called the Behaver, in this case 'she', who is typically a conscious being), and are often rounded off with a word or phrase telling us about the 'how' of the Behavioural process (called a Circumstance of manner), in this case 'beautifully'. The transitivity configuration here is Behaver + Behavioural process + Circumstance of manner. Thus, the example in 1) above and this example, 2), are about different goings-on in the world, and this is captured in their different transitivity configurations.

3) Mental processes

   Example: I think that he hit Mary.

In this sentence there is a Mental process ('think') and the participant is the Senser (namely, 'I'). One important characteristic of Mental processes is that they can project another clause. In the above example, this projection ('he hit Mary') is set up by the word 'that'. The projection is a new clause and can itself be analysed, in this case, in terms of Actor + Material process + Goal. However, in the case of Mental processes, this is not the only transitivity configuration, since we can say, for example, 'I heard the sound'. In this case, in addition to the Senser, we have an additional participant, which is termed the Phenomenon (namely, 'sound').

4) Verbal processes

   Example: I will tell you my little secret.

In this case we have a Verbal process ('tell') and the participant is called a Sayer (namely, 'I'). The other participant is the receiver of the saying (namely, 'you'), and is thus called the Receiver. What is said, is also a participant, namely, the matter that is said or communicated, and is known as the Verbiage (namely, 'my little secret'). Verbal processes are similar to Mental processes in that they can also project: 'I told him that I would be late'. This is only to be expected, since expressing thoughts verbally and mentally are not all that different.

5) Relational processes

   Example: John is a bore.

In the above sentence, the participant is called a Carrier (namely, 'John') who is so named because he is 'carrying', or is endowed with, some attribute, namely the attribute of being a bore. 'A bore' also has a participant function and is known as the Attribute. The process is termed a Relational process. The grammar of Relational processes is quite complicated, with a number of sub-categories, of which this Relational process, in which one of the participants is an Attribute, is but one.

6) Existential processes

   Example: There is an old church next to the pond.

In this sentence the verb is the same as in example 5) (namely, the verb 'be'), but the sentence is not about the church being endowed with some attribute, but rather about the church existing. 'The old church' is thus a participant which is labelled Existent, and the process is an Existential process (namely, 'is'). 'There' supplies the sentence with a subject, but itself is given no participant label. 'Next to the pond', obviously, is not a participant; it is in fact a Circumstance of location. The transitivity configuration here is Existential process + Existent + Circumstance of location.

The question naturally arises as to how we know which verb is an example of a particular process. First, we appeal to common sense. Most of us intuitively know that 'hit' is material 'think' is mental, 'say' is verbal, and so on. Doubtful cases can often be resolved by looking at possible alternative verbs. Instead of the example in 6) above (There is an old church next to the pond), there could be the following sentence, with more or less similar meaning: 'There stands an old church next to the pond'. In this case, 'stand' is clearly not an example of a Behavioural process, but is more or less equivalent to 'be', and is therefore an Existential process. 'Stand', on the other hand, in a sentence like 'John stood in the corner', is an example of a Behavioural process, since it is telling us about John's behaviour. Second, we can look at the grammar itself. The fact that we can say, 'The boy is standing in the corner' (a clear example of a Behavioural process), but we cannot say, 'There is standing an old church next to the pond', since there is a general rule of English grammar that does not permit the use of Existential processes in the '-ing' form, suggests that 'stand' in the case of the church is Existential and not Behavioural.

The fact that only Verbal and Mental processes can project, as mentioned above, is another example of grammatical criteria for distinguishing verbs according to process type. Regarding the difference between 'look' and 'see', perhaps our instinctive feeling is that the former is more concerned with behaviour than the latter. In fact, the former is a Behavioural process and the latter a Mental process. This can be verified by means of checking whether these verbs can project. The fact that we can say, 'I see that it is going to rain' (an example of a projection), but cannot say, 'I look that it is going to rain', supports the categorization of these two verbs into Mental process and Behavioural process.

It is important to mention that the above is only a rough sketch of the system of transitivity. The processes above are divided into a large number of sub-categories.

The system of transitivity is less complicated than it seems at first glance. We ourselves do intuitively feel that the world of experience and existing is divided as sketched out above. In our daily lives we act like functional grammarians when we have conversations like the following, which I overheard recently:

*A*: What is another word that means the same as 'think'?
*B*: Ponder?
*A*: It doesn't quite fit into the sentence. You cannot say, 'I ponder that you are wrong'.

The point here is that 'think' is a Mental process and 'ponder' is a Behavioural process, and this is why 'ponder' cannot be substituted for 'think'. Put differently, 'ponder' cannot project, as 'think' can. Although A might not have been able to express the difference in this way, she nevertheless had a feel for a difference between the two verbs.

Linguistic analyses centring on the transitivity system and the connection between choices from this system and the meanings, including ideological meanings, created have been carried out by a number of linguists. Mills (1995: 145–149) shows that the transitivity choices in a text from a popular romance of a man and woman embracing and then kissing, throws light on who does what to whom. The male generally acts on a body part of the female (e.g. 'he kissed her mouth'), but the female more commonly acts on her own body part (e.g. 'she raised her head'). If we had sufficient data, such an approach to analysing transitivity in texts might allow us to construct a linguistically based argument that could claim, for example, that in romantic or sexual encounters in popular fiction it is not the woman as an individual human being that is valued, but her erotically attractive body parts and that, furthermore, she is frequently acted upon by the man, but seldom acts on him, and thus she is pictured as being powerless. To take some examples made up by me, the following are not all saying the same thing:

| 1 | He | kissed | her | |
|---|----|--------|-----|---|
|   | Actor | Material process | Goal | |

| 2 | He | kissed | her | on the lips |
|---|----|--------|-----|-------------|
|   | Actor | Material process | Goal | Circumstance of location |

| 3 | He | kissed | her lips | |
|---|----|--------|----------|---|
|   | Actor | Material process | Goal | |

In 3 above, (and to a lesser extent in 2) the female body has been fragmented into one of its constituent parts, which is a common technique in sexual or pornographic literature (Mills 1995: 171, 172). Mills argues that such fragmentation not only depersonalizes and objectifies the female, but, because the female is not represented as a conscious human being, her experience is written out of the text, with the focus of the text being solely a male one.

This simple example illustrates how functional grammar, in this case the system of transitivity, can provide us with a tool for analysing the meanings, and more specifically the ideologies, created by texts.

## The system of taxis

The system of taxis is concerned with how clauses are linked together. Clauses can be linked on the same level (coordination, known as paratactic relations in functional grammar), or they can be linked at different levels (subordination, known as hypotactic relations). Thus, in sentence 4 below there are two paratactic clauses, joined by 'and':

4   I opened the door and went into the room.

This is different from sentences like:

5   Opening the door, I went into the room.

6   I went into the room after I opened the door.

7   After I opened the door, I went into the room.

In the last three examples, the relationship between the clauses is a hypotactic one, with 'I went into the room' being the dominant clause in all the sentences, and the clauses ('opening the door', 'after I opened the door') being in a subordinate or lower-level relationship with it.

All four sentences could be about the exact same occurrence in the real world. But that is not to say that the meanings they make are exactly the same. To illustrate this more simply, we can consider the following two sentences, which could be about the same occurrence, or more accurately the same existing, in the real world:

8   Although Henry's English is very good, he has rather a strong German accent.

9   Although Henry has rather a strong German accent, his English is very good.

Probably for most speakers of English the meaning of number 8 is something like, 'I will concede that Henry's English is very good, but his German accent is a problem', and the meaning of number 9 is something like, 'I will concede that Henry has a strong German accent, but this is not really a problem when you consider his overall high level of English'. In number 8, the criticism of Henry's English is in the main clause ('he has rather a strong German accent') and the fact that his English is good is in the subordinate clause. If we were to delete the subordinate clause, which is present in the sentence in a less central way than the main clause, we would be left with, 'he has rather a strong German accent'. In number 9, 'his English is very good', is what we would be left with if the subordinate clause were deleted. Thus, we could argue the main message in number 8 is about his strong German accent; the main message in number 9 is about his good English. The important point is that although both sentences are about the same existing in the real world, the different grammars encode different viewpoints.

Examples 8 and 9 are examples of hypotactic clause relations. We could also express the same general idea paratactically:

10   Henry's English is very good, but he has rather a strong German accent.

11   Henry has rather a strong German accent, but his English is very good.

What are the differences in meaning here? First, in both these sentences, the good English and strong German accent seem to be more evenly balanced against each other than in the previous pair of sentences. There is, however, a difference between the meanings of these sentences, both because of the function of 'but' and because the main 'weight of meaning' seems in both cases to fall on the second clause. Therefore, in number 10, Henry's strong German accent is presented as more of a problem than in number 11, in which his good English is more strongly emphasized.

These examples and the explanations have been somewhat laboured. This is because it is important to stress that when we look at grammar and meaning closely, we almost always find that differences in the grammar reflect differences in the meaning. Or, to express this more carefully: grammar is a resource which is used creatively by speakers (and writers) to make a wide variety of meanings by choosing from a large number of possibilities from within the meaning potential of the language system. A rather naive objection to the type of analyses in this book is something to the effect that 'although these two sentences are different, everyone knows they mean the same thing'. It will be repeatedly shown throughout this book that such objections are not tenable. Indeed, if two different ways of writing about the same occurrence mean the same thing, it would be natural to expect these two ways of writing to occur with more or less equal frequency in the language of the textbooks. In fact, for much of the language analysed, this will be very far from the case.

## *Embedded clauses*

The other clause relationship to consider is that of embedding. This is a type of clause relationship outside taxis, which deals only with paratactic and hypotactic clause relations. In the case of embedded clauses, a clause is moved down to a lower rank within the grammar. Thus, 'the boy who is tall' can also be expressed as 'the tall boy'. In the former case, there is a noun phrase containing an embedded 'who' clause, and in the latter case a noun phrase containing an adjective and a noun. Nevertheless, 'the boy who is tall' and 'the tall boy' behave in the same way grammatically: simply as noun phrases that can be the subject, object, etc. of a sentence:

12  The tall boy is my friend.

13  The boy who is tall is my friend.

14  I like the tall boy.

15  I like the boy who is tall.


The preceding is an outline of the parts of functional grammar that are most relevant to the analysis of the language of the history textbooks. In this section I have attempted to explain the kind of linguistics I will be using and the potential utility of such a model and, in a sense, get as much of the linguistics out of the way as possible so that it does not clutter up the flow of the book and the development of the argumentation. It is very difficult to strike the correct balance with respect to this. Throughout this book, the linguistics will often be in the background, as it were; it will be brought in to the foreground and discussed when this is considered necessary.

## Functional grammar and Japanese

In some of my earlier work using functional grammar as a tool for critical discourse analysis (e.g. Barnard 1998b) one of the difficulties was that, at that time, there was no functional grammar of Japanese. This, itself, is not an insurmountable problem. Functional grammar is a theory of language, not a theory of the grammar of English.

In its particulars, the functional grammar of any one language will vary from that of any other language (Halliday 1994: xxxiii, xxxiv), but the overall shape of functional grammar is not language specific. Halliday sees his book as a functional grammar of English, but also, at the same time, as a functional grammar of language in general, using English as the language of illustration. If functional grammar is a theory of language in society (in other words, a sociological theory of language and not a psychological one), it follows that it is a grammar of human experience. While individual grammatical categories will differ from language to language, the general characteristics of functional grammar will be common to all languages, and this has indeed been shown to be the case with all research into other languages. It would be very surprising if we found a language in which the grammar did not organize clauses into transitivity configurations of participants, processes, and circumstances, and which had no way of expressing tactic clause relations. Rose (1996: 316), in discussing Pitjantjatjara (an Australian language) writes that 'the analysis of experience presented by the grammar of Pitjantjatjara exhibits a number of general resemblances to the English transitivity system, as described by Halliday'. In short, human beings are all broadly the same and live in broadly the same kinds of environments, so we would expect them to have adopted the same ways of reacting to this environment, including the ways in which they use language to interact with that environment.

But this is not to say that what is a Verbal process in English is a Verbal process in another language, or that all languages share the same number of process types. Teruya (forthcoming) shows that in Japanese there are four main process types (Verbal, Mental, Relational, and Material), and that one characteristic of Japanese is that Verbal processes occupy a much larger area of the semantic space than they do in English, incorporating what would be Behavioural processes in English (e.g. laugh: *warau*) and even extending into the domain of Material processes (e.g. push: *oshitsukeru*).

Thanks to recent work by Teruya on the metafunctional profile of Japanese (forthcoming) and by Thomson on the textual metafunction in Japanese (2001), we now have very good functional descriptions of important parts the grammar of Japanese.

Thomson (2001: 48) shows that in Japanese the tactic relationship is usually one of dependency (i.e. hypotaxis). Compared to English, Japanese is a very hypotactic language. The data from the textbooks support this conclusion of Thomson's. If the Japanese had been followed more closely in the translations from the textbooks which follow in this book, I would have given hypotactic translations like:

16   The Japanese army entering Nanking, a great massacre occurred.

rather than paratactic translations like:

17   The Japanese army entered Nanking and a great massacre occurred.

At times I have done so, but in general have found that such a way of translating soon irritates readers.

## A preliminary analysis

The above is nothing more than a brief look at some parts of functional grammar, and in particular those parts which will be most relevant to the analyses and discussion in this book. It is in no way intended to be systematic. All that I am interested in demonstrating at this stage is that, in functional grammar, we have a theory, as well as an extensive background of application, that provides a very useful tool for carrying out a critical discourse analysis of texts, including identifying ideologies which such texts might express, and that this theory is as equally applicable to Japanese as it is to English.

In order to make the discussion more concrete, and at last get to some actual data from the textbooks, I will informally work through three texts, while referring back to the main points of the grammar outlined above. In other words, the aim here is to show how a grammar that privileges meaning can help us find out 'what is going on' in a text.

These following examples are taken from the section of the textbooks that deal with the Mukden (Manchurian) Incident, which is generally seen to be the real beginning of the Asia-Pacific War, and are thus examples that are supplementary to the three main events investigated later on in this book.

The following example is from a textbook describing the reactions of Japanese residents (mostly colonists in one form or another) in Manchuria, who feared for their safety after the Manchurian Incident in 1931. The example is a caption and an explanation under a photograph:

**Text 1.1** (Toriumi *et al.* 2002: 131)

Hooten no zairyuu-Nihonjin no zooheiyookyuu-taikai (1931-nen 11-gatsu):
Manshuu-jihen ga boppatsu-suru to, Kantoo-gun no koodoo o shiji-suru nekkyoo-teki na yoron ga takamatta. Toku ni

Manshuu no Nihonjin-kyoryuumin no aida kara wa, teppei-hantai/zoohei-yookyuu no sakebigoe ga okori, Shidehara gaikoo no jihenfukakudai-hooshin wa kyuuchi ni tatasareta.

Translation: Rally of Japanese resident in Mukden demanding increase in military forces (November, 1931):
When the Manchurian Incident broke out, fervid public opinion supporting the operations of the Kwantung army grew stronger. In particular, loud voices of demand against the withdrawal of military forces and for an increase in military forces arose from among the Japanese residents of Manchuria, and the Shidehara diplomacy of a policy of non-escalation of the incident was placed in a difficult position.

One noticeable characteristic of this text is that there are no people who do anything. In functional terms, there are no people who are Actors, Sayers, Sensers, or Existents. Although we could certainly have a history in which people acted in various ways, in this case this is not so. The people who could be the active participants in the processes are 'swallowed up' by the grammar in various ways. So, in the caption, the Japanese who were living in Mukden did not carry out any actions or behave in some manner; it was the 'rally' (*taikai*) that was demanding an increase in military forces, and the 'Japanese [who were] resident' is modifying 'rally', telling us what kind of rally it was. Likewise, there are no people who supported the military operations of the Kwantung army, rather it was 'public opinion' (*yoron*) that supported it, and 'grew stronger' (*takamatta*). One could well imagine a history in which the Japanese residents in Manchuria demanded in loud voices that military forces be not withdrawn, but should be increased; but this is not what the text tells us happened, since the Japanese residents are a Circumstance of location (indicating motion away from a source (Teruya forthcoming)) from which emanate loud voices of demand ('loud voices of demand ... arose from among the Japanese residents'); the loud voices have their point of origin in this source and then move away from it. In functional terms, we could have a Sayer and a Verbal process ('the Japanese residents of Manchuria in loud voices demanded'), but instead have an Actor, which is not a person, but an abstract noun ('loud voices': *sakebigoe*) plus a Material process ('loud voices arose': *sakebigoe ga okori*), with no Goal since the process 'arise' (*okoru*) does not act on, extend to, or impact on anyone or anything. Shidehara (the foreign minister) did not actually do anything, nor was he even placed in a difficult position, since he figures in this text only insofar as he is modifying 'diplomacy' (*Shidehara gaikoo*) and it is this diplomacy which was placed in the difficult position. We can assume from the text that some people wanted to 'escalate' this incident (since it was presumably in response to them that Shidehara had to adopt a policy of non-escalation), but the text leaves the party or parties behind this escalation up to the reader's assumptions and common-sense interpretations.

In the clause translated as 'the Shidehara diplomacy of a policy of non-escalation of the incident was placed in a difficult position', Foreign Minister Shidehara is rather far removed from being an Actor. We could well imagine a natural sentence in which he were an Actor, such as something like: 'Foreign Minister Shidehara tried to do such-and-such, but was unable to'. The point is, although there are several ways in which Shidehara could exist in the text as a responsible human being who takes, or does not take, certain actions, none of these ways is chosen by the writers of this text.

The policy of non-escalation of the incident was placed in a difficult position. What placed this policy in the difficult position was presumably, judging from the context, the protests arising from the residents in Manchuria. This can hardly be a satisfactory explanation. Surely there must have been more important 'opinions' that exerted pressure on the Japanese government so that it could not carry out its policy of limiting the escalation of the incident, such as the interests of the Japanese-owned South Manchurian Railway, the industrial and commercial interests in Manchuria, sections of the Kwantung army, and so on.

This text is an example of historiography in which human agency and, therefore, human responsibility, has been attenuated or minimized by the grammar; in fact, it is a history in which inanimate entities drive the narrative forward. To use Goldhagen's phrase (1996: 475), this is a history 'robbed of human agency'.

Another example is useful to further illustrate the points made above, as well as to bring up some further points:

**Text 1.2** (Aoki *et al.* 1996: 281)

1931- (Shoowa 6-) nen 9-gatsu 18-nichi, Kantoo-gun sanboo
Ishiwara Kanji/Itagaki Seishiroo wa Hooten-koogai no
Ryuujooko de Mantetsu no senro o bakuha-saseta (Ryuujooko-
jiken). Soshite Kantoo-gun wa issei ni Chuugoku-gun ni koogeki
o kuwae Mantetsu-ensen no shuyootoshi o senryoo-shita

(Manshuu-jihen). 4-gatsu ni hossoku-shita dainiji-Wakatsuki-naikaku wa jihen no fukakudai-hooshin o kettei-shita ga, Kantoo-gun wa senryoochi o kakudai-shita. Shinbun nado masukomi wa gunbu no koodoo o shiji-shi, yoron o yuudoo-shi, kokumin wa haigai-netsu ni ukasareta.

Translation: On 18 September 1931 (Shoowa 6) Ishiwara Kanji and Itagaki Seishiroo, staff officers of the Kwantung army, caused an explosion of the tracks of the Manchurian Railway at Liutiaohu in the suburbs of Mukden (the Liutiaohu Incident). Then the Kwantung army, launching concerted attacks against the Chinese army, occupied the major towns along the Manchurian Railway (the Manchurian Incident). The second Wakatsuki cabinet, which had been inaugurated in April, decided on a policy of non-escalation of the incident, but the Kwantung army expanded the area of occupation. The newspapers and other media, supporting the actions of the military and guiding public opinion, the people were carried away by xenophobia.

The transitivity labelling for part of the above is given below (abbreviated for the sake of simplicity and brevity):

18  *Ishiwara Kanji/Itagaki Seishiroo wa*
Ishiwara Kanji and Itagaki Seishiroo
Actor

*Ryuujooko de*
at Liutiaohu
Circumstance of location

*Mantetsu no senro o*
the tracks of the Manchurian Railway
Goal

*bakuha-saseta*
caused an explosion
Material process

**Ishiwara Kanji and Itagaki Seishiroo caused an explosion of the tracks of the Manchurian Railway at Liutiaohu**

19  *Kantoo-gun wa*
    The Kwantung army
    Actor

    *Chuugoku-gun ni*
    against the Chinese army
    Circumstance of motion towards

    *koogeki o*
    attacks
    Goal

    *kuwae*
    launching
    Material process

    **The Kwantung army, launching attacks against the Chinese army**

20  *(Kantoo-gun wa)*
    (The Kwantung army)
    (Actor)

    *shuyootoshi o*
    the major towns
    Goal

    *senryoo-shita*
    occupied
    Material process

    **(The Kwantung army) occupied the major towns**

21  *Wakatsuki-naikaku wa*
    The Wakatsuki cabinet
    Senser

    *fukakudai-hooshin o*
    a policy of non-escalation
    Phenomenon

    *kettei-shita*
    decided on
    Mental process

    **The Wakatsuki cabinet decided on a policy of non-escalation**

42  *Introduction*

22  *Shinbun nado masukomi wa*
The newspapers and other media
Actor

*gunbu no koodoo o*
the actions of the military
Goal

*shiji-shi*
supporting
Material process

**The newspapers and other media, supporting the actions of the military**

23  *(Shinbun nado masukomi wa)*
(The newspapers and other media)
(Actor)

*yoron o*
public opinion
Goal

*yuudoo-shi*
guiding
Material process

**(The newspapers and other media,) guiding public opinion**

For me, one thing that stands out in this text is the identification of two particular individuals as Actors, but then after these two individuals have been specifically identified, after the spotlight has been turned on them, there is a blurring of human agency. To put this differently, there is no intermediate human agency between the level of specific individuals and that of the Kwantung army (Actor), the Wakatsuki cabinet (Senser), the Kwantung army (Actor), and the newspapers and other media (Actor). Furthermore, these higher level Actors or Sensers are themselves not human beings, but umbrella organizations which in some sense are made up of human beings (e.g. 'newspapers and other media'; 'the Wakatsuki cabinet'). The point I am making here is that there seems to be a disparity, on the one hand, between the two specific named individuals who carried out the acts which were the immediate cause of the Manchurian Incident and, on the other hand, the very much higher-level individuals who are not named but must bear a high level of responsibility for this, but only enter into the historical narrative through being members of umbrella organizations. If one wanted to write a history in which the Japanese government took little or no responsibility for the events that occurred in Manchuria, and if one wanted to make a very limited number of people bear this responsibility, for example as scapegoats, this is how one would write it.

Also, notice that in Text 1.2 the people themselves do not behave in a xenophobic way, but are the passive recipients of a carrying away by xenophobia, the responsibility of which is, directly, public opinion, and, indirectly the newspapers and the media; and also, in some even more indirect sense, the military. This mention of xenophobia is itself especially puzzling. It is difficult to see why xenophobia should enter the historical narrative at this time. Anyway, what is clear is that no mention is made of who the xenophobia was directed against. Was it China itself, the large majority of the people in Manchuria who were not Japanese, or Western countries?

To sum up the two above texts, they narrate a history robbed of human agency, and any deep level causation. The only actions by human beings are limited to those of the two officers who blew up the railway tracks. The actions of these two officers are presented as being the cause of the incident, without any reference being made to deeper or more fundamental causation.

Before concluding this section, I would like to look at one text from the point of clause relations:

**Text 1.3** (Kodama *et al.* 2002: 320)

1931– (Shoowa 6-) nen 9-gatsu 18-nichi, buryoku ni yoru
Manshuu no seiatsu o kuwadateta Nihon no Kantoo-gun wa
Hooten-kinkoo no Minami-Manshuu-tetsudoo no senro o
mizukara bakuha-shi (Ryuujooko-jiken), sensoo no kikkake
o tsukutte Hooten-fukin no Chuugoku-gun e no koogeki o
kaishi-shita.

Translation: On 18 September 1931 (Shoowa 6), the Japanese Kwantung army, which had been planning to gain control of Manchuria by force, having on its own blown up the tracks of the South Manchurian Railway in the suburbs of Mukden (the Liutiaohu Incident) and creating an opportunity for war, started an attack on the Chinese army in the vicinity of Mukden.

This example is useful to look at from the point of view of taxis and embedding (which from now on will be referred to as 'modification'). 'The Japanese Kwantung army' is modified by the underlined clause: The Japanese Kwantung army, <u>which had been planning to gain control of Manchuria by force</u> (*buryoku ni yoru Manshuu no seiatsu o kuwadateta Nihon no Kantoo-gun wa*). Note that in English the modifying clause comes after the noun phrase 'the Kwantung army', but in Japanese it comes before. There then follow a pair of non-finite clauses (i.e. non-main clauses) and a finite clause (main clause). This can be set out as follows, again abbreviating slightly:

24   *Nihon no Kantoo-gun wa Minami-Manshuu-tetsudoo no senro o mizukara bakuha-shi*

The Japanese Kwantung army, having on its own blown up the tracks of the South Manchurian Railway

**non-finite clause**

25   *[Nihon no Kantoo-gun wa] sensoo no kikkake o tsukutte*

[The Japanese Kwantung army,] creating an opportunity for war

**non-finite clause**

26   *[Nihon no Kantoo-gun wa] Chuugoku-gun e no koogeki o kaishi-shita*

[The Japanese Kwantung army,] started an attack on the Chinese army

**finite clause**

This example also illustrates the way clauses can be downgraded, or upgraded, by the grammar. Thus, the modifying clause translated as 'which had been planning to gain control of Manchuria by force' has been downgraded since it does not operate within the sentence at the clausal level (either hypotactically or paratactically) but simply as an element modifying the head of a noun phrase ('the Japanese Kwantung army': *Nihon no Kantoo-gun*). The two non-finite clauses could, in a different writing of this narrative, be finite clauses so, in this sense, they have also been downgraded. The last clause (the finite clause: '[The Japanese Kwantung army] started an attack on the Chinese army') is the only finite clause, so it is present in the sentence at a higher level than all the other clauses. This particular text has been written like this, but it could certainly have been written in many other different ways. For example, it would have been possible to write something like this (slightly abbreviating for the sake of clarity):

**Text 1.4** (rewritten example of 1.3)

... Kantoo-gun wa buryoku ni yoru Manshuu no seiatsu o kuwadate, Hooten-kinkoo no Minami-Manshuu-tetsudoo no senro o mizukara bakuha-shita. Kore ni yotte, sensoo no kikkake o tsukutte Hooten-fukin no Chuugoku-gun e no koogeki o kaishi-shita.

Translation: ... the Japanese Kwantung army, planning to gain control of Manchuria by force, on its own blew up the tracks of the South Manchurian Railway in the suburbs of Mukden. By means of this, the Kwantung army created an opportunity for war and started an attack against the Chinese army in the vicinity of Mukden.

In this rewritten example, the planning by the Kwantung army has been upgraded in the grammar from a modifying clause, which did not operate at the tactic level, to a non-finite clause. The 'blowing up' part of the historical narrative in the original example is present as a non-finite clause, but in the rewritten version as a finite clause, which then in the following sentence becomes a Circumstance of means ('By means of this': *Kore in yotte*) by which the Kwantung army starts the attack.

Part of my argument will be that different clause relations and different patterns of downgrading and upgrading can produce very different messages in the language of the textbooks. If we consistently find that certain types of information have been grammatically downgraded by being, for example, in modifying clauses, when they could just as well have been in other types of clauses, or that information which could be in a finite clause is consistently present in a non-finite clause, we have to enquire why these particular choices have been made.

Using the examples above, simply for the purposes of illustration and without claiming that they are, by themselves, enough to build a convincing case, my argument is that Japan itself or the political and governmental system, or the Japanese people themselves take little responsibility for any of the events or actions that took place in

Manchuria in 1931. Indeed, the role of historical participants who may be, or indeed may not be, responsible for the actions described, is obfuscated by suggesting that inanimate things act or are acted on. Even when in the texts there are actual Japanese people to whom actions or thoughts could potentially be ascribed, we find that they are frequently depersonalized. The exceptions are the two staff officers, Itagaki (executed for war crimes) and Ishiwara (died in 1949), who frequently figure in the textbooks.

The text also appears to adopt a method of writing history in which historical events are seen to occur almost in the natural flow of time, with little or no examination of causation ('the incident broke out', 'opinion grew stronger', etc.). The causation is of a triggering type of superficial surface causation: A causes B and then B causes C. In the texts above, among the reasons for the expansion of Japanese forces in Manchuria is the sabotage of a railway line and the opinions of a rally of Japanese who were resident in Manchuria. But there is surely a bigger picture here involving, for example, domestic Japanese politics and the crisis of the Japanese economy, colonialist and expansionist views held by influential sections of Japanese society, the great financial investments made in Manchuria by Japanese firms, including the South Manchurian Railway, the belief common within Japan that it was necessary for Japan to have control of the resources of Manchuria for economic growth, and so on. Actually, only two of the textbooks currently in use directly link the Manchurian Incident with these important background factors.

## Data and selection procedures

Three events within the period of the Asia-Pacific War form the main subject of this study. It is convenient to briefly outline these now:

a) The Rape of Nanking from 13 December 1937 (when the city finally fell to the Japanese army) to approximately the end of January 1938. (The duration of the Rape of Nanking is itself a subject of controversy, since it is obviously impossible to give a definite starting point and finishing point for such an event.)
b) The Japanese attacks against the Western Allies, comprising Japanese amphibious landings and military action against the British forces on the Malay peninsula, and the subsequent attack on Pearl Harbor on 8 December 1941. The explanation or justification the textbooks give for these attacks will also be examined.

c) The Japanese surrender to the Allied Powers, covering the period from 14 August (the day on which the Japanese government decided to accept the Potsdam Declaration (issued by the United States, the United Kingdom, and Nationalist China), calling for Japan's surrender) to 2 September 1945 (the day on which the instrument of surrender was signed).

In making my selection of these three events, I have been guided by my knowledge of the ideological struggles now taking place in Japan, current public debate concerning the content of history textbooks, and my background knowledge of the textbook screening procedures. For example, as shown earlier, it is not an uncommon view within Japan that the war Japan fought was an unavoidable one of self-preservation. It therefore makes sense to look at the language describing Japan's attacks and the causal explanations, including justification, for these attacks. The language of the Rape of Nanking should also be looked at since, as pointed out by Fogel (2000: 2), it has achieved the status of a 'metonymy' for Japanese aggression in China. The Japanese surrender, an act that led to the collapse of the imperial state, and that set the stage for the new, modern Japanese state is also of crucial significance.

Studying the attacks and surrender also opens up the possibility of carrying out a comparative analysis with the language used to refer to German actions, since Germany also carried out an attack and surrendered to the Allies.

The actual data for this study comprise the 55 officially approved history textbooks currently being used in Japanese high schools. Of these books, 29 are world history textbooks and 26 of them Japanese history textbooks. Given the fact that the events in question are seen both as a part of world history, and as a part of Japanese history, and that all the 55 textbooks deal with all the events, I will approach this as one corpus. My interest is thus on the general totality of meanings produced by all the textbooks, considered as one corpus. In one sense, an indirect question being addressed is: What meanings, created by the language of the textbooks, find their way into Japanese high school history classrooms?

The 55 textbooks are published by a total of 11 publishers, with 12 of the textbooks being published by one publisher. The textbooks almost always come in B5 or A5 size, and are about 230 pages in the former case and 350 pages in the latter case. Textbooks are generally all rather alike in general design and layout. They have very beautifully designed, with colourful soft covers, with several pages of coloured maps, photographs and time charts in the front and back. The body of the book is more austere and business-like, with text and other material on the pages being rather dense and serious looking. Almost every page has one or more footnotes (or marginal notes); maps, photographs and other illustrative material are in black and white.

The textbooks have multiple authorship; seven or eight authors is rather a common number, but sometimes there are as many as 15. The majority of these authors are university professors, with a much smaller number of high school teachers.

There is no flag-waving nationalism in either the illustrations or the titles of the textbooks. In fact, the textbooks having titles equivalent to 'New World History', 'World History', 'World History B (new revised edition)', 'New Japanese History B', etc., means that it becomes almost impossible to distinguish the textbooks solely by their titles.

The discussion and analysis of these 55 textbooks is informed by my previous work on a larger database of 88 textbooks (Barnard 1998b, 2000a, 2000b, 2001) which no longer form the current officially approved set. However, there is a very great degree of similarity between these two sets of textbooks, with particular books in the current set being revised versions in the earlier set.

The previous set of 88 could certainly have been used for this study, and the conclusions arrived at would have been much the same, since one characteristic of the textbooks that will become clear as they are examined is the great similarity among them. They consistently present the same information in the same order, use the same photographs and illustrations, and in very many places use identical or nearly identical language. This is the case even when the publishers are different. Nevertheless, in order to present the most up-to-date material, the data have been limited to the current set.

In a project such as this, the author is free to select the data that support his or her position, while excluding data that do not. The author is thus open to the charge of hunting around in the data in order to select examples that conveniently support his or her position. In consideration of this, the following procedure has been adopted. In selecting the material from the textbooks that is discussed in each chapter, 13 textbooks from among the Japanese history textbooks and 14 from the world history textbooks have been randomly selected (using a playing-card shuffling machine with the number assigned to each textbook written on a card). After making this random selection, and discarding one (or more) of a pair (or more) of the books that use exactly or almost exactly the same language, I have then selected from the remaining textbooks (say 18 or so) those textbooks which contain texts that are relevant to, and conveniently illustrate, the point being discussed (say 8 or so textbooks), and then used material from these textbooks in my presentation of data and argument. This procedure has, at times, prevented me from developing the argument in exactly the direction desired and, at other times, has meant that the example which best illustrates the point being made cannot be used. But, generally, given the great similarity in the language of the textbooks, this procedure of initial random selection followed by that of choice has not been a serious inconvenience. At a few points in this book, in order to make a specific point, texts have been purposefully selected. In such cases, this is made clear by using the words 'purposefully selected'. When statistical data relevant to the whole corpus are given, this naturally means that each individual textbook has been examined.

The selection procedure explained above has meant that texts from 20 of the 55 textbooks (i.e. approximately 36 per cent) are discussed in some detail in this book. Of these 20 textbooks, 8 of them deal with world history and 12 with Japanese history. Of the 11 publishers, selections from 8 of them (approximately 70 per cent) are discussed. It therefore seems fair to claim that the language data analysed in detail in this book provide a very reasonable coverage of the corpus, and that conclusions drawn from these 20 textbooks are applicable to the corpus as a whole. Further strengthening this position is the fact that statistical data for the whole corpus are also presented.

## Overview of the rest of the book

In this book, using functional grammar as a tool, the ideology encoded in the language of Japanese high school history textbooks is examined, and it is shown that these textbooks encode a naturalized ideology which can be divided into two components. First, there is what is termed an ideology of *irresponsibility*, which to a certain extent absolves the Japanese state of 1945 and its lineal successor, the Japanese state of today, as well as Japanese military personnel, for aggressive actions and atrocities committed during the period in question. Second, there is an ideology of *face-protection*, which minimizes the threats to the face of the Japanese state that occurred at the time of the Japanese surrender. When referring to the ideology of the textbooks in general the word 'ideology' will be used in the singular; when it is necessary to stress the subcomponents of this ideology, or to separate the ideology or

50  *Introduction*

irresponsibility and face-protection, the plural form, 'ideologies', will be used.

The following are some of the strange, surprising, and indeed unbelievable, things that an examination of the textbook language reveals:

(1) The fact that although, according to the textbooks, there are Chinese soldiers, Chinese civilians, American people, foreign (i.e. non-Japanese and non-Chinese) journalists, etc. in Nanking at the time of the Rape, Japanese soldiers, with one exception, disappear from the pages of the textbooks – and therefore from the historical record. The textbooks rather clearly tell us who the victims of the atrocity were, but are very reticent and cagey about telling us who the perpetrators were. It will be argued that one effect of this way of writing history is that it makes it difficult for pupils to critically respond to denials of the Rape of Nanking which are so common in modern-day Japan.

(2) The fact that there is not one single example in all the 55 textbooks of Japan attacking another *country* in 1941. It will be argued that this cannot simply be explained away in terms like 'this is how history is written', etc., but can be related to the question of to what extent the present Japanese state is willing and ready to take responsibility for the actions of its predecessor, and to what extent such a way of writing history minimizes the aggressor role of Japan in 1941 – and thereby fits in with the view (which is still widely held today among influential sections of Japanese society) that Japan waged a war of colonial liberation and self-defence. As a preliminary to the section dealing with the Japanese attack, I also discuss one of the explanations, bordering on actual justification, that the textbooks often give for the attack, namely that Japan was being strangled by the economic embargo of the ABCD countries (American, British, Chinese, Dutch). This of course brings us back to the war-as-self-defence argument.

(3) The fact that the surrender of Japan is not directly and forthrightly recorded in the language of a large majority of the textbooks, but a set of grammatical resources are used to actually make it disappear from the narrative or downplay it in various ways, including slipping it in to the narrative through the back-door, as it were. It is argued that this is one means by which the face of the Japanese state is protected.

(4) The fact that the grim reality of the Japanese surrender, together with the needless prolongation of the war, almost completely disappears

from the textbooks, and what we very often have in its place is a stressing of the responsible, statesman-like behaviour of Japan's leaders at the time of the surrender, and the picturing of the surrender as grave ceremonial occasion, rather than, as it was, a national humiliation. Again, the argument will be made that this is another example of an attempt by the textbooks to protect the face of the state.

(5) At several important points in the development of the argument, comparisons will be made with the language of the textbooks as they refer to German actions and Japanese actions. So, just to take one example, it will be shown how the German attack against Poland is regularly expressed in the main verb of the sentence (and thus, I will argue, in what tends to be the main information carrying element of the sentence) but the Japanese attack is expressed at lower levels of the grammar. The argument will be that these consistent differences in the grammar of the texts create messages that are ideologically very different, and the overall effect is to downplay the aggressor role of Japan. This comparison is also used to argue against the 'genre objection' to the analysis (see page 52 below).

Finally, in the concluding chapter, I will argue out from the meanings expressed by the grammar to the ideologies these meanings encode, and seek to link the persistence of these ideologies to social structures (including governmental and bureaucratic structures) within the modern Japanese state.

To argue out from the language to the wider society is by no means an easy task. Nevertheless, what does make this task somewhat easier is the fact that there is one central organization within Japan that is in control of history textbooks, namely, the Ministry of Education. If the ministry insists on authorizing the textbooks, it seems natural that it must take responsibility for the language they use. All roads lead to the Ministry of Education, as it were.

## Potential objections

By now I hope that readers appreciate that this study is not about whether what is in the textbooks is true, or not true – it is about *how* the material is presented. As Simpson (1993: 2) writes: 'The elusive question of the "truth" of what a text says is not an issue here; rather, it is the "angle of telling" adopted in a text'.

There are at least three objections to the kind of approach undertaken in this book. The first of these is what will be referred to as the 'genre objection' or the 'genre argument', namely, the language of the textbooks reflects nothing more than how history is written, and therefore much of the analysis and argumentation which claims there is a particular ideology in the textbooks confuses genre with ideology. This objection can be answered in two ways, both of which I will do in this book: by producing a cumulative wealth of data in order to present a persuasive argument against the genre objection; by producing comparative data (say, comparing similar Japanese and German actions) that show the genre argument does not stand up to examination, since similar kinds of Japanese and German actions are written about in very different ways.

The second objection, which has been mentioned previously, is that in the case of sentences like 'loud voices of demand for an increase of military forces arose from among the Japanese residents of Manchuria' far too much is being read into such sentences. Anyone who reads this text will know that this expression is the same as 'the Japanese residents loudly demanded an increase in military forces'. But once one regards language as a semiotic system, as a system of choosing from within all the meaning-making potential of language, it follows that choices create different meanings according to the situation in which the user of the language finds himself or herself at any particular moment. In other words, between a particular context in which language is used and the actual instance of language use there is a wide range of choice available to the language user. Matthiessen and Bateman (1991: 128) make the point that 'A fundamental assumption of systemic-functional linguistics is that variation in language, unless proved otherwise, carries functional loads that require description'. Adopting this position, I would certainly reject the view that these variations mean the same thing. If we do accept that this choice is not meaningful or think it not worthwhile to seek to explain it, this means that we have no way in which we can link language and the situation in which it is used, but it is precisely this linkage that is at the core of all language use, since, as I have already mentioned, language is the means by which we encode all the happenings and existings in the real world, and our perceptions of these happenings and existings.

Whether or not the choice is conscious is a different matter. In most cases of language used in casual, daily life it will often not be conscious. However, in the case of the textbooks, which have undergone many careful rewritings, have been issued in new editions over the years, and are written with the knowledge that they will have to be submitted to the Ministry of Education for authorization, the amount of conscious choice is very great.

Furthermore, even if this objection could be sustained with reference to one or a few short texts, when we look at a large number of texts and find that the same kinds of meanings are being produced by common patterns of language throughout the textbooks, this suggests that what we have is language being used for ideological purposes. If 'loud voices of demand arose from among the Japanese residents' is the same as 'the Japanese residents loudly demanded', we would expect to see both these expressions used in the textbooks. If we find that one of the expressions is being overwhelmingly used and not the other, this would suggest that the two expressions do not mean the same thing, and that the difference in meaning is worth investigating.

The last objection is that, in looking at, say, the texts dealing with the Manchurian/Mukden Incident, I was doing what any relatively perceptive person could do. In fact, all I am doing is dressing up common sense in fancy linguistic garb. This objection does not hold up for the following reasons:

(1) The approach taken in this book is one in which the meanings created by the texts are explained by reference to a model of language. The analysis is not subjective and personal. Rather, the means by which the language is analysed is clearly stated. The use of such an approach, namely, one of specifying and clarifying the analytical procedures and the method of argumentation, allows those who may want to look at the same data a chance to analyse it using the same, or a different, model of grammar to argue against the analyses and conclusions. My position follows Halliday (1994: xvi, xvii), who writes that:

> A discourse analysis that is not based on grammar is not an analysis at all, but simply a running commentary on a text: either an appeal has to be made to some set of non-linguistic conventions, or to some linguistic features that are trivial enough to be accessible without a grammar, like the number of words per sentence . . .; or else the exercise remains a private one in which one explanation is as good or as bad as another.

The discourse analyst, by allowing others to reach different conclusions based on an explicitly stated grammar, avoids sterile and inconclusive 'my interpretation vs your interpretation' type arguments.

(2)   The approach taken is to both look at the system of language itself, and also to look at the particular instances of language use (namely the texts themselves). It is only when we do this that we can compare one text with another or 'with what it might itself have been, but was not' (Halliday 1994: xxii).

(3)   Functional theory is rather well developed and has been successfully applied to a considerable number of languages and genres, so it has in this sense had its field trials.

## 2 The Rape of Nanking
Processes and participants

In the literature in English on Japanese history textbooks, the claim is often made that censorship by the Ministry of Education ensures that Japanese atrocities do not figure in the textbooks – that, for example, the Rape of Nanking is 'officially killed by silence' (Buruma 1994: 115). The inside cover of Chang's book, *The Rape of Nanking* (1997), states that 'the Japanese have tried for years to erase [the Rape of Nanking] from public consciousness', and, even more inaccurately, 'Amazingly, the story of this atrocity – one of the worst in world history – continues to be denied by the Japanese government'. Gerow (2000: 74) writes that: 'Anyone familiar with Ienaga Saburoo's court case is aware that the Ministry of Education has in the past consistently opposed including any discussion of Japanese war atrocities in school texts'.

Although this view of Japanese history textbooks has become rather widely accepted, it is incorrect. Looking at the space the high school history textbooks devote to the Rape of Nanking and comparing it with the space devoted to other events, it is true to say that as much space is given it as could possibly be desired. To the extent that these textbooks include 'discussion', rather than just a presentation of the 'facts', the discussions on Nanking are often quite satisfactory.

But an examination of the textbooks shows that the language used in relating the events that took place at Nanking is in certain specific ways extremely circumspect. When we examine this circumspect use of language in detail, the existence of a naturalized ideology becomes clear. The question, then, is of a far more subtle nature than material simply being present or not present in the textbooks. The material is almost always there, the question that needs to be addressed is: How is it there? In other words, I am interested in what Simpson (1993: 2), quoted previously, calls the 'angle of telling'.

56  *The Rape of Nanking*

In this chapter the focus will be on the processes and participants in the textbook narratives of Nanking. It will be argued that the way the textbooks write about the Rape of Nanking is an example of a naturalized ideology, and one which contributes to the deniability of the Rape within modern Japanese society.

## Historical background

On 13 December 1937, Nanking, the capital of the Nationalist Chinese Government, fell and Japanese troops entered the city. Although, as previously mentioned, some Japanese, often influential ones in the political, bureaucratic, academic, and journalistic fields, hold the view that the Rape of Nanking is a fabrication (e.g. Matsumura 1998; Nakamura 1990: 430–456), or at least a gross exaggeration, it is generally recognized that an atrocity did take place in Nanking. Nevertheless, there is still controversy today regarding the extent of that atrocity and the degree to which it was either planned or encouraged by those in authority. (See, for example, Askew 2002: 77–82; Buruma 1994: 112–135; Chang 1997; McCormack 1996: 227–229, 236–237; Nozaki and Inokuchi 2000: 96–126 for discussions of the Nanking controversy in modern Japan.)

Regarding the first point, there are widely differing figures, often based on different methods of calculation, for those killed in and around Nanking at this time; low figures are in the tens of thousands; Chinese sources give figures as high as 300,000. Bergamini (1971: 44) writes that at least 200,000 men murdered (at least a quarter of them civilians) is the figure accepted by the International Military Tribunal for the Far East. Calvocoressi *et al.* (1995: 803) suggest a figure somewhat less than 250,000 dead. Ienaga (1978: 186) describes the horror:

> The documents and testimony prepared by the International Committee for the Nanking Safety Zone, organized by neutral foreigners and by other unbiased observers and survivors, tell a ghastly tale of mass slaughter. Tens of thousands of Chinese – prisoners of war, stragglers who had discarded their weapons and mingled with civilians, women and children – were massacred. Countless women were raped. Stores and homes were systematically plundered and burned.

Regarding the second point, whether the Rape was planned, or at least abetted, by the Japanese authorities, Calvocoressi *et al.* (1995: 803) write that: 'The massacre was done for the most part by Japanese conscripts, unfamiliar with war, perhaps neurotically working out of their system the extreme repressions in which they had passed so much of their lives'.

Even Ienaga (1978: 187), who is generally highly critical of the Japanese army and sympathetic to the Chinese, writes that the Rape of Nanking may have been a reaction to the fierce resistance the Japanese army had up to then been receiving from the Chinese.

## Analysis and discussion

The following extract from a textbook seems to be a rather reasonable portrayal of the Rape of Nanking:

**Text 2.1** (Nitani *et al.* 2002: 138)

Nankin o kanzen ni hooi-shite Chuugoku-gun o senmetsu-saseru sakusen o totta Nihon-gun wa, 12-gatsu 13-nichi ni Nankin o senryoo-shi, hikitsuzuite shinai no sootoo-sen o okonotta. Kono aida ni Nihon-gun wa tairyoo no horyo ya shimin o gyakusatsu-shita no o hajime, fujo e no bookoo, hooka/ryakudatsu nado zangyaku-kooi o kurikaeshita (Nankin-daigyakusatsu)*.

*Nankin-daigyakusatsu wa, Nankin ni todomatte ita gaikokujin no hoodoo ni yotte hayaku kara kaigai de wa shirasare, 'Nankin-atoroshitiizu' (gyakusatsu) toshite sekai no hinan o abita ga, tooji no Nihon-kokumin ni wa issai shirasarenakatta.

Translation: The Japanese army, which had completely invested Nanking and had adopted a strategy of annihilating the Chinese army, on 13 December occupied Nanking, and following this carried out mopping-up operations in the city. During this time, the Japanese army above all killed great numbers of prisoners-of-war and citizens, and repeated the cruel acts of raping women, arson, plunder, and so on (the Great Nanking Massacre)*.

*The Great Nanking Massacre was soon made known overseas by the reports of the foreigners who had remained in Nanking, and as the 'Nanking Atrocities' (massacre) received worldwide criticism, but the Japanese of the time were not informed of this at all.

In this textbook, the section on Nanking is four lines long, and the marginal notes are the equivalent of three lines of main text. This certainly shows that there is no cover-up of Nanking in the sense that information is not present. It is not difficult to read this narrative of the atrocities that took place at Nanking and be persuaded that it is a reasonable telling of history. All the main points seem to be in the text: the date, the atrocities, who the atrocities were directed against, the international reaction, and so on. However, a careful reading of all the textbooks reveals a writing of history which is extremely circumspect. This circumspection is examined below under the headings of absence of perpetrators, locating the knowledge of Nanking, types of criticism, naming the atrocity, and semantically neutral verbs.

## *Absence of perpetrators*

A more careful reading of Text 2.1 reveals a pattern that is common throughout the textbooks. The victims of the atrocities are rather carefully described. If one were to pick up at random half-a-dozen of these textbooks one would soon learn that surrendered soldiers, prisoners of war, women, children, citizens of Nanking, and so on, were killed. In contrast, if we try to find out who the perpetrators were, we notice that they only exist at the organizational level ('the Japanese army'), and thus are faceless. There is some disparity here. After all, it would be perfectly natural to say that Japanese soldiers killed Chinese people. We would at least expect such a writing of history to exist in some reasonable number of the textbooks. But this is not the case – in not one single textbook is it stated that Japanese *soldiers* killed Chinese people. The textbooks relate a history in which an organization commits atrocities against individuals. In functional grammar terms, the Actor in the Material process of massacring is an organization, but the Goal of the process is made up of individuals.

The following text has been purposely selected from a textbook, of which Ienaga is one of the authors. This section of this textbook is almost identical to Ienaga's *Shin Nihonshi* (1964), which was reprinted and issued in new editions for many years, but which is no longer in print, which, as far as I can ascertain (Nozaki and Inokuchi 2000: 96–126), is the same textbook that had long been the object of dispute between the Ministry of Education and Ienaga:

**Text 2.2** (Ienaga *et al.* 2002: 281)

Nihon-gun wa Nankin senryoo no sai, tasuu no Chuugoku-gunmin o satsugai-shi, Nihon-shoohei no naka ni wa bookoo ya ryakudatsu nado o okonau mono mo sukunaku nakatta. Nankin-daigyakusatsu to yobareru.

Translation: The Japanese army, during the occupation of Nanking, killed a large number of Chinese soldiers and civilians, and among the Japanese officers and men, also those who carried out rape, pillage, and the like were not a few. This is called the Great Nanking Massacre.

Actually, this is the only textbook that puts Japanese perpetrators in the text at the non-organizational level (i.e. as 'Japanese officers and men'). But when we look at this text closely we find that the presence of Japanese soldiers in this text, and the actions they carry out, are highly attenuated or downplayed by the grammar.

What immediately strikes the reader about this text, in both the English translation and the original Japanese, is the great awkwardness of the language. In the first sentence, which is of rather average length, we find that 'Japanese soldiers' occur in three different guises, but never simply as 'Japanese soldiers' – the normal and expected way we would expect their presence to be recorded. These guises are: Japanese soldiers expressed as 'Japanese army' (*Nihon-gun*), the slightly military term 'Japanese officers and men' (*Nihon-shoohei*), and 'those' (*mono*).

I have seen loose English translations of this particular text. In these translations the rape and pillage is attributed to 'the Japanese officers and men'. This is not what the text says at all. The 'officers and men' are a Circumstance of location within which the 'those' exist, as is clear if we label for transitivity. The transitivity configuration of this sentence has to be analysed at two levels. The labelling of the first clause, which modifies 'those' (*mono*), is as follows:

1   *Nihon-shoohei no naka ni wa*
    Among the Japanese officers and men
    Circumstance of location

   *bookoo ya ryakudatsu nado o*
   rape, pillage, and the like
   Goal

> *okonau*
> carry out
> Material process
>
> *[mono]*
> [those]
> ----
>
> **Among the Japanese offices and men [those] who carried out rape, pillage, and the like**

The noun phrase, of which 'those' is the head, then functions as an Existent, with the process being an Existential one (Teruya forthcoming), as shown here:

2  > ... *mono mo*
> also those [who did such-and-such]
> Existent
>
> *sukunaku nakatta*
> were not a few
> Existential process
>
> **also those [who did such-and-such] were not a few [literally: also those existed in a not small number]**

To summarize, the text is not about Japanese officers and men carrying out heinous acts. Some very vaguely defined 'those' are the party who carried out these heinous acts; the presence of 'officers and men' in this text serves as the location in which the 'those' can be placed. This is a very different matter from the officers and men carrying out the heinous acts.

Sometimes, when carrying out a critical discourse analysis of a text, we find that the writer seems to have put a lot of effort into some part of the text. This is often a hint to the analyst that that part merits special attention. The effort we see being put into this one sentence is primarily in terms of the repetition of 'Japanese soldiers' in three different guises, but not in the most straightforward form, 'Japanese soldiers'. This effort is an example of what Fairclough (1989: 115) calls 'overwording', when he writes that:

> We sometimes have 'overwording' – an unusually high degree of wording, often involving many words which are near synonyms.

Overwording shows preoccupation with some aspect of reality – which may indicate that it is a focus of ideological struggle.

It seems likely that what we have here is the result of a series of compromises between Ienaga and the Ministry of Education regarding how to portray Japanese soldiers as guilty of a range of heinous and shameful acts: the Japanese soldiers are sort of in the text, but then, on the other hand, they are not really there if we look at the text more closely.

Then, we also have the effort put, not into repetition, but into the inflections of the Japanese adjective ('be a few': in its basic form *sukunai*), 'were not a few' (*sukunaku nakatta*), a wording that uncomfortably sticks out in the Japanese sentence as it does in the English translation.

It is hard not to conclude that this sentence is bending this way and that way to avoid saying 'Japanese soldiers' carried out pillage and rape, but at the same time gets as near to saying this as possible, without actually saying it. Not only is there this avoidance of the term 'Japanese soldiers', but the nature of the atrocity is played down in the way the different acts of atrocity are distributed around the sentence in various ways. The most general act (that of killing a large number of Chinese soldiers and civilians) is attributed to the Japanese army, but the act of rape is downgraded in the grammar by virtue of being present in a modifying clause ('those who carried out rape'), by being carried out by a very vague, non-specific noun ('those'), and by the 'those' being present in some vaguely defined number (less than 'many' but more than 'a few').

The heinous act of killing people is a depersonalized act that takes place in war, perhaps in the heat of battle, or even if it involves planned killing of individuals (who may even have surrendered), this is often difficult to prove and easy for any one particular soldier to deny. Even if civilians are killed by a soldier, it is rather easy for that soldier to offer plausible explanations, such as to claim the civilian was a guerrilla, and so on. Rape, by its very nature, is an individualized, personalized act, which, in some sense, is more shameful and far less easily excusable than killing the enemy, or killing men who might be soldiers dressed as civilians. Interestingly, what we find in the above text (Text 2.2) is that the more easily explicable and excusable heinous act of killing soldiers and civilians is attributed to the all-encompassing, organizational term 'Japanese army'. When it comes to the act of rape, this is attributed to the vague 'those' (*mono*), who the text portrays as existing in some vaguely defined number.

To examine, and at least try to understand, an atrocity we have to look at the motivation of the people who perpetrated the atrocity. Looking closely at the victims may give the impression that the horrific details are being dealt with. But actually, to look closely at only the victims diverts attention from the perpetrators. The victims are, in a sense, victims because of bad luck – anyone, anywhere can be a victim. But killers and rapists, on the scale on which killing and rape occurred at Nanking, are not produced by bad luck. They are surely products of particular societies, cultures, educational systems, or political systems.

To say that the 'Japanese army' did such-and-such is to obfuscate the issue. What kind of soldiers committed the atrocity? Were they conscripts, volunteers, seasoned fighters, elite troops? Were they hungry, or drunk? Were they from particular parts of Japan? Had they been in China long? Had they been taught to despise the Chinese? Was the Japanese army one in which the officers could not control their men? What kinds of people were in positions of authority in Nanking?

To give answers to these kinds of questions would ensure that the Japanese soldiers who committed the atrocity and their Chinese victims would be in the pages of history in approximately the same detail.

### Locating the knowledge of Nanking

In Text 2.1 above also, there is a part of the grammar into which a lot of effort has been put. For me, at any rate, what jumps out from the above text is the 'was not made known' (*shirasarenakatta*). This is derived from the verb *shiru* ('know'), which has then been turned into a causative ('make known'), which has then been passivized ('is made known') and negativized ('is not made known'), and, since we are dealing with a historical event, it has been obligatorily put in to the past tense ('was not made known'). This verb itself is preceded by an adverbial expression (*issai*) which emphasizes the negative element ('was not made known *at all*'). In the textbooks, the historical narrative does not generally, perhaps hardly ever, involve verbs with such complex inflections – verbs into which such great effort has been put.

By picking up on this use of language, we can then start to ask some interesting questions about the text. For example, does it make sense to say that the events at Nanking were not made known to the Japanese people when the perpetrators of the Rape of Nanking were themselves Japanese? Also, there must have been many Japanese within Japan, who because of their positions of authority or access to accurate information from the front in China, knew about what happened at Nanking (see Bix 2000: 336). Surely also there must have been some leakage from the perpetrators of the Rape to their colleagues, families, and so on back in Japan. There were many Japanese journalists in and around Nanking at the time of the Rape. When their stories and photographs came back to Japan, what happened to them? Weren't they censored by the authorities in Japan? There must have been various elites in Japan who knew about the Rape. Hirohito's uncle by marriage, Prince Asaka, was the commander on the ground in Nanking when the troops entered the city. Didn't he tell anyone what happened? Indisputably, Japanese people, including almost all the Japanese people in Nanking, and at least some Japanese people in Japan and elsewhere, knew about the Rape, or were informed about it. Y. Yoshida (1999: 28–37) discusses who knew about what happened at Nanking, and concludes that the knowledge at the time was far more widely spread in Japan than was claimed after the war, and argues that, while there is no definite proof, it is not unlikely that Hirohito himself knew about the Rape of Nanking. Instead we get a solid wall of ignorance built up between the Japanese people and the knowledge of Nanking.

In historical writing, as in many other forms or writing, it is normal to avoid categorical statements which admit to no exception whatsoever. It cannot be literally true, and certainly cannot be verifiable, that the Japanese people were not informed about the Rape of Nanking *at all*. The authors who wrote this were surely not wearing their historians' hats at the time. Such a categorical negative seems rather out of place in historical writing concerned with the dissemination and state of people's knowledge more than 60 years ago.

Furthermore, by using this 'make known' (*shiraseru*) in its passive form, the authors are spared the task of telling us who was responsible for not conveying this information. In other words, a potential Sayer has disappeared from the historical narrative. Why does this text tell us the means by which the incident was made known internationally (i.e. by the reports of the foreigners who were in Nanking), but does not tell us the means by which the incident was not made known to the Japanese people? It seems to me that what we have hidden below the surface of this text is 'the military and governmental authorities covered up/tried to cover up the events at Nanking from various sections of the Japanese population'. This is a crucial point, because once we, or one hopes pupils using the textbook, realize that there was someone or some organization which tried to cover up the facts about the Rape of Nanking, then it becomes possible to critically respond to denials within modern Japanese society that this atrocity did not take place.

Examining Text 2.1 above from the point of view of the location of knowledge of Nanking, an interesting pattern reveals itself. The text tells us that the possessors of the knowledge of Nanking were: the people 'overseas' (but presumably excluding any Japanese who were overseas), and 'the foreigners who had remained in Nanking'; the people who certainly did not possess knowledge of Nanking were 'the Japanese of the time'. This strains credibility.

Part of the denial of Nanking in modern-day Japan (either the occurrence of the atrocity itself, or its scale) centres around the argument that it could not have happened since the people in Japan at the time did not know about it; that Japanese only knew about it after the war, at the Tokyo trials (see Fujiwara's reply to this argument (1999: 14–25)). Y. Yoshida (1999: 28) writes (my translation) that:

> Among the deniers of the Nanking Incident, there are those who strongly argue that at the time no one knew about the Nanking Incident, and therefore the incident itself never occurred. For example, the 'classic work' on the denial of the massacre, Tanaka Masaaki's 'The Fabrication of the "Nanking Massacre"' [' *"Nankin-gyakusatsu" no kyokoo'*] ... states that it was at the postwar Tokyo trials that the Japanese first knew about the incident.

The following (which is drawn from a detailed footnote, rather than the main text) deals with post-war knowledge of the Nanking atrocities:

**Text 2.3** (Tsurumi *et al.* 2002: 318)

Nihon-gun wa, senryoo-ji no suushuukan ni, sentooin bakari de naku, josei/kodomo o fukumu hisentoo-in ya buki o suteta heishi o mo gyakusatsu-shita. Satsugai-sha wa 20-man-nin ijoo to iwareru ga, Chuugoku de wa sono kazu o 30-man-nin ijoo to shite iru. Nao, kooshita gyakusatsu/hakai/ryakudatsu nado no kooi wa, tooji tsuyoi kokusai hihan o abita. Shikashi, ippan no Nihonjin ga kono jiken no koto o shitta no wa, sengo no Kyokutoo-kokusai-gunjisaiban ni yotte de atta.

Translation: The Japanese army, in the several weeks of the occupation [of Nanking], killed not only combatants, but also non-combatants, including women and children, and soldiers who had laid down their weapons. Those killed are said to be more than 200,000, but in China that figure is reckoned to be more than 300,000. Moreover, such acts of massacre, destruction and pillage at the time received strong international criticism. However, it was due to the post-war International Military Tribunal for the Far East that ordinary Japanese people knew about this incident.

This example seems to me more reasonable in that there is not a complete categorical denial (as in Text 2.1) that Japanese people did not know about the atrocity. There is no definition of 'ordinary Japanese people' (*ippan no Nihonjin*), but at least the possibility that certain people in Japan knew about this atrocity is left open. But again, of course, there must have been some leakage of information from the not ordinary Japanese people (including, presumably, the Japanese soldiers in Nanking) to the ordinary Japanese people.

When we look at who actually, according to the textbooks, have knowledge of what happened at Nanking, we find that the people who the textbooks depict as having detailed knowledge of the atrocities in almost all cases can be assumed to be anti-Japanese. Thus in Text 2.1 above the 'foreigners' presumably refers to the mostly American journalists, doctors, and missionaries who were in Nanking at the time. In Text 2.3, the textbook suggests that the knowledge of Nanking was common knowledge internationally (but not within Japan) and then only became common knowledge within Japan at the Tokyo war crimes trial. This was held by the victors, and the judges were drawn from the Allied countries, so the trials can be assumed to be anti-Japanese in character – nothing more than victors' justice. In fact, the criticism that these trials served the purpose of vengeance rather than that of seeking justice is a position widely accepted both inside and outside Japan (Bergamini 1971: 47: Minear 1972). Therefore, by locating the revelation of knowledge of Nanking in what can very reasonably be argued were biased legal proceedings, this text gives those who claim that there was no major atrocity at Nanking good grounds for denying the atrocity.

Together with the knowledge of Nanking being attributed to anti-Japanese foreigners, it is not attributed to either Japanese people or Chinese people who were the witnesses of the events. (Exceptions to this are two textbooks by the same publisher which quote the same diary entry from a Japanese soldier at Nanking.) This is truly remarkable. The participants of the atrocity, the owners of the knowledge of the atrocity, as it were, are overwhelmingly Chinese people and Japanese people. How on earth can the knowledge they possessed, and still do possess, be considered not worthy of including in almost all the history textbooks?

One result of all this is that knowledge of the atrocity is precluded from being something that existed in Japan from 1937 to now (laying aside the knowledge revealed at the Tokyo trials, which, as I have said, are commonly reckoned to have been biased). In other words, there is no point going around Japan trying to find witnesses to the atrocity, since the knowing of the atrocity is confined to a small number of probably anti-Japanese foreigners.

Readers might think I am putting forward an eccentric or extreme point of view here. But when the diaries of John Rabe (1998), a German and a member of the Nazi Party, who witnessed the atrocity, and recorded it in terms similar to those of the other foreign witnesses, were recently discovered, their importance in Japan was often assessed in terms of their lending credibility to the American reports on the event. Here, for example, are the words (presumably excluding the headings to the articles) of two history professors as quoted in the *Asahi Shimbun* newspaper. First, Professor Hata Ikuhiko (*Asahi Shimbun*, 8 Dec. 1996a):

### Value Above That Of The American Witnesses

A German from a country friendly to Japan, objectively depicted the conditions at the time. From this point of view, I think it is of greater historiographical value than the evidence of the American clergymen who were considered to bear animosity towards Japan.

Second, Professor Kasahara Tokushi (*Asahi Shimbun*, 8 Dec. 1996b):

### Support For The Occurrence Of A Great Massacre

The very fact that someone in a position like Rabe's dared appeal to the leader [Hitler, CB] of a country allied to Japan supports the occurrence of a great massacre.

Without wishing to cast aspersions on the motives of the two professors, or to question their good intentions, it is possible that many readers of these articles would be left with the impression that the occurrence or non-occurrence of the Rape of Nanking is itself open to doubt, and that the recognition of the Rape of Nanking as a historical event had hitherto hinged on the credibility of a handful of Americans.

What is important about Rabe's testimony is not that it *supports* the Americans, but that it is *the same* as that of the Americans, and thus further *destroys* the credibility of those who over the years have based part of their arguments against the occurrence of the Rape of Nanking on the fact that the witnesses are anti-Japanese Americans, or the anti-Japanese Allied victors who were intent on administering victors' justice at the Tokyo war crimes trials.

My point is that the absence of Japanese people from Nanking not only allows a history to be written in which Japanese people do not carry out heinous acts, but also the absence of Japanese people precludes the possibility of Japanese existing as witnesses to the atrocity. This goes a long way towards creating and maintaining what may be called the climate of deniability regarding the Rape of Nanking that exists within various influential sections of modern-day Japanese society.

Of all the textbooks, seven of them state that the (ordinary) Japanese of the time did not know (at all) about the atrocities at Nanking. Ten textbooks locate the revelation within Japan of knowledge of Nanking to the Tokyo trials. The textbooks therefore do show a preoccupation with the patterns of distribution of knowledge discussed in this section, although the pattern is not a very common one when considering the textbooks as a whole. Nevertheless, when one considers that the argument against the Nanking atrocities includes the view that these atrocities could not have occurred since no one in Japan knew about them at the time (as shown in the quote from Y. Yoshida on page 64) it would seem that the textbooks should not allow any room to manoeuvre for those who deny the atrocity on grounds of a lack of knowledge of the atrocity.

## *Types of criticism*

Since the presence of Japanese soldiers per se (with the exception of Text 2.2) is not recorded in the textbooks, not surprisingly they cannot be criticized for their behaviour. When the textbooks do record criticism, it is either directed to the behaviour (as in Text 2.3 above: 'such acts of massacre, destruction and pillage at the time received strong international criticism'), or to the atrocity (as in 2.1 above: 'as the Nanking Atrocities (massacre) received worldwide criticism'). The nearest that Japanese soldiers get to being criticized is when the Japanese army itself receives criticism, as in Text 2.4 below:

**Text 2.4** (Bitoo, Masuda, *et al.* 2002: 227)

Nihon-gun wa, 1937 (Shoowa 12) nenmatsu ni wa shuto Nankin o senryoo-shita. Sono sai, josei ya kodomo o fukumu ooku no Chuugokujin o satsugai-shita tame (Nankin-daigyakusatsu), shogaikoku kara hinan o abi, Chuugoku-gunshuu no koonichi ishiki o sara ni takameru koto ni natta.

Translation: The Japanese army at the end of 1937 (Shoowa 12) occupied Nanking, the capital. At this time, because of [the Japanese army] having killed a large number of Chinese, including women and children (the Great Nanking Massacre), [the Japanese army] received criticism from foreign countries, and it came about that the anti-Japanese feelings of the mass of Chinese people were heightened.

In all the textbooks, there are 24 books in which criticism, in one form or other, concerning the Rape of Nanking is present. In four of these cases, the criticism is directed to the Japanese army, in one case to Japan itself, and in all the other cases (i.e. 19 cases) to the atrocity or the behaviour which constituted the atrocity. According to the textbooks, the criticism emanates from the foreigners who were in Nanking at the time and the international community. If these sources of criticism actually overwhelmingly did criticize the atrocity itself and the behaviour of the Japanese army, rather than the Japanese army or the soldiers of that army, I would be obliged to concede that the textbooks were dealing with the matter of criticism fairly. However, it is not very difficult to find contemporary reports of the Rape of Nanking in which the criticism is overwhelmingly of the Japanese army and the soldiers of that army, rather than of the atrocity itself or of the actions which constitute it. Thus, strictly speaking, in order to give a fair account of the contemporary criticism of Nanking, the textbooks, considered as a whole, should specifically and frequently mention that the Japanese army and its soldiers were criticized.

### *Naming the atrocity*

In this section, the manner in which the Rape of Nanking receives its name, and, related to this, how it comes into being as a historical event will be examined.

The following is a rather typical example from the textbooks:

**Text 2.5** (Ikeda *et al.* 2002: 195)

Nihon-gun wa kahoku no shuyoobubun o osaeta nochi, 12-gatsu ni wa shuto Nankin o senryoo-shi, Nankingyakusatsu-jiken o hikiokoshita.

Translation: The Japanese army, after gaining control of the main parts of north China, in December occupied the capital Nanking, and caused the Nanking Massacre Incident.

In Japanese writing there are no capital letters and the distinction between proper and common nouns is not as clear-cut as in English. Nevertheless, this text is clearly teaching pupils the name of this event.

What is interesting about this example is that the event receives its name at the exact same instant that it occurs. One result of this is that the people who killed and were killed are not in the text. Or rather, instead of being plainly on the surface of the text, for all to see, they are, by inference only, inside the event translated as 'Nanking Massacre Incident'. Thus, the naming of the event simultaneously with the occurrence of the event means that there is no narrative space for actions and behaviour to take place, and also no space for those who carried out the actions to be present. The Japanese army, let alone soldiers of this army, are not perpetrators of an atrocity; but the Japanese army is the cause of an incident which *encapsulates* heinous acts – what these heinous acts are is not fully stated, but left up to the inferences of readers. Labelling the relevant clause (slightly abbreviated) for transitivity makes this clear:

3  *Nihon-gun wa*
   The Japanese army
   Actor

   *Nankingyakusatsu-jiken o*
   the Nanking Massacre Incident
   Goal

   *hikiokoshita*
   caused
   Material process

**The Japanese army caused the Nanking Massacre Incident**

The heinous act (namely, 'massacre': *gyakusatsu*) is nothing more than part of a noun phrase which fulfils the participant function of Goal. However, the party who committed the massacre is in the text by inference (namely, 'the Japanese army'); the party who was massacred has actually disappeared from the story.

When we name something at the same time as it occurs, this means that there is no space left in the text for explanation (on the writer's part), and interpretation (on the reader's part). The event, has, as it were, been taken care of by the author of the text, without allowing readers to have any space for reflection and questioning.

If we look at Text 2.2 above, we find something rather different. The actions that constitute the events are recorded in the text, and then the event is given a name ('and among the Japanese officers and men, also those who carried out rape, pillage, and the like were not a few. This is called the Great Nanking Massacre.')

This allows readers to enter the text and then question it. They can for example ask questions like: Does this name summarize fairly what happened? Who gave it this name? When was it given this name? I do not say that this kind of text necessarily gives an answer to these kinds of questions, but it at least allows readers to ask these kinds of questions.

Among the options available to the authors of this textbook (Text 2.5) was that of expanding the noun phrase ('the Nanking Massacre Incident') by modification so that we have an Actor (the people who carried out the massacre), a Goal (the people who were massacred), and a Material process (the actual act of massacring). Thus, in Text 2.5 the verbal/process part of the 'Nanking Massacre Incident', namely, 'massacre' (*gyakusatsu-(suru)*), could be taken out of this noun phrase and be part of a noun phrase which, having been expanded by modification, has a transitivity configuration as follows: Actor + Goal + Material process. This would look something like, 'the Nanking Massacre/Incident, in which a large number of people were killed by the Japanese army', similar to Text 2.6 below, in the next section.

A nominalization tends to have a subtle effect, as pointed out by G. Thompson (1996: 170):

> By 'nouning' a process, the writer can reflect the fact that s/he has negotiated the meaning of the clause centred around the process – in other words, that meaning can now be treated as existing, as a kind of abstract 'thing'.

In other words, the name has been presented to readers as a sort of fait accompli, and one with which it is very difficult to argue since, for most of the pupils, the history textbooks are seen as being a sort of fount of knowledge which should be imbibed, but not questioned.

## Semantically neutral verbs

One result of the process of nominalization is that, since what could be the process in a full clause, has been subsumed within the noun phrase, the process slot of the clause then becomes vacant, and can be occupied with a range of different verbs. Sometimes these verbs are rather innocuous, neutral, or devoid of any concrete or specific meaning, as in Text 2.5 above ('caused': *hikiokoshita*), in which the story has become one of 'causing', rather than of 'massacring'.

In the following example (Text 2.6) the nominalization is what may be called a reasonably full nominalization in that it tells the story in some detail, in contrast with the nominalization in Text 2.5 above, which certainly does not tell anything like the full story.

**Text 2.6** (Tanaka *et al.* 2002: 101)

Kooshita Chuugoku-gun no tsuyoi teikoo o ukenagara mo, Nihon-gun wa, kahoku/kachuu no shuyootoshi ni tsuide shuto Nankin o senryoo-shita. Kono toki, <u>hisentoo-in o fukumu tasuu no Chuugokujin o satsugai-shita</u> Nankin-jiken ga okite iru.

Translation: Even while receiving this kind of strong resistance from the Chinese army, the Japanese army occupied the capital, Nanking, following the occupation of the main cities of northern and central China. At this time, the Nanking Incident <u>in which [the Japanese army] killed a large number of Chinese, including non-combatants</u>, occurs.

In Japanese, as in English, the equivalent to 'the Nanking Incident in which [the Japanese army] killed a large number of Chinese, including non-combatants' is one large noun phrase. The head of this noun phrase is 'the Nanking Incident' (*Nankin-jiken*) which is, in the original Japanese, modified by the material preceding it. This is shown in the underlining. The noun phrase is, therefore, filled out (in contrast with the non-filled out noun phrase in Text 2.5 above) in that the clause which modifies it contains a Goal ('a large number of Chinese, including non-combatants') and a Material process ('killed'); the Actor ('the Japanese army') is named in the previous sentence and is by clear inference present in this nominalization. (This may seem strange to English speakers, which is why the square brackets are used in the translation above, but is very normal and common in Japanese, where a noun marked by the topic particle *wa* can extend its 'reach' over a whole paragraph.)

The whole story is, as it were, packed into the nominalization. This has the effect of freeing the process slot of the finite verb of the sentence. This process slot is then occupied by the more or less semantically empty verb 'occurs' (*okirite iru*). This is an intransitive verb, with 'the Nanking Incident in which . . .' as its subject. The story is thus one in which, admittedly, nasty things happen in the nominalization, but this nominalization itself comes into existence in a more or less self-willed and automatic manner, by simply 'occurring'.

Also, notice that the verb is in the present tense. This shifts the narrative from a historical narrative in which events occur in their proper chronological order as the events unfold in time. What has happened in this text is that the authors have insinuated themselves into the story with an omniscient voice. The text could have been the following:

**Text 2.7** (rewritten example of 2.6)

. . . hisentoo-in o fukumu tasuu no Chuugokujin o satsugai-shita Nankin-jiken ga <u>okita</u>.

Translation: . . . the Nanking Incident, in which [the Japanese army] killed a large number of Chinese, including non-combatants, <u>occurred</u>.

This switching from the voice of chronological narrative to that of the omniscient historical voice is not a common enough pattern in the textbooks to allow one to draw conclusions about it. However, I have only noticed this use in ideologically sensitive parts of the texts.

## The nature of closed texts

Much of the analysis of the texts and the accompanying discussions in this chapter can be thought of from the point of view of the positioning of readers of the textbooks. It would be crude and simplistic to think that ideologies are baldly stated in texts. For, as Fairclough (1989: 85) writes, 'Texts do not typically spout ideology. They so position the interpreter through their cues that she brings ideologies to the interpretation of texts – and reproduces them in the process!' Thus, the positioning of the reader is crucial to the creation, maintenance, and reproduction of an ideology.

One way to position readers is to create texts that are almost impervious, at least to the casual reader, to critical examination; the text can block the reader from getting inside it. This view is related to Eco's (1979) distinction between open and closed texts. Open texts encourage the reader to engage with the text and interpret the text in potentially a range of different ways. Closed texts, on the other hand are constructed in such a way that they block engagement with the reader and only allow one, or a very limited number of interpretations. Closed texts have a tendency to reconfirm of reinforce what is the commonsensical and accepted way of looking at the world. In terms of the way in which the term ideology is used in this book, closed texts restate, reinforce, and reconfirm naturalized ideologies.

Luke (1989: 74) makes use of Eco's distinction in discussing the language of textbook narratives:

> Closed texts flatten out relationships between, and structure within possible worlds, ruling out the invocation of other possible worlds and meanings. Denoting rather than connoting, stating rather than alluding, delimiting rather than expanding temporal and spatial deixis, such texts offer an airtight kind of cohesion which reinforces rather than expands known lexicon and syntax.

In the examples above, we have examples of an airtight kind of cohesion: the absence of Japanese people as perpetrators, the barrier erected between the Japanese army in Nanking and (ordinary) Japanese people, the way knowledge of Nanking is something that anti-Japanese foreigners, but not Japanese people themselves, possess, the use of 'was not made known' without telling the reader by whom it was not made known, the way criticism of Nanking is never directed towards Japanese soldiers and very seldom towards the Japanese army, the way in which the event is named at the same time that it comes into existence, the way the story of the atrocity (sometimes the full story, and sometimes less than the full story) is encapsulated in noun phrases, and the way the process slot can be filled by a semantically empty verb, etc. Some of the questions that pupils could ask about the Rape of Nanking – indeed should be encouraged to ask – are:

- Why is this called the Nanking Massacre?
- What kinds of Japanese people were at Nanking?
- How did the Chinese people of the time feel about this?
- Who knew about the events at Nanking at the time?
- If I ask my grandmother if she knew about the massacre, what will she tell me?

- Are there books on Nanking written by Japanese and Chinese people who witnessed the event?
- Is it possible to hide information so perfectly that no one in one particular country knows about it, but it is common knowledge internationally?
- If such a hiding of information was possible in 1937/1938, what does this tell us about the government, media, and education in Japan at that time?
- What are the arguments for and against the Rape of Nanking in Japan, and how does this textbook help me to counter or support such arguments?

It seems to me that these are the questions that the textbooks should be encouraging pupils to ask, instead of blocking such questions. What we have in the textbooks regarding the Rape of Nanking is an airtight kind of cohesion, and one which reinforces a naturalized ideology – a way of writing about the events in question which has become the accepted common sense.

## A partial answer to some objections

Certainly, there is the genre objection to the analysis and discussion above. It is possible to argue that all the examples given above are nothing more than normal ways of writing history, and therefore genre has been confused with ideology – that the ways of writing about the Rape of Nanking illustrated above are simply the way history is written. One possible reply to such a view would be to turn the genre objection on its head and argue that, within the genre of history writing, authors have access to a large number of linguistic resources, and among those resources there are some that *enable* the naturalized ideology to exist and be reproduced.

The objection can also be raised that far too much has been made about the textbooks not mentioning the presence of Japanese soldiers at Nanking. It can certainly be argued that everyone knows that 'Japanese army' means the same as 'Japanese soldiers'.

As I develop my argument, analyses, and discussion in this book, as well as producing a wealth of data to support my positions, I hope that I can convincingly counter these objections. Nevertheless, at this stage I can give some evidence that supports my position. The two following texts are from the same textbook:

**Text 2.8** (Nunome *et al.* 1995: 328)

Nihon-gun wa Shanhai ni mo gun o susume, 12-gatsu, Nankin o kooryaku-shita ga, kono toki ni Nankingyakusatsu-jiken ga okotta.

Translation: The Japanese army, advancing its forces as far as Shanghai, in December captured Nanking, and at this time the Nanking Massacre Incident occurred.

**Text 2.9** (Nunome *et al.* 1995: 328)

1919-nen 4-gatsu, Indo-hokuseibu no Amurittosaru de Igirisu-hei ga daigunshuu ni mukete happoo, 1500-nin no shishoosha ga deta.

Translation: In April 1919, in north-west India at Amritsar, British soldiers shot into a large crowd, and there were 1,500 dead and wounded people.

This textbook is no longer in the current set of 55 approved textbooks; it has been purposefully selected by me from among the previous 88 that were approved.

It is strange that in one of the few books that deals with the Amritsar Massacre, the perpetrators are people ('British soldiers'), but in none of the 88 textbooks previously issued, nor in the current set, do we have Japanese people as perpetrators at Nanking (excluding, in total, three texts that are almost identical versions of Text 2.2, discussed above). It is difficult to believe that this is merely a coincidence. Surely it cannot be because of the nature of the historical events themselves, or because of educational considerations, or because of the editorial or organizational requirements of the textbooks, or because of certain characteristics of the Japanese language. I do not believe that in a disinterested, objective relating of history those killed can be identified frequently, but the killers almost never.

This same textbook also has illustrations of Nanking and Amritsar, on immediately following pages. There is the famous photograph of the triumphal entry into Nanking by General Matsui Iwane. He leads the procession on horseback, and is followed by about half a dozen officers, also mounted. Lining the route of the procession are two rows of soldiers standing at attention, with their backs to the camera. In the middle distance there are some parked cars and soldiers standing and looking at the procession. Next to them there is a flagpole with a Japanese flag flying. In the background, there are the imposing city walls of Nanking with three large arches, presumably gates. In this picture there is not a single rifle visible. The only face that is recognizable is that of Matsui. There is nothing in the picture that tells us it is not a military review on a parade ground.

When we look at the Amritsar illustration (which appears to be an anti-British black-and-white drawing locally produced, cameras being rare in Amritsar in 1919), we do not see any of the faces of the British soldiers, but their rifles with fixed bayonets are pointed towards a crowd of Indians. The most visible people in this crowd are women and children, and an old man who is holding up on a pole an early version of what will later become the Indian national flag. The ground is littered with stones, which presumably have been thrown at the British soldiers; there is a little child bending over her prostrate mother. A British officer is mounted on a rearing horse, which seems to be trampling down people in the crowd. The officer is brandishing a riding crop with which he is about to strike some of the protesters.

These two texts are very different and this difference is so clearly repeated in the illustrations that it is difficult to believe that what we have here is not a conscious attempt to obfuscate what happened in Nanking, but give the graphic details of what happened at Amritsar. The texts and pictures perfectly fit in with the view that Japan was fighting in China to bring stability to Asia and was not waging a war against Asians, but Britain was a cruel white colonial power suppressing Asians who were craving freedom from colonial rule.

In the next two chapters I will show by comparing the language used with reference to the German and Japanese attacks and the German and Japanese surrenders that this genre argument does not stand up to examination. But even in this chapter, I believe that both the data themselves, and these two purposefully selected examples go some way towards showing this.

## A note concerning Prince Asaka

In order to give an idea of the extreme delicacy with which the Nanking problem is handled in Japan today, particularly with reference to knowledge and responsibility, some data from outside the textbooks will be briefly examined. In the *Asahi Shimbun* (16 May 2000) there is an article about the renovation of what was the former palace of Prince Asaka, which is now an art gallery. This article includes a potted biography of

Prince Asaka and tells us when he was born, his position within the imperial family, the fact that he studied in Paris from 1922 to 1925, where he was interested in art deco, that he renounced his imperial title in 1947 (forcibly, as part of occupation policy of abolishing aristocratic titles) and died in 1971. Since Asaka was in command in Nanking up to 17 December (on which day General Matsui, his military superior, arrived) and since he was on active military service during the war years, one would have thought that the *Asahi Shimbun* might have considered this worthy of mention. This is especially so since millions of Japanese have seen his picture, almost certainly without knowing who he is, in the famous photograph of the Japanese entry into Nanking described above. In this photograph, he is on horseback immediately behind General Matsui. However, if we look at not the exact same photograph, but one that was taken at almost exactly the same time and from only a slightly different angle, and published in the *Tookyoo Asahi Shimbun* (18 Dec. 1937), there is a tension between the photo itself and the explanatory caption. Since Matsui was leading the procession, it is clear that he was in command, and he did indeed have the higher military rank. But the fact that in the caption Asaka is mentioned first, with the use of honorific language, tells us that in some sense he was superior to Matsui, by virtue of his birth:

**Ceremonial Entry Into Nanking**

His Highness Prince Asaka on the august right, with Commander-in-Chief Matsui in the front.

The disagreements that arise in war and on the battlefield between military commanders and aristocrats of higher social, but lower military rank, are not exactly unknown in history. This picture and its caption certainly raise this question and thereby lead us to ask who was really in command in Nanking, during all or part of the time the atrocities occurred.

I do not believe that the *Asahi Shimbun* simply forgot about this period of Asaka's life. This is almost certainly an attempt to massage his biography so that it does not raise questions of members of the imperial family possessing knowledge of Nanking.

As a footnote, I will add that Matsui was executed for war crimes committed by his troops in Nanking. Bergamini (1971: 46, 47, 182, 1,057) strongly argues that he was the scapegoat for what happened at Nanking, and Minear (1972: 210) expresses doubt about the justice of sentencing him to death. Asaka lived on to enjoy life in post-war Japan.

## Summary and conclusion

One aim of this chapter has been to identify patterns of language use in the data. The claim has not been made that there is anything intrinsically wrong with writing that 'the Japanese army killed civilians in Nanking', or with omitting Chinese or Japanese as witnesses to the events in question in some number of textbooks. What I am saying is that when we have virtually no reference in all 55 textbooks to Japanese soldiers being present in Nanking at the time of the Rape, and when the witnesses of the atrocities are consistently people who may be assumed to be anti-Japanese, we have strong grounds for suspecting there are ideological reasons for what at the beginning of this chapter was termed 'circumspect language'. We are told that the foreigners in Nanking at the time made the events known worldwide, but the (ordinary) Japanese were not told about these events. Surely in some cases we would expect to be told who was responsible for not telling the Japanese people about these events, and whether this constituted a cover-up.

The people who were responsible for the atrocities could at least in some of the textbooks be clearly identified and criticized. Only if this is done can they stand in the court of history. If the grandfathers and grandmothers of the children who are studying the history textbooks knew about the atrocity at the time, either through having been at Nanking or by means of information leakage from the front to the people in Japan, should not, then, these children be told?

Naturally, a close look at the soldiers who carried out the atrocities is likely to lead to a questioning of the educational system that produced such people. This was an educational system in which textbooks were controlled by bureaucrats and children were taught lies in order to further the aims of the state. If Japanese children are to be truly taught about the history of their country, it would seem that they need to be told this.

What we see in the language of the textbooks with reference to the Nanking atrocities is certainly not a crude censorship of the language of the textbooks. The textbooks describe the Rape of Nanking in what appears to be reasonable detail. And it would be difficult to criticize any one textbook for presenting a false or even biased picture of the Rape of Nanking. It is only when we examine all the textbooks in the corpus that a clear picture emerges.

The question arises here as to what kind of ideology we see being expressed in the language of the textbooks. I do not think that the language used to refer to the Rape of Nanking, considered as a whole, constitutes examples of normal historiography. Something is clearly going on as far as these textbooks are concerned. I think that what we have here is an example of an ideology that may be called naturalized in that it seems to be almost the only way, the common-sense way, of writing about the events in question; and also this has probably been the way of writing about these events for many years. The ideology itself may be called an ideology of lack of responsibility, or, as it is termed in this book, an ideology of irresponsibility. The findings of this chapter can be summarized in terms of this ideology. According to at least a significant number of textbooks:

a) There were no Japanese soldiers who were responsible for carrying out atrocities at Nanking.
b) (Ordinary) Japanese people did not know about the atrocity until after the war, and are therefore absolved from any moral duty that human beings might have which requires them to protest against great injustice.
c) No military or governmental organ bears responsibility for covering up, or trying to cover up, the atrocities.
d) There was international criticism of the atrocities, but this criticism never extended to Japanese soldiers, therefore they are spared the obligation (i.e. the responsibility) of having to respond to such criticism, for example by apologizing (i.e. by taking responsibility) to their victims.

If one *had* to write about Nanking but did not want readers to ask any questions about responsibility and did not want them to trace the historical thread that leads from 13 December 1937 to today, this is how one would write this history.

If we look at the denial of the Rape of Nanking in modern Japan, among the general arguments against a large-scale massacre are the following (see T. Yoshida 2000: 87, 88; and the several essays by different authors in *Nankin-jiken Chuusa Kenkyuukai* [Research Group on the Nanking Incident] 1999):

a) The Japanese people did not know until after the war, so it could not have occurred.
b) The Japanese heard about 'the Rape of Nanking' after the war because it was a fabrication, or at least an exaggeration, which was part of victors' justice.
c) Soldiers who were in Nanking at the time deny it.

d) Evidence from people who claim to be witnesses to the atrocities is based on hearsay.
e) It was a post-war Chinese plot that has been repeatedly used over the years to bring various kinds of diplomatic pressure to bear on Japan.

One would have hoped that since the Rape of Nanking is a very well documented event, the writers of the textbooks and the Ministry of Education would have made every effort to present a clearly written and well-balanced account of this event. But far from this being the case, what we have is a writing of history that allows denials like those listed above to flourish. The brief digression regarding the career of Prince Asaka and his biography given in the *Asahi Shimbun* show that not only are the textbooks circumspect with regard to Nanking, but this circumspection probably extends to one of Japan's most prestigious newspapers, and one which is usually regarded as being liberal in outlook.

# 3 The attacks by Germany and Japan
## The ideology of irresponsibility

This chapter will first discuss the ways in which many of the textbooks provide an explanation, bordering on justification, of Japan's actions which started the Pacific War. This explanation or justification is, itself, one version of the view that Japan fought an unavoidable war of national survival. In this preliminary section of the chapter, I will move away from the ideational part of the grammar, which has been my focus up to now, and discuss the area for which the overall term 'evaluation' is sometimes given. This covers some part of the field known as appraisal in functional grammar (Coffin 1997: 196–230; J. R. Martin 2000b: 142–175) and, considering recent work only, is related to Hunston's evaluation (2000: 176–208), Conrad and Biber's stance (2000: 56–73), and Hyland's work on hedging (1998). In looking at the explanation for Japanese actions, the distinction between averral and attribution (Hunston 2000: 178–181) will be discussed and, applying these concepts to the data, it will be shown how some of the authors of the textbooks tread the fine line between teaching pupils the ABCD line (the Allied economic sanctions against Japan) as a historical 'fact' worthy of remembering, while at the same time avoiding committing themselves to the historical reality of this ABCD line. In short, the writers of the textbooks succeed in having it both ways, while leaving any pupil who happens to be thoughtful and questioning confused about the historical events in question.

The discussion of the ABCD line is, however, only a preliminary section to this chapter. The remainder of the chapter examines the language used to describe the attacks by Germany in 1939 and Japan in 1941. It will be argued that when the language the textbooks used in writing about these attacks is compared, it becomes clear that the textbooks, considered as a whole, downplay the aggressive nature of the Japanese attacks.

The analysis of the language of the textbooks relevant to this part of the chapter will be in terms of transitivity (i.e. participants and processes), as well as taxis. However, the role that the participants and processes play in the grammar of the texts will be examined from the point of view of grammatical metaphor, a concept that will be developed later in the chapter.

The naturalized ideology that will become clear in the analysis and discussion is again one of irresponsibility.

## Historical background

The Second World War started with the German invasion of Poland on 1 September 1939, and the subsequent declaration of war against Germany by Britain and France. The German attack on Poland was not preceded by a declaration of war.

The Pacific War phase of the Asia-Pacific War (that is to say the war against the Western Allies) started on 8 December 1941, with Japanese amphibious landings in northern Malaya (which were preceded by landings in southern Thailand in order to outflank the British forces in northern Malaya (Bix 2000: 434)), which were shortly followed by the attack on Pearl Harbor. Neither of these attacks was preceded by a declaration of war or an ultimatum. In the period leading up to these attacks there had been ongoing negotiations between Japan and America. America, Britain, and the Netherlands had already implemented a series of economic sanctions against Japan in response to Japan's aggression in China and entry into the southern part of Vietnam, then a Vichy-French colony, in July 1941.

The attack on Pearl Harbor has achieved a special significance in folk memory in both the United States and Japan: in America as a day of infamy, in Japan as a brilliant coup de main that demonstrated the daring and resourcefulness of the Japanese.

Calvocoressi *et al.* (1995: 943) take a pragmatic view regarding the alleged perfidious nature of the Japanese attacks:

> The idea that the Japanese attacks on 7–8 December 1941 were dastardly acts should be laid to rest: the notion of a Japanese 'Day of Infamy' has outlived its usefulness. Surprise attacks, as we have seen, has [*sic*] been the customary practice of states throughout modern times: they were not the exception, but the general rule.

It is often said that decoding and typing problems at the Japanese embassy in Washington were responsible for the delay in informing the United States government of the breaking off of diplomatic relations. Thus Ienaga (1978: 1365) writes that:

> The Japanese government had intended to inform the US Department of State immediately before the attack on Pearl Harbor that diplomatic relations were broken. There were delays in Washington, however, because the embassy staff had difficulty with the last long message from Tokyo. ... The charge that Japan planned a perfidious attack without any prior warning is incorrect. The Nomura-Kurusu note, however, simply declared that relations were severed; it was not an explicit declaration of war. Furthermore, British forces were attacked without any advance notice. The Imperial Rescript declaring war was not issued until 11 a.m., December 8 (Tokyo time), several hours after the raid on Hawaii. This clearly violated the provisions of the Hague Convention of 1907 on the commencement of hostilities, which Japan had ratified in 1911.

It is difficult to know exactly what Ienaga means, for even if the note stating that diplomatic relations were severed had been delivered before the attack on Pearl Harbor, the attack surely would have been perfidious? Likewise, Ienaga himself seems to imply that the attack on British forces was perfidious.

Guillain, a French journalist who spent the war years in Japan and was present at the press conference held at the Foreign Ministry after the Japanese attack and declaration of war, suggests that, even at this early stage, the Japanese government felt that it had acted improperly (Guillain 1981: 5):

> ... in the weeks that followed, the Japanese government would shroud the facts in a prudent fog, carefully concealing from the people that the attack on Pearl Harbor had been made without warning. In the enthusiasm of victory, the 75 million people would swallow official propaganda with the unreflecting credulousness typical of the Japanese at that time and would honestly suppose that Pearl Harbor had been a proper engagement in which Japan had exploited the element of surprise to win the 'battle.' Only those in the leadership class, perhaps, had some doubt about this; they were careful to keep it to themselves.

## The ABCD line

Within Japan today, the self-preservation argument (namely, that Japan had no choice but to go to war in self-defence), as previously mentioned, is not an uncommon one. This argument goes back to at least the period before the start of the war in Manchuria. This view is also present in Hirohito's surrender broadcast of 15 August 1941 (for the full English translation see Weintraub 1996: 594, 595) in which he said:

> Indeed, We declared war on America and Britain out of Our sincere desire to ensure Japan's self-preservation and the stabilization of East Asia, it being far from Our thought either to infringe upon the sovereignty of other nations or to embark upon territorial aggrandizement.

One of the clearest versions of this self-preservation argument is that known as the ABCD (American, British, Chinese, Dutch) line, or the ABCD encirclement of Japan. This view holds that Japan was being economically strangled by these countries and thus had no choice but to go to war. The following is a typical textbook reference to the ABCD line:

**Text 3.1** (Toriumi *et al.* 2002: 139, 140)

Nihon no Toonan-ajia e no seiryoku-kakudai ni taishite,
Amerika wa zenmen-teki na tainichi keizai-seisai de taikoo-shi,
zaibei Nihon shisan no tooketsu, tainichi sekiyu-yushutsu no
kinshi o dankoo-suru to tomo ni, Igirisu/Chuugoku/Oranda
to kyooryoku-shite tainichi keizai-fuusa o tsuyometa
(ABCD-hooijin).

Translation: In response to Japan's expansion of power in South-East Asia, America resisted with thoroughgoing economic sanctions against Japan, and as well as the freezing of Japanese assets in the United States and enforcing the prohibition of exports of oil to Japan, cooperated with Britain, China, and the Netherlands to strengthen the economic blockade against Japan (the ABCD encirclement).

When I first started reading the textbooks, I accepted the term ABCD line/encirclement rather uncritically. But it was not long before it was not making very much sense. After all, if Japan had set up the puppet state of Manchuria in northern China, had been waging a very aggressive war of expansion in China for a decade (1931 to 1941), was occupying large areas of China, and had already captured the Chinese capital of Nanking, how could it make sense to say that China was party to an economic blockade directed against Japan? It is a bit like saying the Soviet Union was instituting an economic blockade of Germany while German troops were in Stalingrad. This claim is not only against common sense, but is actually historically untenable, or at the very least open to dispute, as shown by the following quotation from a standard Japanese dictionary of historical terms (*Kokushi Daijiten* 1980: 242):

> The ABCD Encircling Countries: This refers to the American, British, Chinese, and Dutch anti-Japanese encirclement that was established in response to Japan's advance south [entry into southern Vietnam, CB] immediately prior to the start of the Pacific War in 1941. It was not an official term, but a term of incitement used by the Japanese media, under the guidance of the military, in order to stir up the Japanese people's sense of crisis ... the Japanese military authorities added China [to America, Britain, and the Netherlands] and claiming that an anti-Japanese encirclement was being formed, manipulated the media to incite the people and lay the psychological basis for legitimatizing the coming Pacific War as a war of self-defence.

In fact, while it is reasonable to talk of an ABD encirclement of Japan, an ABCD encirclement does not make very much sense at all. But at least in Text 3.1, the writers have given some sort of explanation of why China gets into the historical narrative – namely through cooperation with America. This is not so with the following example:

**Text 3.2** (Mayuzumi *et al.* 2002: 318)

Shikashi, 7-gatsu no nanbu-futsuin shinchuu ni Amerika wa hanpatsu-shi, zaibei-hoojin shisan tooketsu to tainichi sekiyu-yushutsu teishi no hoofuku-sochi o totta. Kono ugoki ni, Igirisu/Oranda mo doochoo-shi, iwayuru ABCD-hooimoo ga umareta.

Translation: However, America, reacted to [Japan's] advance in July into southern French-Indochina, and took the retaliatory measures of freezing the assets of Japanese in America and stopping the export of oil to Japan. Britain and the Netherlands also conforming with these steps, the so-called ABCD encirclement came into being.

According to the above, Britain and the Netherlands cooperated with America, and then the ABCD, not ABD, encirclement came into being, without any explanation of what C stands for, and how and why China joined ABD. Some rather necessary information seems to be missing from this text.

But more revealing than this is the way in which, when writing about the ABCD line, there is a use of language that is extremely common throughout the corpus. Authors of the textbooks give their readers information about the ABCD line, but do not commit themselves totally to the historical reality of this line of encirclement. Or, they leave the readers (more probably a small number of perceptive readers) wondering if the authors have, or have not, committed themselves to this term. Or, finally, if there is still a genuine historical controversy regarding the economic encirclement of Japan, and the suitability of using the term ABCD, they do not let readers know that this is the case. The fact that this is done in various ways suggests that what we are seeing here is, to use Fairclough's words (1989: 115), a 'preoccupation with some aspect of reality'.

In the above example, *iwayuru* has been translated as 'so-called'. Note that the English translation is ambiguous in the same way as the Japanese. Does it mean 'so-called by the people at the time', or does it mean 'so-called by the authors of this textbook (and other authors as well)', or does it mean both of these: 'so-called by the people of the time and by the authors of this textbook (and other authors as well)'? Furthermore, is this 'so-called' to be interpreted as 'so-called, but that is not really a suitable name'? This is one of the natural interpretations in Japanese: 'We call it this, for reasons of economy of space or ease of presentation, and so on, but wish to point out that this term is not one hundred per cent accurate or suitable'. This allows several question marks to hang over the historical status of the ABCD line: What is a better or more accurate term? What would a more suitable term be? How does this term differ from a more accurate or suitable term? Why are you calling it this term? and so on. Whether the pupils studying these textbooks will actually notice these question marks is very doubtful.

## The attacks by Germany and Japan 87

To summarize the above, there is a two-fold problem regarding the interpretation of 'so-called' (*iwayuru*). First, whose voice is this 'so-called', and, second, what does this 'so-called' tell us about the status of the ABCD line in terms of it being a historiographically accepted term – in other words a reasonable name in a school history textbook for the economic blockade of Japan?

By distinguishing between attribution and averral (Hunston 2000: 178) it is possible to go some way towards identifying the effects of this ambiguity of voice. By presenting language as attributed, the writer (or speaker) is saying that it derives from someone other than him or her and, thus, the writer will not take responsibility for its truth-value. On the other hand, if the writer avers something, the responsibility for its truth-value lies with the writer. It is useful to distinguish between these using a concrete made-up example. If I say, 'John says he was born in London', I am making an attribution to John, and it is John who must take responsibility for the truth-value of his being born in London; if John was not born there, I cannot be accused of telling a lie. If I say, 'I was born in London', I am averring that that is where I was born, and the responsibility for the truth-value of this statement lies with me.

In the example of 'the so-called ABCD encirclement' above, the reader simply does not know whether this is a case of attribution or averral. In the case of attribution, the interpretation is 'so-called by the people of the time and it is they who must take responsibility for the truth-value of this term'. This naturally raises the question of whether the term was, even at that time, a reasonable one, and brings to the fore such matters as government censorship of the media, propagandization of the mass of Japanese people by the media, the teaching of ultra-nationalistic history at school, and so on, and thus could lead to the conclusion (for any pupil, or teacher, perceptive enough to notice this) that this term is unsuitable and out of place in a modern history textbook when presented in this manner.

In the case of averral, the interpretation by a pupil is likely to be 'the authors are taking responsibility for the suitability of this term, therefore it is a reasonable term which I can remember and use in my study of history'.

But then, if anyone were to take the authors of this textbook to task for presenting a term about the suitability of which there is some doubt, they can always escape from this charge by pointing out that they used the term 'so-called' when introducing it, and that they were thereby themselves expressing doubt as to whether this was a suitable and accurate term, and have made this clear to the pupils precisely so that these pupils do not accept it uncritically. In other words, even if it is an averral, it can be claimed to be a hedged averral.

'Hedged averral' refers to an averral regarding which the writer (or speaker) leaves himself or herself some 'escape route' if challenged. Thus if I aver that my dog is 'a sort of labrador', the responsibility for the truth-value of this clearly lies with me. This truth-value, however, lies not in 'labrador', but in 'a sort of labrador'. Thus, if I am challenged about the dog being a labrador, I can rightly point out that I did not say it was a labrador, only 'a sort of labrador', and thus do not claim one hundred per cent labradorhood for the dog. I have, in other words, used a hedge when describing the labrador-like quality of my dog. Hedges within averrals can be difficult to disentangle.

Thus, to summarize the above, this 'so-called' does not discriminate between averral and attribution and, furthermore, if it is an averral (which we could well claim would be an irresponsible and inaccurate representation of the historical facts), the writers of the textbooks have an escape route since the averral has been hedged.

This is all very confusing; the term is presumably judged by the authors to be worth teaching, and in this sense has been given the imprimatur of historical reality. But what are pupils learning? There was something called the ABCD line, and it was called that at the time or is called this now. But exactly what it was and what its status is in terms of the range of generally accepted historical scholarship is glossed over. Yet no one can accuse these authors of introducing wartime language and wartime propaganda into the textbook, since the lack of distinction between averral and attribution, and the use of a hedge means that the status of this ABCD line is by no means clear and it is impossible to pin down the authors to exactly what they mean.

When the textbooks are examined from the point of view of the justification for the Japanese attacks, we find that it is not simply a question of whether 'so-called' is in the text or not. There are, in fact, a set of grammatical resources that produce a pattern of related meanings. By this, I mean that if I claim that one specific resource of the grammar creates one particular meaning, my interpretation can be disputed. But this is not the case; what we see in the textbooks is a set of copatterning resources of the grammar which also obfuscate the degree of historical acceptability of the ABCD line. When such is the case, it becomes harder to dispute the interpretations made here. The following example demonstrates this:

## Text 3.3 (Sakamoto *et al.* 2002: 291)

Nihon wa Amerika (America)/Igirisu (Britain)/Chuugoku (China)/Oranda (Dutch) ga Nihon o hooi-shite iru toshite, kore o ABCD-hooijin to shooshita.

Translation: Japan, regarding America, Britain, China, and the Netherlands as encircling it, called this the ABCD encirclement.

First, we are told that Japan regarded the four countries as encircling it. The authors are attributing the feeling of encirclement to the Japan of that time, and thus this is an example of an attribution. This leaves open the question of whether Japan was actually being encircled. (It also leaves open the important question of who or what 'Japan' stands for. Whether 'Japan' represents the government, the armed forces, industrial and business interests, or the Japanese people as a whole, or the land-mass that is called 'Japan' – these are all different stories which the textbook does not tell us about.) The word translated as 'called' (*shooshita*) tells us what the people of the time called the encirclement of Japan. This is, therefore, another example of an attribution. The word *'shooshita'* carries very much the same nuance as its English translation equivalent, 'called', namely: 'Japan at the time called this the ABCD encirclement (*although such a term may not be entirely accurate*)'. So, in this case, the attribution, not the averral (as above in Text 3.2), is hedged. Summarizing this, in this text we have two attributions, both attributed to the 'Japan' of the time, with the second attribution hedged by the use of 'called'. Finally, the authors themselves do not let the reader know where they stand regarding the status of the ABCD line.

A number of textbooks tell us somewhat more frankly what was going on. The following example does make clear that there was a media campaign aimed at whipping up war-fever, as mentioned in the above quote from the encyclopaedia (*Kokushi Daijiten* 1980: 242):

## Text 3.4 (Bitoo, Fujimura, *et al.* 2002: 304, 305)

Shikashi, Nihon no nanshin-saku no kyookoo ni taido o kooka-saseta Amerika wa, Nihon no zaibei-shisan o tooketsu-shi, sara ni Nihon e no sekiyu-yushutsu o kinshi-shita.*

*Nihon no masukomi wa, A (Amerika), B (Igirisu), C (Chuugoku), D (Oranda) to eigo no kashiramoji o totte, ABCD-hooimoo to hoodoo-shi, kokumin no kaisen-netsu o aotta.

Translation: However, America, which had hardened its stance against Japan's forceful implementation of its policy of advancing south, froze Japanese assets in America and also forbade exports of oil to Japan.*

*The Japanese media, taking the initial English letters of A (America), B (Britain), C (China), and D (the Netherlands), and reporting this as the ABCD encirclement, fanned the Japanese people's fever for starting war.

But even so, limiting ourselves to the parts of the above text that are central to the discussion here, a close examination of the text reveals an interesting pattern. Among the averrals that the authors make are as follows: 'America froze Japanese assets'; 'America forbade exports of oil'; 'the Japanese media took the initial English letters of A (America), B (Britain), C (China), and D (the Netherlands)'; 'the Japanese media reported this'; 'the Japanese media fanned the Japanese people's fever for starting war'. All these averrals are very reasonable and most historians would readily agree with them. The historiographically problematic part of the textbooks, namely, the status of the ABCD line, in fact, and scholarship, comes into the narrative by means of being an averral followed by an attribution: 'the Japanese media reported this [averral] as the ABCD encirclement [attribution]'. The authors take responsibility by averring that the media reported this. Then they make an attribution to the media, but without taking a stance regarding the reasonabless of this attribution. In other words, they do not take responsibility for the attribution. But it is exactly this attribution which is the crux of the text and its most ideologically sensitive part; for whether or not Japan had reasonable grounds for going to war partly hinges on this. This attribution, precisely with reference to the most ideologically sensitive part of the text, surrounded by five averrals, is not something that can be separated out by the pupils reading this text. In fact, 'ABCD encirclement' is the only item printed in bold in this text. The text thus gives a high level graphological status to the least historically tenable part of the narrative, and the only part for which the authors of the textbook do not have to take responsibility for its truth-value.

All pupils, almost certainly, and probably most teachers, will interpret this to mean that the ABCD encirclement is a recognized and well-established historical term. This is a truly remarkable piece of historical writing. As was mentioned above, there are a set of copatterning grammatical (and in this case a graphological resource) which produce the same kinds of meanings; this text flutters between according or not according the ABCD line recognized historical status, as does Text 3.2, but in different language. This ambiguity regarding the ABCD line must, nevertheless, be regarded as being closer to the historical reality than Text 3.1, which presents the ABCD line as a simple historical fact that is beyond dispute and beyond questioning.

Text 3.4 also intimates that the responsibility for starting the war lies with the media and the ordinary Japanese people. Surely the role of the government was more important than that of the ordinary Japanese people. Furthermore, what this textbook, and almost all others neglect to mention was the strict government censorship of the media.

Somewhere between Text 3.2 and Text 3.3 (which in their use of attribution averral and hedging leave the question of the status of the ABCD line unresolved) and Text 3.1 (which presents the ABCD line as a fact), is the following example, which presents it as an *exaggerated* fact:

**Text 3.5** (Miyaji *et al.* 2002: 66)

Kono yoo na Nihon no koodoo ni taishite, doogatsu, Amerika/ Igirisu/Oranda wa jikoku ni aru Nihon shisan o tooketsu-shi, 8-gatsu ni Amerika wa, sekiyu no tainichi yushutsu o zenmen-teki ni kinshi-shita. Kono tainichi keizai-fuusa, toku ni sekiyu no kin'yu wa Nihon ni totte chimei-teki na dageki de ari, ABCD-rain* no kyooi ga sakan ni kyoochoo-sareta.

*America/Britain/China/Dutch no yonkakoku no kashiramoji o totte nazukerareta.

Translation: In response to these kinds of Japanese actions, in the same month, America, Britain, and the Netherlands froze Japanese assets within their own countries, and in August America completely forbade exports of oil to Japan. This economic blockade of Japan, in particular the prohibition of oil exports, was a fatal blow to Japan, and the threat of the ABCD line* was widely exaggerated.

*This was named by taking the initial letters of America, Britain, China, Dutch.

This falls into the category of accepting that there was such a thing as the ABCD line, but explaining to pupils that it (or more accurately its threat) was an exaggeration, and thus holding it up to some degree of examination or questioning. But again the authors have not disentangled attribution and averral. There was something at the time that was named the ABCD line; this is clearly an attribution, although since the verb is in the passive we do not know by whom this attribution was made. But the authors insert themselves into the narrative and tell us, the readers, that this attribution was itself an exaggeration; this is clearly an averral on the authors' part. All this can be untangled as follows: 'Some unnamed people or organizations at the time said there was a threat from the ABCD line, but we, the authors, are telling you, the readers, that this was an exaggeration on the part of these unnamed people or organizations'. Nevertheless, at the end of the day, this still leaves the main question unanswered: What, according to modern scholarship would be a reasonable interpretation of the ABCD line such as would be present in school history textbooks? Since the ABCD line, in this case also, is printed in bold, this would suggest that it is deemed to be something worth remembering.

This is all a bit confusing, especially as the above text does not give any explanation of the entry of China; 'America, Britain, and the Netherlands' becomes 'ABCD', without explanation. This text is adding China to the ABD countries in the same way that the encyclopaedia entry states that the military authorities added China.

Throughout the textbooks, the common presence of averral and attribution, and the likely confusion between the two of these in the minds of pupils studying the textbooks, together with the presence of hedging, means that both the status of the ABCD line and the authors' position with regard to this are vague and unresolved. The use of language that produces this effect does not exist in other parts of the textbooks that I have looked at. When there is a genuine disagreement, as for example with the number of Chinese dead at Nanking, the textbooks tend to present several sides of the case (the numbers accepted at the Tokyo trials, the numbers put forward by Japanese historians, and the numbers put forward by the Chinese government).

The patterns being discussed here are common throughout the textbooks. Thirty-four of the 55 textbooks specifically mention the ABCD economic encirclement of Japan, and among these 34, 19 either present it as an exaggeration, but nevertheless as a fact, or employ a use of language (hedging, averral, or attribution) that leaves its status unclear (to at least perceptive readers). In eight of the mentions, ABCD line (or encirclement) is printed in bold, which suggests that it is deemed important for the pupils to remember.

The Ministry of Education had, in the past, frequently blocked mention in history textbooks of, for example, the sex slaves, on the grounds that there was no reliable and well-established scholarship on it. In fact, the lack of a commonly accepted position within the field of history scholarship has been one of the ministry's main grounds for excluding material, or asking for revisions or alterations in the textbooks, or for insisting that both sides of a controversial question be treated in the textbooks. Such a position clearly does not apply to the 'ABCD line' in modern Japanese textbooks.

The question arises as to how we can interpret this use of the ABCD line in a more focused way in terms of ideology and, more precisely, in terms of naturalized ideology. The ideology is of Japan being pushed into a corner by the actions of the white races and China, who were attempting to constrain its very reasonable behaviour. This is precisely what we see in Hirohito's surrender broadcast, which I will quote here once more for ease of reference:

> Indeed, We declared war on America and Britain out of Our sincere desire to ensure Japan's self-preservation and the stabilization of East Asia, it being far from Our thought either to infringe upon the sovereignty of other nations or to embark upon territorial aggrandizement.

The way of writing about the ABCD line discussed above can be seen as representing an ideology that serves the interests of certain powerful groups – namely, the people who were responsible for leading Japan into war, in that justification is given for their actions, and it also bolsters Hirohito's position in so far as it is a reaffirmation of the self-preservation view of the necessity of going to war advanced in his broadcast. The way of writing about the ABCD line clearly represents the accepted common sense of the textbooks, goes back 60 years to Hirohito's broadcast, and is, itself, one of the main justifications given by the revisionists in modern Japan for Japan's decision to go to war. In short, this ideology has come down in time, is still with us, and is being uncritically repeated, and thus may be properly regarded as being naturalized.

The reason we have this ambivalent way of writing about the ABCD line is precisely because it is historically a very weak claim, but it is one of the key ideological justifications for the Pacific War being an unavoidable struggle of national self-preservation. The inclusion of China in the ABCD line, also provides Japan with a reason for waging war against China for the same sort of reasons that it waged war against the Western Allies, namely, for its self-preservation, and neatly side-steps the fact that the war against China had been continuing for ten years prior to the attacks against Britain and the United States. As I have already pointed out, the different phases of the Asia-Pacific War tend to get muddled up in modern Japan.

The reality is that Japan needed great quantities of oil, iron, steel, and other strategic material in order to pursue its aggression in China. This is mentioned in any meaningful manner in five textbooks, among which it is specifically and clearly mentioned in only one textbook (Ienaga et al. 2002: 285). Laying aside these exceptions, as far as readers are concerned, the oil that was cut off because of the embargo could well have amounted to what Japan needed for its normal transport and industrial needs. But this was far from the case. After the imposition of the embargoes, Japan had the three alternatives of continuing the war in China while being under an embargo, stopping the war and having the embargo lifted, and going to war against the Western Allies before the embargo started to bite and strategic stockpiles were depleted. The last option was the one chosen. Such a view is well within the range of reasonable and accepted historical scholarship within Japan and abroad, as Bix (2000: 439) writes:

> Confronted with military strangulation by oil embargoes and the choice of admitting defeat in China, thereby abandoning a large part of his continental empire and probably destabilizing the monarchy he had inherited, Hirohito opted for his third alternative [It is not clear to me why Bix calls this the 'third' alternative, CB]: war against the United States and Britain. ... If certain strategic schedules were quickly achieved, Japan would be able to counter superior American productive capacity and force at least a standoff with the United States.

In other words, as long as Japan continued the war in China it had no alternative but to go to war against the Western Allies, a point with which Ienaga is in agreement (1978: 132):

> Director of the Planning Board Suzuki Teiichi, a member of the cabinet that decided for war, has said that 'although some people have charged that Japan went to war despite a lack of resources,' the decision was actually made for the opposite reason: Japan went to war *because* its resources were insufficient. [emphasis in original]

We would expect this view of the start of the war by Japan to be at least present in some form in a considerable number of the textbooks.

But this is not the case. Instead, what the textbooks have done is to adopt the ABCD line rhetoric of the time; they have failed to discriminate between averral and attribution, and by the use of hedging, together with a lack of explanation of how China could have been carrying out an economic embargo against Japan and how China came to join the ABD countries so that an entity known as the ABCD line came into being, thoroughly clouding the issue.

In conclusion, when it comes to the ABCD line, what we see in the textbooks is a writing of history that allows the revisionist self-preservation argument to flourish, and directly echoes the logic of Hirohito's broadcast of 15 August. It is also the explanation or justification that sets the stage for the Japanese attacks that started the Pacific War.

## The German and Japanese attacks: a comparison

In this section it will be shown that the German attack that started the Second World War and the Japanese attacks that started the Pacific War are described in significantly different language, and such differences cannot be explained in terms of the differences in the historical events themselves. In the previous chapter I could not present a convincing case to counter what has been called the genre objection, namely, that I am confusing the history textbook genre with a particular ideology. However, in this chapter, by means of a comparative analysis of the language used to describe the German attack on Poland and the Japanese attack on Pearl Harbor, it will be shown that the genre objection is not tenable. In order to do this, it will be necessary to present statistical data from all the textbooks.

Here, the analysis will involve looking at the data from two different points of view:

a) the participants and the processes in the German attack on Poland and the Japanese attack on British forces in Malaya and on the United States at Pearl Harbor;
b) clause primacy, which is a general term that will be used to refer to taxis and the modification, by a clause, of the head of a noun phrase.

In this section, the means by which there can be slippage or incongruency between actual events and the language which is used to describe these events will be examined. It will be shown that there is a consistent pattern of slippage in the language used to describe the

Japanese attacks that started the war against the Western Allies. The idea of slippage or incongruency will be dealt with from the point of view of what is termed grammatical metaphor (Halliday 1994: 342–367; Halliday and Matthiessen 1999: 227–296; G. Thompson 1997: 166–172).

The argument will be that this slippage creates an ideology in which the responsibility of the Japanese state of the time and also, to a certain extent, its lineal successor, the Japanese state of today, is downplayed or diminished. In this section, especially when considered in conjunction with the preceding one on the ABCD line, it will be argued that the language of the textbooks encode an ideology of reasonable and justifiable actions, and of behaviour for which Japan has to take little responsibility – in other words, an ideology of irresponsibility.

## *Participants and processes: grammatical metaphor*

This concept of grammatical metaphor needs some explaining. We can regard it as being the natural or the usual case when the relationship between the state of affairs in the real world (all the happenings, goings-on, existings, etc.) and the way a text expresses this state of affairs is close. In such cases of a close relationship, nouns will encode people and things and verbs encode happenings, etc. (Coffin 1997: 217, 218; Halliday 1994: 342–367; Halliday and Matthiessen 1999: 227–296). In such cases, we can speak of a congruent realization in that the semantic categories are mapped onto natural grammatical categories. For example, consider a sentence like:

1    Peter hit John.

In this sentence, the doer (the Actor) is Peter and the person to whom the action (the Material process) is directed is John (the Goal). Peter is also the subject of the sentence and John the object. Furthermore, the actual process is straightforwardly expressed by the verb 'hit'. Thus we can say the actual occurrence, the grammar, and the semantics all fit together in a natural and expected way.

But we could express the occurrence of Peter hitting John in either one of the following ways:

2    John received a blow from Peter.

3    John was the recipient of a blow from Peter.

In both these cases, the natural congruency of sentence 1 has been lost. In sentence 2, the 'hit' of sentence 1 becomes 'received a blow', but with the direction reversed, so that what was the object of sentence 1 (John) becomes the subject of sentence 2, with the former subject, 'Peter', an indirect object, which can be deleted from this sentence and the sentence can still be well-formed (since we can say 'John received a blow'). In sentence 3, the only verb is 'was', and 'received' is recast into its noun version ('recipient'), with appropriate changes made in the rest of the grammar of the sentence.

The term 'metaphor' is used with reference to sentence 2 and sentence 3 on the previous page. Thus, a sentence like 'John received a blow from Peter' is another way of saying 'Peter hit John', but is not really about John *receiving something* from Peter, as this sentence is: John received a present from Peter. This sentence, in which 'receive' is used in its 'real' meaning, is not metaphorical. In order to describe these metaphors, which operate within the grammar of the language, and to distinguish them from the more usual metaphors, the term 'grammatical metaphor' is used.

An even more obvious example will further help to illustrate the concept of grammatical metaphor. Consider the sentence, 'Sunrise saw us at the top of the mountain'. This is certainly not about the sunrise seeing us in a specific location, since a sunrise obviously cannot see. It is a grammatical metaphor which means, 'We arrived at the top of the mountain at sunrise'.

Some examples of grammatical metaphor are so common and so natural that it is difficult to think of them as such. Consider the sentences:

4   I think it is going to rain.

5   John thinks it is going to rain.

The first of these illustrates the concept of grammatical metaphor; it is not a sentence about 'thinking', as the second is. We can verify this by adding a question tag to each sentence:

6   I think it is going to rain, *isn't it*?

7   John thinks it is going to rain, *doesn't he*?

Sentence 6 is about 'it' and 'going to rain', not about 'I' and 'think', and it is these that the tag is echoing. 'I think' is a grammatical metaphor for some word like 'perhaps', as in 'Perhaps it is going to rain', which is the meaning of sentence 6. Sentence 7 is truly about 'John' and 'thinks', as shown by the tag, which picks up these words.

Grammatical metaphor arises in a variety of ways, one of which is nominalization. The process element is the central part of the clause. Depending on the particular process, there are a number of other elements in the clause, namely, one or more participants, and perhaps Circumstances. What these elements are depends on the process itself. If it is the Material process of hitting, we would expect to see an Actor and a Goal, and perhaps a Circumstance telling us what kind of hitting took place, or where the hitting occurred, etc. In the case of nominalization, what could be a full transitivity configuration (say of Actor + Material process + Goal) all becomes encapsulated within a noun. Once the process is nominalized, this means there can be a realignment of all the other participants and Circumstances in the clause. One consequence of this is that the process slot becomes available to be filled with a verb different from the verb that would have been occupying this slot in the non-nominalized alternative. The points being made here were discussed in Chapter 2 on the Rape of Nanking (see page 71).

We often make fun of bureaucratic language because one characteristic of such language is to carry grammatical metaphor to extremes, often in terms of nominalization, as in an example like this, in which the nominalizations have been underlined:

> Owing to <u>an increase in unemployment benefit applications</u>, there will be <u>a corresponding increase in application processing times</u>.

If, in order to create a non-metaphorical (a congruent) version, we unpack these noun phrases, we get something like this:

> Because more people are applying for unemployment benefits, it will also take longer to process their applications.

Or perhaps this:

> Because more people are applying for unemployment benefits, we will also need more time to process their applications.

These congruent versions tell, as it were, the full story. There are processes in the clauses that explicitly state the goings-on and the behaviours (who does what to/for whom, etc.). Comparing these versions with the original version, it is clear that all these goings-on and behaviours have been encapsulated within the noun phrases in the original and that the only process slot that exists is occupied by the very neutral or semantically empty verb 'be'. The grammatical structure of this original version is very simple: 'Owing to such-and-such there will be such-and-such'. This contrasts with the two congruent examples which, as a result of telling us the full story, are both composed of three clauses.

Grammatical metaphor is a very natural part of the way we make meanings in our daily lives. Sometimes, in certain types of speaking or writing, we may feel that it has been taken too far, at other times it seems to be the more natural way of saying something. If we continue to unpack the above already unpacked sentence, we find that the language becomes unnatural and needlessly circumlocutory:

> Because more people are applying for benefits they get when they lose their jobs, we will need more time to process their applications.

'Unemployment benefits' certainly seems to be a more normal wording than 'benefits they get when they lose their jobs', which sounds very much like a definition we would give a child or a learner of English who did not know what 'unemployment benefits' meant.

Thus, grammatical metaphor is neither all nor nothing, and is not a case of good or bad; it is simply one of the resources of the language system of which speakers and writers can avail themselves. The claim in this section is that grammatical metaphor is a means by which we can create ideological representations of the real world, and that this occurs in the textbooks.

In order to give an idea of language of the textbooks with reference to the German attack and the Japanese attack, two typical examples, both from the same textbook, follow:

### Text 3.6

**Germany** (Kanda et al. 2002: 302)

1939-nen 9-gatsu tsuitachi, Doitsu-gun wa totsuzen Poorando shinryaku o hajimeta. Kore ni taishi Ei/Futsu wa 9-gatsu mikka Doitsu ni sensen-shi, Dainiji-sekaitaisen ga hajimatta.

Translation: On 1 September 1939, the German army suddenly started the Polish invasion. In response to this, on 3 September, Britain and France declared war on Germany, and the Second World War started.

**Japan** (Kanda *et al.* 2002: 304)

Sekiyu no ketsuboo o osoreta Nihon wa kaisen o isogi, doonen 12-gatsu Hawai no Shinjuwan o kishuukoogeki-shi, Bei/Ei ni sensen-shita. Kooshite Taiheiyoo-sensoo ga hajimatta. Sara ni Doku/I mo Amerika ni sensen-shi, sensoo wa zensekai ni hirogatta.

Translation: Japan, which feared for a shortage of oil, hastened to start hostilities, and in the same year in December surprise-attacking Pearl Harbor in Hawaii, declared war on America and Britain. Thus the Pacific War started. Furthermore, Germany and Italy also declared war on America, and war spread to the whole world.

Looking at the processes and participants in the above two texts, while bearing in mind the concept of grammatical metaphor, there are several points worth mentioning. First, the doer of the action (the Actor) in the German example is the German army, but the Actor in the Japan example is Japan. In the Japan example, Pearl Harbor is in the story congruently (as the Goal of the attack) but in the German example Poland is in the story non-congruently, since it is not a Goal, but part of the noun phrase 'Polish invasion' (*Poorando shinryaku*). Not only do the parties attacked get into the stories in different ways, they are also different kinds of parties, with 'Poland' being a country, and 'Pearl Harbor' being a place. The process in the German example is rather an innocuous or empty one, namely, 'started' (*hajimatta*), that does not by itself directly tell us much about what actually happened. But the process in the Japanese example is 'surprise-attacked' (*kishuukoogeki-shi*), a phrase that tells us more about what happened. As an aside, but also as an illustration of grammatical metaphor, notice that this verb, 'surprise-attacked', has within it the meaning of 'suddenly/without warning'; the 'suddenly/without warning' part of the historical narrative has been encapsulated, in this case, in the verb, not in the noun phrase. The German example contrasts with this, in that the 'suddenly/ without warning' (*totsuzen*) part of the story is in the sentence, with an independent existence for all to see.

One way of clarifying the possible ideological uses of grammatical metaphor is to give semantic labels to the participants and processes, and then examine how these labels are related to the transitivity labels. The party that carried out the attack can be given the label 'Attacker'

(Germany, Japan, or the armed forces of either of these countries), the party who was attacked 'Attackee' (Britain, the United States, colonies of these countries or geographical expressions located within these countries or their colonies, or the armed forces of these countries), and the process of attacking can be semantically labelled 'Attack' (the actions of 'invading', 'entering militarily', 'attacking', 'carrying out military landings', 'surprise-attacking', 'air-attacking', etc.).

First, looking at the Japan example in Text 3.6, there is a congruent relationship between the real world, the semantics, and the grammar such that both Attacker and Actor map on to 'Japan', Goal and Attackee map on to 'Pearl Harbor', and process and Attack map on to 'surprise-attacking':

8  *Nihon wa*
   Japan
   Attacker
   Actor

   *Shinjuwan o*
   Pearl Harbor
   Attackee
   Goal

   *kishuukoogeki-shi*
   surprise-attacking
   Attack
   Material process

   **Japan, surprise-attacking Pearl Harbor**

In the case of the corresponding German example, something rather different happens:

9  *Doitsu-gun wa*
   German army
   Attacker
   Actor

   *Poorando*          *shinryaku o*
   Polish              invasion
   Attackee            Attack
   – – – – Goal – – – –

*hajimatta*
started
Not Attack
Material process

**The German army started the Polish invasion**

Here, we have a case in which there is a lack of congruency. Actor and Attacker map on to German army, but after this the congruency breaks down, with what could be Attackee (namely Poland) and what could be the Material process of Attack being joined together in one noun phrase, which itself then becomes the Goal of the Material process 'started' (*hajimatta*).

It is important to stress that these examples are only given as illustrations of how we can approach the question of congruency and grammatical metaphor. It can certainly be argued that 'started the Polish invasion' accurately captures the fact that the German invasion of Poland was an ongoing process, of which the above sentence only records the beginning, and thus it is the normal and expected way of writing about the German invasion. As I say, I am, at this stage, only trying to explore the idea of grammatical metaphor.

To further clarify the point being made here, I will give one more pair of examples:

**Text 3.7**

**Germany** (Tanigawa *et al.* 2002: 308)

Kooshite Doitsu wa, 9-gatsu tsuitachi Poorando ni shinkoo-shi, Ei/Futsu ryookoku mo futsuka-go ni Doitsu ni sensen-shi, koko ni Dainiji-seikaitaisen ga hajimatta.

Translation: Thus Germany invaded Poland on 1 September, and both Britain and France two days later declaring war on Germany, the Second World War thus started.

**Japan** (Tanigawa *et al.* 2002: 309, 310)

Nichibei-kankei wa akka-shi, tsui ni 41-nen 12-gatsu yooka, Nihon no Shinjuwan-koogeki ni yotte Taiheiyoo-sensoo ga hajimatta.

Translation: Japan–American relations worsened, and finally on 8 December 1941, by means of Japan's Pearl Harbor attack, the Pacific War started.

Again, Germany is the Attacker and the process is Attack. In the English translation, Poland appears as the Goal of the Material process of attacking. However, in the Japanese it is a Circumstance of location, and not a Goal, since the Japanese verb for 'invade' (*shinkoo-suru*) does not occur with a Goal, but a Circumstance of location in that it is obligatorily followed by the directional particle *ni* plus a noun (Teruya forthcoming), so that if we translate the Japanese literally it is 'invade *into* Poland'. Once the writers of the textbook make the choice of using this word for 'invade', which is the natural and obvious choice, the option of Poland being present in the text as a Goal no longer exists. This German example is therefore best regarded as being congruent:

10  *Doitsu wa*
    Germany
    Attacker
    Actor

    *Poorando*
    into Poland
    Attackee
    Circumstance of location

    *shinkoo-shi*
    invading
    Attack
    Material process

    **Germany invaded Poland**

But if we look at the Japan example, we can see that something very different happens. The really important part of the narrative (the Attacker, the Attackee, and the Attack) have all been encapsulated in to one large noun phrase, which is itself functioning as a reason or a means by which the Pacific War started:

11  *Nihon no Shinjuwan-koogeki*　　　　　*ni yotte*
    Japan's Pearl Harbor attack　　　　　by means of
    Attacker/Attackee/Attack

    – – – – Circumstance of means – – – –

    *Taiheiyoo- sensoo ga*
    the Pacific War
    Actor

    *hajimatta*
    started
    Material process

    **By means of Japan's Pearl Harbor attack the Pacific War started**

Thus the part of grammar that tells us the really dramatic and important part of the story, namely, the actions that Japan carried out that started the war, does not exist in the sentence as a clause in its own right, with its own transitivity configuration, in which the who did what to whom and how is clearly expressed in the grammar of the clause, but as a noun phrase that functions as reason for explaining why the war started.

There is one other way to look at the process of nominalization. If there is a part, or parts, of a sentence that can be deleted, but the sentence still remains well-formed, this is a strong argument that the deletable part is less central to the sentence; it is existing as an optional 'tag-on', as it were. This is the case with the noun phrase translated as 'Japan's Pearl Harbor attack' (together with the Japanese translated as 'by means of') which is present as a non-obligatory element in the sentence; we could say 'on 8 December 1941 the Pacific War started', and the equivalent in Japanese.

Furthermore, looking at the noun phrase itself, elements of it are not obligatory. The head of the noun phrase ('attack': *koogeki*) is preceded by the modifying elements 'Japan's Pearl Harbor' (*Nihon no Shinjuwan*), with the structure of the modification being Pearl Harbor modifying 'attack' and 'Japan' modifying 'Pearl Harbor attack'.

Thus, because the elements that come before this head are modifying the head, they are present as extra or optional elements. This is shown by the fact that they can be deleted. We could say, 'Japan's attack' (*Nihon no koogeki*), thereby deleting 'Pearl Harbor', or the 'Pearl Harbor attack' (*Shinjuwan-koogeki*), thereby deleting 'Japan's', and, less contextually natural in this particular case, but certainly grammatically possible, we could simply say 'attack' (*koogeki*), thereby deleting the two modifiers of 'Japan's' and 'Pearl Harbor'. Thus, both at the sentence level and at the level of the noun phrase there is a high degree of grammatical optionality with respect to the manner in which the sentence refers to Japan's attack on the United States. It is the realization of what could be a fully fledged clause in its own right as a grammatical metaphor which makes this possible.

When we have to unpack a large noun phrase in order to arrive at a congruent realization, this is often a signal that there is 'something going on' in the text and, therefore, it perhaps merits careful examination.

One result of the noun phrase encapsulating Attacker (Actor), Attackee (Goal), and Attack (Material process) is that what would be the process (verbal) slot in the congruent realization then becomes empty and can be occupied by other potential processes (verbs), which can then enter into transitivity configurations with other potential Actors. With 'Japan's Pearl Harbor attack' functioning as a Circumstance of means (or more strictly, as part of a Circumstance of means) there is the opportunity to introduce different Actors, together with different processes, into the sentence. The Actor in this sentence is 'Pacific War' (*Taiheiyoo-sensoo*) and the process is 'started' (*hajimatta*). This process is the main verb, in fact the only verb, in the sentence. It, thus, is the main meaning-carrier of the sentence. The sentence becomes not primarily about 'Japan attacking', but about 'the Pacific War starting'. These are rather different stories.

What the Japan example above in Text 3.7 and this discussion illustrate is the concept of downgrading within the grammar, in this case downgrading from a clause to a noun phrase (from 'Japan attacked Pearl Harbor' to '(by means of) Japan's Pearl Harbor attack').

In conformity with my rejection of the view that these kinds of differences in the structure of the sentence do not realize meaning differences, and that 'everybody knows that they mean the same thing', the claim being made here is that what we see in the texts is language encoding meaning differences. As a further argument, besides the general theoretical one on page 52, Halliday and Matthiessen (1999: 231, 235) assign some semantic naturalness to congruent realizations in which all the main participants and processes are plainly there on the surface of the sentence.

To give an example of this, let us consider the following made-up sentences, which illustrate how downgrading can lead to a loss of information:

12  I got the letter which Peter sent to me.

13  I got the letter which Peter sent.

14  I got the letter from Peter.

15  I got Peter's letter.

Let us imagine that the above series of sentences are all about the same event that occurred in the real world. As we go down this series of sentences, the possibility for different interpretations of the meanings increases because of losses of clarity of meaning within the different sentences. In sentence 13, it may be assumed that Peter sent the letter to me, but this interpretation is open to dispute, since he could have sent it to someone else. Sentence 14 could mean that I received the letter by hand, and it might not be Peter's letter, but have been simply delivered by him. Sentence 15 has all the above interpretations, as well as the interpretation that the letter belongs to Peter, not me, and also the interpretation, in informal English, in which 'got' can mean 'possess' as well as 'receive', that I am the possessor of Peter's letter, rather than its recipient.

Congruent and non-congruent modes are not simply free variants (Halliday and Matthiessen 1999: 238) – nothing more than saying the same thing in different words. When we use language, we are always presented with a series of choices, and these choices are motivated. If we regard language as a semiotic system, it is legitimate and relevant to enquire why particular choices have been made.

In another textbook, purposefully selected, there are the following two noun phrases (underlined below), which also function as a Circumstance of means, as in the Japan example in Text 3.7 above:

**Text 3.8** (Esaka, Takeuchi, *et al.* 2002: 314)

1941-nen 12-gatsu yooka, <u>Eiryoo Maree-hantoo no Kotabaru e no Nihon-rikugun no kishuu-jooriku</u> to, <u>Hawai Shinjuwan e no Nihon-kaigun no kishuu-koogeki</u> ni yotte, tsui ni Taiheiyoo-sensoo ga kaishi-sare, Nihon wa Amerika/Igirisu ni sensenfukoku-shita.

Translation: On 8 December 1941, by means of <u>the Japanese army's surprise-landing at Kota Baharu on the British territory of the Malay peninsula</u> and <u>the Japanese navy's surprise-attack on Pearl Harbor</u>, the Pacific War was finally started, and Japan issued a declaration of war against America and Britain.

The second of these underlined noun phrases is somewhat more expanded or filled out than the one in Text 3.7 ('by means of Japan's Pearl Harbor attack') in that some extra information is provided regarding the aim and the dynamic nature of the attack. This is done by including the directional particle *e* ('towards', literally, 'the Japanese navy's surprise attack towards Pearl Harbor') as part of the noun phrase. This illustrates the point that congruency itself is not a question of either/or, but in fact constitutes a cline or a continuum, from the fully congruent, to the less congruent, to the incongruent. Thus, in writing about this attack, among the choices that exist, there are the following, of which I will give only the English:

16  Japan/The Japanese navy attacked Pearl Harbor and the war started.

17  By means of Japan's/the Japanese navy's attack on Pearl Harbor the war started.

18  By means of Japan's/the Japanese navy's Pearl Harbor attack the war started.

The first example (sentence 16) is fully congruent, but the congruency decreases in the subsequent examples, with sentence 17 telling us more of the story in that the direction or target of the attack is mentioned ('*towards/on* Pearl Harbor'). Thus, there is some directionality, dynamism, or Goal-like quality in sentence 17 that is absent from sentence 18. The point is the same as with different sentences about 'Peter's letter' above: as the congruency breaks down, and the grammatical metaphor becomes denser, some information is lost from the surface of the sentence – although it might be retrievable based on background knowledge and common-sense interpretations.

This might seem to be rather insignificant nit-picking. The claim is certainly not that there are necessarily different ideologies encoded in these three sentences, or that sentence 18 is hiding some important information that is more clearly present in sentence 16, and also present, but less so, in sentence 17. What I am doing here is to explore the connection between grammar as a system of choice and the meanings that are created by these choices. The grammars of the three sentences are different because different choices have been made from the language system. The question is: What different meanings do these different grammatical choices create?

Naturally, if the third type of sentence were overwhelmingly present in the textbook data, when the other two types of sentences could be present equally frequently, then one would want to look at the different meanings produced by these different examples and then tie it to the question of ideological encoding in the textbooks. Or, again, if we find that the German attack on Poland is frequently written about using congruent realizations, but this is not the case with the Japanese attack, then the question naturally arises as to why this should be so. Answering this question involves a statistical analysis of all the textbooks, and such will be undertaken later in this chapter.

## *Clause primacy*

In this section, the relations of taxis and of modification of clauses within sentences that deal with the German and Japanese attacks will be considered. The term I will use for this is 'clause primacy', which is a shorthand way of referring to primacy of meaning as encoded by the clausal relations within the sentence.

I will assume that it is rather natural for the main or most important event within the narrative to be encoded in the main verb of the sentence, which in the case of Japanese is the sentence final verb, immediately preceding a full stop. In other words, if we have a sentence that is composed of a group of clauses, one or some of which are not main clauses (referred to as beta, gamma, delta, etc. clauses), but one of which is the main clause (the alpha clause), and we consistently do not have certain actions or events encoded in this main clause, although there is no identifiable narrative, stylistic, or pedagogical reason why not, then it seems natural to ask why. Note that a strong claim is not being made. I am not saying that when the most important part of the narrative is not in the main verb this *necessarily* means that there is something fishy going on. What I am saying is, to make it more concrete, that if we look at all 55 textbooks, and we find that the German attack is very often encoded in the main verb, but the Japanese attack is very infrequently so encoded, then we might have grounds for supposing that the textbooks are using one resource of the grammar in order to be in some way circumspect about the aggressive nature of Japanese actions.

In the data analysed in this book, the usual pattern is for one or more hypotactic clauses to precede the main clause, and this is indeed an important characteristic of Japanese, which is heavily hypotactic. The verbs in these beta clauses are in the *te*-form or in the *shi*-form (in the case of the prototypical verb *suru* ('do')), or in S. Martin's terminology (1975: 577) the 'gerund' or the 'infinitive'). So, looking at Text 3.6 above, we find that the alpha, beta, and gamma clauses are organized as follows:

19  Germany

> ... *Doitsu-gun wa Poorando shinryaku o hajimeta.*
> ... the German army started the Polish invasion.
> **alpha clause**
>
> ... *Ei/Futsu wa Doitsu ni sensen-shi,* ...
> ... Britain and France declaring war on Germany ...
> **beta clause**
>
> ... *Dainiji-sekaitaisen ga hajimatta.*
> ... the Second World War started.
> **alpha clause**

20  Japan

> ... *Nihon wa kaisen o isogi,* ...
> ... Japan hastening to start hostilities ...
> **beta clause**
>
> ... *Hawai no Shinjuwan o kishuukoogeki-shi,* ...
> ... surprise-attacking Pearl Harbor in Hawaii, ...
> **gamma clause**
>
> ... *Bei/Ei ni sensen-shita.*
> ... declared war on America and Britain.
> **alpha clause**

In order to make this clear, I will give one more example, with the clause labelling immediately below the relevant country:

### Text 3.9

**Germany** (Toriumi *et al.* 2002: 137)

Sara ni, 1939 8-gatsu ni wa Soren to no aida ni fukashin-jooyaku o musubi, 9-gatsu tsuitachi, Poorando shinkoo o kaishi-shita. Kore ni taishite Igirisu/Furansu wa Doitsu ni sensen o fukoku-shi, Dainiji-sekaitaisen ga hajimatta.

Translation: Furthermore, in August 1939 [Germany] concluded a non-aggression treaty with the Soviet Union, and on 1 September started the Polish invasion. In response to this, Britain and France issued a declaration of war against Germany, and the Second World War started.

21  *[Doitsu wa] fukashin-jooyaku o musubi,*
[Germany] concluding a non-aggression treaty,
**beta clause**

*Poorando shinkoo o kaishi-shita.*
started the Polish invasion.
**alpha clause**

*Igirisu/Furansu wa sensen o fukoku-shi,*
Britain and France issuing a declaration of war,
**beta clause**

*Dainiji-sekaitaisen ga hajimatta.*
The Second World War started.
**alpha clause**

**Japan** (Toriumi *et al.* 2002: 140)

1941- (Shoowa 16-) nen 8-gatsu, Nihon-rikugun wa Igirisu-ryoo no Maree-hantoo ni jooriku-suru to tomo ni, kaigun wa Amerika no kaigun-kichi Hawai no Shinjuwan o kishuukoogeki-suru nado, Nihon wa toonan-ajia/taiheiyoo shochiiki de gunjikoodoo o kaishi-shi, Amerika/Igirisu ni sensen o fukoku-shita. Kooshite Taiheiyoo-sensoo ga hajimari, tsuzuite Doitsu/Itaria mo Amerika ni sensen-shite, Dainiji-sekaitaisen wa zensekai ni hirogatta.

In August 1941 (Shoowa 16), together with the Japanese army landing on the British territory of the Malay peninsula, the navy surprise-attacked the American naval base of Pearl Harbor in Hawaii, and so on, and Japan commenced military operations in various areas of southeast Asia and the Pacific, and issued a declaration of war against America and Britain. Thus the Pacific War started, and following this Germany and Italy also declared war on America, and the Second World War spread to the whole world.

22  *Nihon-rikugun wa Maree-hantoo ni jooriku-suru to tomo ni*
Together with the Japanese army landing on the Malay peninsula
**beta clause**

*kaigun wa Shinjuwan o kishuukoogeki-suru nado*
the navy surprise-attacking Pearl Harbor, and so on
**gamma clause**

*Nihon wa gunjikoodoo o kaishi-shi*
Japan commencing military operations
**delta clause**

*[Nihon wa] sensen o fukoku-shita.*
Japan issued a declaration of war.
**alpha clause**

It is possible for the Attack verb to be in the alpha clause, or, alternatively, it can be in the beta clause (or gamma, etc. clause), and therefore downgraded in the grammar. When this happens, particularly if it happens frequently, this suggests that it is also possibly downgraded in the semantics – in terms of the weight of meaning that it is carrying within the sentence. Consequently, it is not unreasonable to claim that in the Japan example of Text 3.9 above the focus of the historical narrative is on Japan declaring war on America and Britain, since this is encoded in the alpha clause; in the equivalent German example, the focus is on Germany starting the Polish invasion and on Britain and France issuing a declaration of war, both of which occurrences are encoded in alpha clauses.

This consideration of clause primacy also brings us once more to the matter of deletability. As argued above, an element of a sentence which is deletable is, in some sense, a less central part of the narrative. The hypotactic clauses (beta, gamma, etc. clauses) are thus giving the reader, not core information, but supplementary, and optional, information. Looking at Text 3.9 from this point of view, in the German example deleting all but the alpha clause leaves 'Germany started the Polish invasion' and 'The Second World War started'; doing likewise in the Japan example, we are left with 'Japan issued a declaration of war'. The alpha clauses, which contain the skeletons of the story, as it were, encode, in the case of Germany, a narrative of 'invading' and 'the Second World War starting'; in the case of Japan, a narrative of 'Japan issuing a declaration of war'. The different clause relations thus are related to potentially different weights of meaning.

Again, and I cannot stress this too strongly, I am using illustrative examples here for purposes of exemplification. The claim is not that certain information is not in an alpha clause and therefore a particular textbook is trying to hide or downplay such information. To make such a claim it is necessary to look at all the data, which I will do later.

### Textbooks echoing wartime language?

In this section, I briefly take up a point that will be looked at in more detail in the next chapter, namely, the manner in which the textbooks uncritically echo the language of the war years.

If we look at all the textbooks, we find examples like the following purposefully selected example:

> **Text 3.10** (Egami *et al.* 2002: 173, 174)
>
> Kore in taishi Amerika wa, Igirisu, Chuugoku, Oranda to tomo ni sekiyu kyookyuu no teishi nado no keizai-teki appaku o Nihon ni kuwaeta (ABCD hooi-rain). Kono tame Nichibei-kankei ga akka-shi, 1941-nen 12-gatsu, Nihon wa totsujo Hawai no Shinjuwan o koogeki-shite, Amerika/Igirisu ni sensen-shi Taiheiyoo-sensoo ni totsunyuu-shita.
>
> Translation: In response to this [the Japanese advance into southern French Indochina, CB], America, together with Britain, China, and the Netherlands applied the economic pressure on Japan of stopping the supply of oil, and so on (the ABCD line of encirclement). Because of this, Japanese–American relations worsened, and in December 1941 Japan suddenly attacked Pearl Harbor in Hawaii, and declaring war on America and Britain, plunged into the Pacific War.

This is an example in which Japan plunges into war. Since there are only six such examples it cannot be said to be a common pattern. But nevertheless, although it is not a common pattern, it is one specific to Japan. In all the textbooks there is not one other example of another country plunging into war; China, Britain, France, Germany, Italy, the Soviet Union, the United States – none of these countries plunges into war. Then why should Japan be the only country to do this plunging? It is difficult to see that there is some special characteristic of the historical events themselves that would limit the use of this expression only to Japan.

I think that there are two reasons why Japan is the only country which, according to the textbooks, plunged into war. First, referring to Teruya's discussion of Material processes (Teruya forthcoming), I take 'plunge' (*totsunyuu-suru*) to be a Material process and 'war' (*sensoo*) is a Circumstance of location, even though it is not an actual physical place that one can see and touch. This Material process is not in the subclass of Material processes concerned with the Japanese equivalents of making, creating, starting, or bringing about something; such Material processes occur in transitivity configurations with an Actor and a Goal (Actor + Goal + Material process). The process thus extends to, or in some way impacts on, the Goal. 'Plunge' (*totsunyuu-suru*), on the other hand, in both English and Japanese, does not occur with a Goal. As a consequence of this, when Japan is recorded as 'plunging into war', the war is not something that has been created by the Material process or something to which the Material process extends itself or impacts on.

Thus, this use of 'plunge' removes Japan from the story as a party which is responsible for creating a particular state of affairs by acting in a certain way. Rather, Japan attacks Pearl Harbor and then plunges into a situation. In a sense, the war receives no true identity or independent existence, since it is simply a kind of non-concrete, non-physical location into which Japan enters. The entry into this location itself is unavoidable and beyond the control of Japan, just as plunging is, after a certain critical moment, caused by the natural and unavoidable force of gravity. In the Japanese case, the unwilling and uncontrollable manner of plunging is clearly shown by the context: the negotiations with America are failing, the ABCD line is exerting economic pressure on Japan, the situation is out of control; and then Japan plunges into war.

But there is another reason why this use of 'plunge' is interesting. I would suggest that this use of plunge is a recycling of wartime language, particularly the announcement to the Japanese people of the start of hostilities against America and Britain by the Imperial General Headquarters on the morning of 8 December (*Oosaka Mainichi Shimbun*, 9 Dec. 1941a):

> The Imperial Army and the Imperial Navy have today, the eighth, in the early hours of the morning, entered into a state of hostilities with American and British forces in the western Pacific.

The plunging into war is perhaps a reworked version of the entering into hostilities (*sentoo-jootai ni ireri*) of this announcement. (This is not clear in the romanization, but the second ideograph with which *totsu-nyuu* is written (namely, *nyuu*) is the same ideograph used to write *ireri* (minus its verbal inflections).) This one bit of evidence might not seem very conclusive, but interestingly enough, when referring to Pearl Harbor, all the textbooks give the calque translation by writing the two ideographs for *Shinjuwan* (literally 'pearl' plus 'harbour') rather than give the syllabic transliteration of the name (*Paaruhaabaa*), with two exceptions in which *Paaruhaabaa* is written either above or after *Shinjuwan*. This is entirely contrary to modern Japanese usage (which long ceased, for example, to write 'Greenland' with the ideographs for 'green' and 'island', but syllabically '*Guriirando*') and entirely consistent with wartime usage. In the initial announcement quoted above, Pearl Harbor is not mentioned for reasons of military security, but after the site of the attack became known, this event and the words the 'Pearl Harbor (surprise-)attack' ('*Shinjuwan-(kishuu)koogeki*') were an expression of Japanese triumphalism. Perhaps what we see, even now, is an echo of this triumphalism in the textbooks used today.

Japanese informants will say that this is a perfectly normal and natural way of talking about the start of the Pacific War. I would suggest it is an example of an ideology that has become thoroughly naturalized over the more than 60 years since the event.

## Statistical analysis

Up to now the discussion of the data has been with reference to specific examples. But it is necessary to identify consistent patterns of language use in order to show that there is some naturalized ideology in operation in the textbooks. Here, by examining all the data, I will argue that there is a consistent pattern of language use that works towards lessening the responsibility of the Japanese state for the attacks, and thereby downplays the aggressive nature of these attacks. We can do this by comparing the German and the Japanese data for the two attacks (in the Japanese case limiting ourselves only to the Japanese attack on Pearl Harbor, since this is always seen as *the* attack – rather than the attack on the British in Malaya).

In order to elucidate the ideology encoded in the language of the textbooks, data from all the 55 textbooks which form the corpus will be examined in this section. Looking at the whole corpus, we can separate out those examples in which the Attacker figures congruently (i.e. is an Actor), and also those examples in which the Attack verb is in the alpha clause. Looking at the Attacker more closely, we can

*The attacks by Germany and Japan* 115

also identify which party carried out the attack (e.g. the country itself, or the armed forces of the country).

In terms of responsibility, the 'worst case scenario', from the point of view of the grammar encoding an ideology of irresponsibility, would be something equivalent to:

23   Germany attacked Poland.

24   Japan attacked Pearl Harbor.

In these cases the Attacker is Actor, the Attacker is a country, and the Attack is in the alpha clause. The text is thus plainly about who did what to whom.

The 'best case scenario' would be something equivalent to:

25   By means of t*he Polish attack by the German army*, the war started.

26   By means of *the Pearl Harbor attack by the Japanese navy*, the war started.

In sentence 25 and sentence 26, the nominalizations (italicized above) encapsulate what could be a full transitivity configuration describing the most important or crucial parts of the historical narrative, namely, the parts for which these countries take responsibility; there is thus a move away from congruency. Furthermore, in these examples the responsibility for the attacks accrues to the armed forces of the respective states, rather than to the states themselves. The states have been let off the hook, as it were, by virtue of the responsibility for their aggressive actions being shifted to their armed forces.

In order to get a profile of this, and in order to ascertain if there are significant differences in language between the way the textbooks write about the German attack and the Japanese attack, the following data from all the textbooks have been tabulated (Table 3.1):

a)   Country as Actor: this tells us if the country takes primary responsibility for attacks and also, at the same time, whether the country that carried out the attack is an Actor (in other words there is a degree of congruency in that the country is Actor and Attacker).

b)   Armed forces as Actor: this also is a measure of congruency (in that armed forces are Actor and Attacker), but the responsibility for

## 116  The attacks by Germany and Japan

Table 3.1 Language forms in the German and Japanese attacks

| Language form | Germany | Japan | Totals |
| --- | --- | --- | --- |
| Country as Actor | 41 | 16 | 57 |
| Armed forces as Actor | 11 | 26 | 37 |
| Attack verb in alpha clause | 19 | 4 | 23 |
| Totals | 71 | 46 | 117 |

Note: N = 55; $p$ = 0.0000 (chi-square = 22.5147; d$f$ = 2).

the attack accrues to the armed forces, and not the state itself. This scenario is thus a 'better' one than country as Actor.

c) Attack verb is in the alpha clause: this captures the tactic relationship of the sentence in which the attack is mentioned, and, according to the argument above is a measure of the meaning weight of the verb that describes the attack in the sentence. It is, at the same time, a measure of congruency, since the attack verb being in the alpha clause excludes it from being present in a nominalization, which is an incongruent encoding of the events.

There is a significant statistical difference ($p$ = 0.0000) in the language used to describe the German attack against Poland and the Japanese attack against the United States. To summarize this table:

a) In the case of the German attack, the country as Attacker and as Actor is the most common pattern, with 41 occurrences, 74.5 per cent (compared to 16 occurrences, 29.1 per cent, in the case of Japan).
b) In the case of the Japanese attack, the armed forces as Attacker and as Actor is the most common pattern, with 26 occurrences, 47.3 per cent (compared to 11 occurrences, 20 per cent, in the case of Germany).
c) Comparing the German attack and the Japanese attack from the point of view of Actor being Attacker (irrespective of whether Actor is country or armed forces), we find that Germany (including its armed forces) is Actor in 52 cases, 94.5 per cent, and that Japan (including its armed forces) is Actor in 42 cases, 76.4 per cent.
d) With respect to the use of the verb in the alpha clause to relate the attack, this is far more frequent in the German case (19 occurrences, 34.5 per cent) than in the Japanese case (4 occurrences, 7.3 per cent).

In summary, the German state takes responsibility for attacking and this attacking is what the main message of the texts is about. On the other hand, the Japanese armed forces take responsibility for attacking, and this is not what the main message of the texts is about.

## Summary and conclusion

The conclusion of this chapter is that the textbooks, with reference to the Japanese attack against Pearl Harbor, encode an ideology of irresponsibility, and this ideology because of its prevalence, both in Japan today, and going back to the pre-war and wartime periods, can be regarded as being naturalized.

In addition to the data included in the statistical analysis, there is the additional fact that there is not a single case of Japan attacking another country in all the textbooks, but in the case of Germany the attack is directed against another country in all the cases. I realize that the argument can be made that 'Pearl Harbor' has some symbolic significance and this is what the textbooks are reflecting. But one would have thought that, at least in some number of textbooks, the fact that Japan attacked the United States would be mentioned. It goes without saying that the Japanese attack against Thailand, which was actually the first attack in the Pacific War, is not mentioned in the textbooks. If this attack were mentioned in the textbooks, it would of course greatly weaken the 'Asian liberation' argument of the revisionists.

We must also consider the expression of 'plunging into war', used only with reference to Japan, and which I have argued is an example of irresponsibility and perhaps an echo of wartime language, and also the anachronistic use of the calque translation of Pearl Harbor, which I have suggested is an example of Japanese wartime triumphalism. All these linguistic data of the Japanese and German attacks must be taken together with the data and discussion regarding the language used with reference to the ABCD line, which I have argued also shows an ideology of irresponsibility. And they must also be taken together with the Nanking data, analysis, and discussion.

It is important to stress that what we have in the textbook data is not one or two language forms which I have happened to latch onto, and then built an argument around in order to claim that there is a particular ideology present in the language of the textbooks. Instead of this, we have different parts of the grammar that copattern to create a particular ideological construction of the historical events in question. What we see is a set of linguistic resources that pattern in the same way and produce the same ideological message – namely, lessen the responsibility of the Japanese state for the attack against the United States.

The argument and claims do not hinge on a simplistic view of language. I am not saying: 'This is an example of a grammatical metaphor, therefore this means that someone is trying to hide some information within this sentence. This important action is not in the main verb, so the writer of this sentence is trying to downplay this particular action for ideological purposes'. What I am saying is that if we have a large body of data and we have a range of language resources that have been utilized to create a range of meanings, and that this range of meanings tends to point in the same ideological direction, then we have grounds for claiming there is a particular ideological encoding in the language of the textbooks.

Certainly, this use of a set of copatterning linguistic resources protects the leaders of Japan who led the country into war from criticism that they acted foolishly and started a war without giving proper thought to the international realities of the time. There must be people in Japan who lost relatives and loved ones in this war who would like to know more about its true nature. The causal relationship between the nature of pre-war and wartime Japanese society (including the educational system), on the one hand, and the decision to go to war and the nature of this war, on the other hand, has to be examined if any meaningful history is to be taught to pupils. Ienaga (1978: 138) puts much of the blame on starting the Pacific War on the educational system within Japan at the time and the lack of any analytical ability or foresight on the part of the leaders of the country:

> Why was Japan so tragically wrong? The reasons were twofold: (1) an educational system and internal security laws that prevented Japanese from developing the ability to perceive the historical and social relations of the world and their own country; and (2) the emasculation of academic freedom, without which objective and scientific knowledge could not be acquired and diffused. Surrounded by inaccurate information and opinions tailored to their prejudices, Japanese leaders tied the blinders over their own eyes and rushed lemming-like toward the precipice. Destruction on the rocks below was the only possible outcome.

Furthermore, the examples and discussion, and in particular the statistical analysis, all show very plainly that what has been called the genre objection to my analysis is not tenable. It is not a question of nominalization, for example, being a feature of historical writing such that it occurs frequently in the textbooks. If this were the case we would find that it occurred with roughly equal frequency in the case of Japan and Germany.

# 4 The surrenders of Germany and Japan
## The ideology of face-protection

The analysis and discussion in this chapter will stay within the ideational area of the grammar, but the interpretation of the findings will be in terms of face theory (Brown and Levinson 1987), which takes us in to what is generally regarded as a rather different area of linguistics, that known as pragmatics.

The aim here will be to show that the textbooks, considered as a whole, downplay the face-threatening nature of the Japanese surrender. I will also look at the language of Hirohito's radio broadcast of 15 August and suggest that some of the face-saving strategies we see in this broadcast are uncritically being recycled in the textbooks. This is another example of recycling wartime language, which was briefly brought up in the previous chapter.

This broadcast is extraordinary in its complete denial of the aggressive nature of the war Japan fought from 1931 to 1945, the denial of responsibility on Hirohito's part, and the way, in looking to both the recent historical past and the mythical past, it reaffirmed and legitimized the nature of the imperial state, while at the same time, by the way it looked to the future, prepared the Japanese people for occupation of their sacred land by foreigners. As Dower writes (1999: 36), 'Despite its chaotic genesis, the rescript emerged as a polished ideological gem'.

This broadcast is still given a special name in Japanese, *gyokuon-hoosoo*, usually translated simply as 'Imperial Broadcast', but written with the ideographs for 'jewel' and 'sound'. In Japan today, it is not infrequently referred to by the older generation with something bordering on embarrassed reverence. The resolutions passed by prefectural assemblies and the comments made by various politicians regarding the just nature of Japan's war bear striking similarities to parts of this broadcast. Dower captures something of the manner in which this broadcast continues to resonate in modern Japan when he writes (1999: 36), 'Like insects in amber, lines and phrases from the broadcast soon became locked in popular consciousness'. In the conclusion of this chapter, it will be argued that the ideology and actual words of this broadcast have become so locked in consciousness that they find their way into current history textbooks. In the terminology adopted in this book, the broadcast has become part of a naturalized ideology that we can still see in the textbooks. It will, therefore, be necessary to quote this broadcast in full, and examine it in some detail

In this chapter, a comparison between the language used to describe the German surrender and the Japanese surrender will also be made.

## Historical background

There is a genuine historical debate that concerns two questions: What kind of surrender took place in 1945? and, Was it the Japanese state that actually surrendered in 1945?

The war aims of the Allies involved the unconditional surrender of the three Axis Powers. In the case of the Italian surrender, both because of the course of events and because of the view of the Allies that Italy was less culpable than Germany, there was some compromise.

Some Allied governments wanted to try Hirohito as a war criminal (e.g. Australia and New Zealand) but it was realized by the American and British governments, although it was only the American one that really counted, that it was necessary for Hirohito to retain his position in order to bring about the surrender of widely scattered, still intact, military forces throughout the Pacific, South-East Asia, and China, and in order to effect an orderly occupation and post-war administration of Japan. Villa (1976: 66) writes that:

> On August 10, 1945, the Japanese government finally announced its willingness to surrender on the sole condition that the imperial institution not be prejudiced. In roundabout ways, the American government met the request, one which virtually everyone had anticipated and which many in Washington had long been prepared to make.

The Japanese reply to the Potsdam Declaration, after lengthy discussion, was that they were willing to accept it 'with the understanding that the said declaration does not compromise any demand which prejudices the prerogatives of His Majesty as a sovereign ruler' (quoted in Bergamini 1971: 90). The reply from Washington to the Japanese request (quoted in Bergamini 1971: 91) stated that:

> From the moment of surrender, the authority of the Emperor and the Japanese government to rule the state shall be subject to the Supreme Commander of the Allied Powers, who will take such steps as he deems proper to effectuate the surrender terms. ... The ultimate form of government of Japan shall, in accordance with the Potsdam Declaration, be established by the freely expressed will of the Japanese people.

In other words, the reply to the Japanese request for one condition was a vague and ambiguously worded compromise. Whether this constitutes unconditional surrender, seems hard to say. According to Campbell (1995: 1176), 'it was the Japanese who succeeded in laying down one condition of surrender, the continued rule of Hirohito, in spite of the fact that many in the west regarded him as a war criminal'. As far as Bix (2000: 498–500) is concerned, the unconditional nature of the surrender remained intact.

The question also arises as to whether the Japanese state itself surrendered or only the Japanese armed forces, or whether there is any real difference between these two. Behr (1990: 296) writes of the Potsdam Declaration that, 'Without outlining any specific concessions, it fell short of the earlier (Cairo summit) request for Japan's unconditional surrender, calling instead for "the unconditional surrender of all Japanese armed forces," which was a very different proposition'. Weintraub (1996: 265) agrees that from the Japanese point of view there was a large and significant difference between Japan itself surrendering and its armed forces surrendering. Bix, however, writes (2000: 748 (note 44)) that it was the official American position that Japan's surrender was unconditional, and applied to Japan, including its armed forces and government.

The arguments for and against any of the above positions are historically and legally complex, and they do not really concern us here. Nevertheless, it is easy to see that there is enough in all this to argue the case that Japan itself never lost the war, since it was the Japanese armed forces that surrendered, not Japan itself, and that this surrender was not an unconditional surrender, but a negotiated one. In other words, in 1945 Japan negotiated the surrender of its armed forces. Thus Miller (1982: 207) is not joking when he writes that there is an 'important segment of contemporary Japanese intellectual opinion that now argues to the effect that Japan did not, in actual fact, lose the war, and that also claims Japan did not actually surrender to the Allies in August 1945'. In its extreme forms, such an argument leads to the conclusion that many of the actions of the occupation authorities, including the Tokyo war crimes trials, were illegal.

It is necessary to bear in mind this controversy or remaining ambiguity regarding the Japanese surrender since we will, perhaps, see it appearing implicitly in the language of the textbooks.

At noon on 15 August 1945, Hirohito's pre-recorded message was broadcast to the Japanese people. The English translation (in Weintraub 1996: 594, 595) is quoted in full below, with paragraph numbering added for subsequent reference:

To our good and loyal subjects:

1. After pondering deeply the general trends of the world and the actual conditions obtaining in Our Empire today, We have decided to effect a settlement of the present situation by resorting to an extraordinary measure.
2. We have ordered our Government to communicate to the Governments of the United States, Great Britain, China, and the Soviet Union that Our Empire accepts the provisions of their Joint Declaration.
3. To strive for the common prosperity and the happiness of all nations as well as the security and well-being of Our subjects is the solemn obligation which has been handed down by Our Imperial Ancestors and which lies close to Our heart.
4. Indeed, We declared war on America and Britain out of Our sincere desire to ensure Japan's self-preservation and the stabilization of East Asia, it being far from Our thought either to infringe upon the sovereignty of other nations or to embark upon territorial aggrandizement.
5. But now the war has lasted for nearly four years. Despite the best that has been done by everyone – the gallant fighting of the military and naval forces, the diligence and assiduity of Our servants of the State, and the devoted service of Our one hundred million people – the war situation has developed not necessarily to Japan's advantage, while the general trends of the world have all turned against her interest.
6. Moreover, the enemy has begun to employ a new and most cruel bomb, the power of which to do damage is indeed incalculable, taking the toll of many innocent lives. Should

We continue to fight, not only would it result in an ultimate-collapse and obliteration of the Japanese nation, but also it would lead to the total extinction of human civilization.

7  Such being the case, how are We to save millions of Our subjects, or to atone Ourselves before the hallowed spirits of Our Imperial Ancestors? This is the reason why We have ordered the acceptance of the provisions of the Joint Declaration of the Powers.

8  We cannot but express the deepest sense of regret to Our Allied nations of East Asia, who have consistently cooperated with the Empire towards the emancipation of East Asia.

9  The thought of those officers and men as well as others who have fallen in the fields of battle, those who have died at their posts of duty, or those who met with untimely death and all their bereaved families, pains Our heart night and day.

10  The welfare of the wounded and the war-sufferers, and of those who have lost their homes and livelihood, are the objects of Our profound solicitude.

11  The hardships and sufferings to which Our nation is to be subjected hereafter will be certainly great. We are keenly aware of the inmost feelings of all of you, Our subjects. However, it is according to the dictates of time and fate that We have resolved to pave the way for a grand peace for all the generations to come by enduring the unendurable and suffering what is insufferable.

12  Having been able to safeguard and maintain the structure of the Imperial State, We are always with you, Our good and loyal subjects, relying on your sincerity and integrity.

13  Beware most strictly of any outbursts of emotion which may engender needless complications, or any fraternal contention and strife which may create confusion, lead you astray, and cause you to lose the confidence of the world.

14  Let the entire nation continue as one family from generation to generation, ever firm in its faith in the imperishability of its sacred land, and mindful of its heavy burden of responsibility and the long road before it.

15  Unite your total strength, to be devoted to construction for the future. Cultivate the ways of rectitude, foster nobility of spirit, and work with resolution – so that you may enhance the innate glory of the Imperial State and keep pace with the progress of the world.

This is how the Japanese people learnt that they had lost the war. It took some time for this to sink in since Hirohito spoke in a court language somewhat different from that of his subjects, and in many places the radio reception was poor.

This broadcast has been criticized for mendacity and lack of frankness (e.g. Bix 2000: 487–530; Dower 1999: 34–45). Guillain, who was in Japan at the time of the surrender, writes (1981: 269–271):

> How odd the proclamation was, and how Japanese in spirit! How prudently it dealt with the future, how careful it was not to tarnish the book of Japanese history with the forbidden word 'surrender'.
> . . .
> Not once was the word 'defeat' mentioned. Should the military, in the future, have occasion to rewrite history to their liking, they will be able to cite the proclamation as witness that Japan had ended the war only because of the inhumanity of her enemies and that, even though her armies were intact, her Emperor had agreed to end the carnage because he wished to be not only the savior of Japan but the defender of human civilization.

## The surrender and the threat to face

It is difficult to convey the effect that the Japanese surrender had on the Japanese people. Much of Japanese education had for many years served the interests of the imperial state. The foundation myths of the Japanese race and the descent of the imperial family from the Sun Goddess had been taught as facts to children (Bix 2000: 31, 32, 71, 283; Brownlee 1997: 8–10; Wray 1983), with history scholars more or less cooperating with such perversions of their academic field (Brownlee 1997: 8–10).

The belief in the Japanese as a unique race, inhabiting a sacred land, and set apart from the rest of humanity, was a major tenet of education, and indeed was restated in Hirohito's broadcast (paragraph 14: 'the imperishability of its sacred land'). In the *Oosaka Mainichi Shimbun* of 9 Dec. 1941 (the day after the start of the Pacific War), we find reference to 'we will not let [the enemy] touch with even one finger the sublime sacred land of Japan' (*suukoo-naru shinkoku Nippon ni isshi mo furesasete naranu*) (*Oosaka Mainichi Shimbun*, 9 Dec. 1941b). And in the same article 'the day the Yamato race [a nationalistic term for the 'Japanese race', CB] rises up has finally arrived' (*Yamato minzoku ga agatte tatsu hi ga tsui ni kita*). On the first page (but not subsequent pages) of newspapers of the time, the mythical year of the foundation of Japan (year 2601(!) in 1941) was given. (It goes without saying, that the self-conscious, bombastic repetition of this kind of rhetoric creates nothing more than the impression that the people who were responsible for it really did not believe it themselves, but were quite happy to use it for their own purposes.)

Throughout the war, official propaganda had stressed the impossibility of the Japanese being defeated because of the very fact of being Japanese; any industrial or material inferiority in the face of the Allies could always be cancelled out by the superior Japanese spirit.

Ienaga, who was born in 1913, captures the Japanese people's feelings at the time of the surrender, when he writes (1978: 232, 233; originally published in Japanese in 1968):

> Defeat had been unthinkable, surrender inconceivable. Neither rulers nor ruled were prepared for the humiliation of national failure and occupation by foreign troops. Minds recoiling from reality sought scapegoats or fantasies of revenge. Persons in authority tried to shift responsibility to the public. .... The government avoided the word 'surrender' and used such euphemisms as 'acceptance of the Potsdam Declaration' or 'the end of the war.' But no words were adequate to express or conceal the national trauma of defeat.

As the above discussion makes clear, the defeat that Japan faced was traumatic. The saving of face was a major consideration of the Japanese government as it became obvious that Japan could not stave off defeat for much longer. The army minister and others vainly tried to attach additional conditions, apart from the one concerning the position of Hirohito, to the Potsdam Declaration. These were that the Japanese armed forces should be allowed to disarm themselves, that there should be no occupation of Japan, and that Japan itself should be allowed to try those accused of war crimes (Behr 1990: 298, 299; Bix 2000: 512; Weintraub 1996: 549). What was of paramount importance to the leaders of Japan was how to lose as gracefully as possible after their world had collapsed around them, as Bix writes (2000: 520, 521):

> The wartime Emperor ideology that sustained their morale made it almost impossibly difficult for them to perform the act of surrender. Knowing they were defeated, yet indifferent to the suffering that the war was imposing on their own people, let alone the peoples of Asia, the Pacific, and the West whose lives they had disrupted, the

Emperor and his war leaders searched for a way to lose without losing – a way to assuage domestic criticism after surrender and allow their power structure to survive.

There was a large vocabulary of euphemism connected with the subsequent Allied occupation of Japan. A Japanese word equivalent to the 'stationed army' (*shinchuu-gun*) was used, instead of one equivalent to the 'occupying army', because the Japanese could not readily bring themselves to use the latter term (Iokibe 1995).

The idea of foreigners moving about Japan just as they pleased and inquiring into whatever they wished had been one of the worst fears of the rulers of Japan for 500 years. 'Expel the barbarians' had been a rallying cry of conservative forces in Japan up to the time of the Meiji Restoration of 1868. One of the priorities of the government of the Meiji Emperor (Hirohito's grandfather) had been the abolition of the extra-territorial rights of foreigners in Japan. It was only with the accomplishment of this that Japan could see itself in its own eyes as a modern, internationally accepted country, and the Japanese themselves would no longer have to bear the humiliation of foreigners living in their own country with special legal protection.

But in 1945, thousands of foreigners were going to be setting foot in Japan, without so much as a by-your-leave; and they were going to be actively digging for evidence regarding war responsibility and war crimes; they were going to be confiscating documents, apprehending people for questioning, arresting some of them, and almost certainly conducting war crimes trials. The possibility of putting Hirohito on trial as a war criminal was real. At the very least, it seemed likely that he, or a close member of the imperial family, would have to suffer the humiliation of signing the instrument of surrender. The abdication of Hirohito was very much on the cards.

All this was a serious threat to the face of the country, and especially the rulers, who were responsible for the war and the defeat. How could these leaders, who had consistently lied about the progress of the war to the ordinary Japanese people, and who were responsible for leading the people into this terrible disaster, possibly hope to maintain any power, influence, authority, loyalty, or respect?

## Face theory

Face theory (Brown and Levinson 1987) affords us a convenient way of thinking about the period in question and how it is handled in the history textbooks. The idea of face is not very different from the commonly accepted use of the word 'face' in such expressions as 'saving face'. The wish that the Japanese forces should disarm themselves is an example of an army, and its leaders, trying to save face at the time of military defeat. Hirohito's broadcast is an example of his trying to save his own face, and also that of the defeated Japanese people. According to Hirohito, Japan's policies over many years had not finally come home to roost, and left her in a position in which the only alternative was to surrender. Far from Japan waging a disastrous war and having to take responsibility for this, Hirohito blamed the situation on the general trends of the world (paragraph 5) and the development of a situation. There was no mention of Japan having run out of all options, with the only course left being to surrender in the face of overwhelming military superiority; or rather, the military superiority that the Allies had achieved by this stage of the war was judged to be 'cruel' (paragraph 6) – the Japanese bombing of the many cities in China, and the years of atrocities there and elsewhere, being conveniently forgotten. Far from being pushed into a corner, Hirohito decided to settle everything after careful consideration of the international situation (paragraph 1). He accepted no responsibility for anything (paragraph 4), but decided to make great and unselfish concessions (paragraph 1) in order to save humanity from destruction (paragraph 7). The war Japan fought for 15 years was, as far as Hirohito was concerned, a war of nearly four years (paragraph 5), and had nothing to do with territorial expansion (paragraph 4). According to Hirohito, the people of East Asia were working hand-in-hand with the Japanese in order to liberate themselves from western colonialism (paragraph 8). At the end of the day, as far as this broadcast was concerned, he had maintained his position (paragraph 11) and the people he was addressing were still his subjects (paragraph 11), with the duty of enhancing the Imperial State (paragraph 14), in which all Japanese were members of one family (paragraph 13), of which of course he was the head.

Since the aim of Hirohito's broadcast was to convey to the Japanese people what had happened in the best possible terms, provide an honourable reason for both having fought, and now ending, the war, and preserve as much of the state and governmental structure (including the imperial system) as possible, it is easy to understand the content and the language of this broadcast.

We can think of the above discussion in terms of face theory – a theory of how considerations of face are expressed in language. In this section, face theory will be briefly introduced and outlined, and then its relevance to the language of the textbooks will be discussed. The following draws heavily on Brown and Levinson.

Brown and Levinson (1987: 61) define negative face as 'the basic claim to territories, personal preserves, rights to non-distraction – i.e. to freedom of action and freedom from imposition'. Actions that constitute threats to negative face include (Brown and Levinson 1987: 65, 66):

a) Threats or warnings that put pressure on the addressee to carry out or not carry out certain acts, in the face of possible sanctions.
b) Expressions of anger or disapproval that suggest the speaker intends to harm the addressee or his possessions.

As Brown and Levinson write (1987: 62), negative face is 'the want of every "competent adult member" that his actions be unimpeded by others'.

Positive face is defined by Brown and Levinson as (1987: 61) as 'the positive consistent self-image or 'personality' (crucially including the desire that this self-image be appreciated and approved of) claimed by interactants'. Actions which constitute threats to positive face include (1987: 66, 67):

a) Expressions of disapproval, criticism, or contempt, or accusations, or expression of the view that the speaker does not like the addressee's beliefs, values, or personal characteristics.
b) The bringing of news that is good for the speaker, or bad for the addressee.

As Brown and Levinson write (1987: 62), positive face involves 'the want of every member that his wants be desirable to at least some others'.

So, to sum this up: if I carelessly or willingly infringe on your territory, either literally or psychologically, I am threatening your negative face. If I threaten your negative face, you can seek to protect it in a variety of ways (such as, for example, by threatening my negative face in turn, or by pretending not to notice that any face-threat has been made, and thus simply ignoring either me or the face-threat). If I make clear that I do not value what you value, I am threatening your positive face; if I make clear that I value what you value, I am respecting (in Brown and Levinson's terminology (1987: 101), 'making redress to') your positive face.

## Applying face theory to the surrender

Face theory provides a useful way of looking at the Japanese surrender in 1945. Japan was being threatened by the Allies in that Japan's basic claim to territories (the physical territorial possessions of Japan and its overseas empire) was being increasingly disputed and encroached upon by the Allies as the war progressed. The Japanese government well knew (despite the propaganda to the general populace) that there was only one end to this conflict, namely, the defeat and almost certain occupation of Japan. Japan's freedom of action was being increasingly restricted, and, furthermore, both at the time of the surrender and in any post-war settlement there were going to be severe restrictions placed on the Japanese state and the Japanese people. There was certainly pressure on the Japanese government to carry out certain acts (namely, surrender) in the face of sanctions. These sanctions included the steadily mounting military pressure (including the entry into the war by the Soviet Union on 8 August) and the diplomatic impasse in which Japan found itself, as well as the two atomic bombs that had recently been dropped on Hiroshima and Nagasaki. Also, it was clear that the Allies regarded Japan as a dangerous militaristic country and would, from the Japanese point of view, be harming its possessions, both within Japan and by confiscation of Japanese overseas possessions, assets, and so on. Thus Japan's negative face was being seriously threatened as the war drew to a close, and would be further threatened at the time of, and after, the actual surrender.

The Allies also threatened the positive face of the Japanese state by announcing that they rejected Japanese values, particularly the leadership and the system of government. As well as this, the Potsdam Declaration was, in effect, bringing the bad news that there was no chance of Japan winning the war (although, of course, those in the leadership class had known this for a long time) and that, from the Allies' point of view, the good news that although the fighting had not ended, they nevertheless, would certainly be the victors.

As the discussion regarding the historical events themselves and the content of Hirohito's broadcast make clear, at the time of surrender the Japanese state was acutely aware of the threat to its face. The question that will be examined here is, to what extent did the Japanese state's desire to protect its face in 1945 (as seen in the attempt to attach face-saving conditions to the Potsdam Declaration and in the language and content of Hirohito's broadcast) carry over to the textbooks of today.

Face theory is generally thought of as applying to person-to-person verbal interactions occurring in real time. When I write of the textbooks protecting the face of the Japanese state, the time lapse between the face-threating event (i.e. the surrender) and the textbooks writing about it is more than five decades. The face of an organization (namely, the Japanese state) is being protected by the people and organizations responsible for writing, authorizing, and publishing the textbooks (i.e. the authors, Ministry of Education, and publishers). This does not invalidate the application of face theory to the present data since neither the channel of communication (written vs spoken language) nor the time lapse between the event and the language used to refer to it, conflicts with face theory.

Neither does the application of face theory to organizations invalidate the analysis and conclusions. I myself am not familiar with any work that applies face theory to organizations, such as countries or the governmental or bureaucratic organs of such countries. However, when one considers that any organization is a collection of individuals who, by virtue of being members of that organization, have group interests and loyalties, that often conflict with the interests of those outside the organization, then it seems to me that applying face theory to organizations does not conflict with the theory. Indeed, in our daily lives it is not that uncommon for any individual to come into conflict with some organization whose main aim seems to be to protect its face; perhaps many readers of this book will have had the thought, 'Such-and-such a government department will never admit that it is wrong'. In face theory terms, this can be expressed as, 'Such-and-such a government department will not allow its negative face to be threatened by ordinary citizens encroaching upon what is seen as the authority, decision-making power, etc. of that department'.

What we see in the language of the textbooks is a consistent use of language that strives to show that the Japanese state and its leaders acted in a way such that their actions were unimpeded by others. In other words, they were acting relatively freely from any imposition. Readers might not readily accept this claim of mine; it is difficult to think of a state that has ever been driven into a corner in the way that Japan had been in 1945. In history, few states had been so thoroughly defeated in such an unwise war. The overwhelming military and industrial might of the Allies (principally the Americans of course – but not forgetting that the greatest number of Japanese forces had always been committed to China), the huge technological gap, the rapid advances of the Allies in the Pacific and in Asia, the recent entry of the Soviet Union into the

*The surrenders of Germany and Japan* 133

war and the collapse of Japanese resistance in Manchuria, and the growing number of deaths from starvation of the Japanese within Japan itself, all showed that Japan was very much on its last legs.

The following text is a rather typical example from the textbooks:

**Text 4.1** (Ishii *et al.* 2002: 325)

Nihon-seifu ga taioo ni kurushinde iru aida ni, Amerika wa 8-gatsu muika Hiroshima ni, tsuide kokonoka Nagasaki ni genshi-bakudan o tooka-shita. Mata 8-gatsu yooka, Soren wa mada yuukookikan-nai ni atta Nisso-chuuritsujooyaku o mushi-shite sensenfukoku-shi, Manshuu/Choosen ni shinnyuu-shita. Kooshita joosei no moto de, seifu to gun shunoobu wa gozenkaigi de, Shoowa Tennoo no saidan ni yori Potsudamu-sengen no judaku o kettei-shi, seifu wa juuyokka kore o Rengookoku-gawa ni tsuukoku-shita. 8-gatsu 15-nichi, Tennoo no rajio-hoosoo de sentoo wa teishi-sare, 9-gatsu futsuka, Tookyoowan-nai no Amerika gunkan Mizuuri-goo joo de, Nihon-seifu oyobi gun-daihyoo ga koofuku-bunsho ni shomei-shita. Kooshite yaku 4-nen ni wattata Taiheiyoo-sensoo wa shuuryoo-shita.

Translation: While the Japanese government was agonizing over the response [to the Potsdam Declaration], America dropped an atomic bomb on Hiroshima on 6 August and then on Nagasaki on the 9th. Furthermore, on 8 August the Soviet Union ignored the Japanese–Soviet neutrality treaty while it was still in force and declaring war, invaded Manchuria and Korea. Under these conditions, at an imperial conference the government and military leadership decided on acceptance of the Potsdam Declaration in accordance with the decision of the Shoowa Emperor [i.e. Hirohito, CB], and on the 14th the government informed the Allied side of this. On 15 August the fighting was stopped by the Emperor's radio broadcast, and on 2 September on board the American warship *Missouri* in Tokyo Bay, the Japanese government [representatives?, CB] and military representatives signed the surrender document. Thus the Pacific War, which had lasted for about four years, came to an end.

At this time, the Japanese state's negative face was being seriously threatened due to the fact that it had no choice but to surrender. But interestingly enough, no surrendering takes place in the above text.

Of course, there is a 'surrender' in the narrative, but this is in the form of a piece of paper ('the surrender document': *koofuku-bunsho*) that Japan signed, not in the form of the face-threatening *act* of surrendering (i.e. not expressed verbally). Surrender gets into the story only by the back-door, as it were. This is a very common pattern throughout the textbooks. What enables surrendering, as an act, not to take place is the fact that the Potsdam Declaration stands for surrendering, and then the Potsdam Declaration becomes a main focus of the narrative, with the actual surrender never taking place, but being alluded to in terms of the 'surrender document'. This is exactly in conformity with the point made by Ienaga, quoted above (page 127), about the Potsdam Declaration standing for surrender, and is also in conformity with the way in which 'joint declaration' is made to stand for surrender in Hirohito's broadcast (paragraph 2).

In my discussion of functional grammar being a grammar of choice on the paradigmatic axis of language, I said that behind 'I would like a beer' there are many other possibilities hovering in the background, as it were. If we look at the stressing by this textbook, and the textbooks generally, of 'accepting/acceptance of the Potsdam Declaration', we find something similar happening. Once 'accepting' (either in its verbal form, 'accept', or in its nominal form, 'acceptance') is set up as a main part of the historical narrative, the text is then able to suggest that 'not accepting/rejecting' existed. Thus, the textbooks are intimating that the possibility of not accepting the Potsdam Declaration was a real one and, in this way, the textbooks are saying that the state was not being seriously imposed on by having been driven into a corner. In other words, the textbooks of today are minimizing the threat to the negative face of the state at the time of surrender in 1945.

The last point I will bring up with regard to this example is the way in which the story is carried forward by a group of verbs that show mature deliberation and freedom of choice ('decided': *kettei-shi*), statesmanlike action ('informed': *tsuukoku-shita*), wise, unselfish use of authority and power ('was stopped': *teishi-sare*), and ceremonial behaviour ('signed': *shomei-shita*). The exception to this is the 'agonizing' (*kurushinde iru*) of the Japanese government. But this is not true agony – only the agony of making a response.

This attribution of a feeling of agony to the Japanese government in the same sentence that reports the dropping of the atomic bombs on Hiroshima and Nagasaki, the citizens of which suffered indescribable agony, is astonishingly callous, especially when one considers that the Japanese government by this time knew that the war was lost and that if Japan's leaders had managed to get over their agonizing more quickly, hundreds of thousands of Japanese citizens would have been saved from death and terrible suffering. What we see here is an extreme example of a 'government-centred history' that totally ignores the general Japanese people.

In Text 4.1 above, Japan is certainly in a difficult position, but nevertheless it is portrayed as preserving its freedom of choice and having a wide area of manoeuvre. This is the prevalent pattern in the textbooks. In terms of negative face, the textbooks consistently minimize the negative face-threat to the Japanese state of the time; in the terminology used here, the textbooks are protecting the negative face of the state. But also, the textbooks are actually respecting the positive face of the state. The argument for this is a little less obvious than in the case of negative face, but the textbooks, by uncritically writing in this manner show that they are valuing what the Japanese state valued at the time, namely, that its decision-making power and its authority, both internationally and nationally, should be recognized. The textbooks are, in Brown and Levinson's terminology (1987: 103) 'claiming common ground' with the Japanese state of 1945.

In studying the history of Japan's surrender, what strikes one more than anything else is certainly not the decisiveness of the leaders, but the lack of a clear policy and firm resolution, as mentioned by, for example, Dower (1999: 22):

> Long after it had become obvious that Japan was doomed, its leaders all the way up to the emperor remained unable to contemplate surrender. They were psychologically blocked, capable only of stumbling forward.

In Chapter 3, it was argued that noun phrases are one important resource by which the aggressive nature of Japan's attacks is minimized in the language of the textbooks. This was specifically discussed in terms of grammatical metaphor. In this chapter, when 'accept the Potsdam Declaration' (*Potsudamu-sengen o judaku-suru*) is nominalized to 'acceptance of the Potsdam Declaration' (*Potsudamu-sengen no judaku*), as in Text 4.1 above, we find this results in a range of uses of language which respect positive face, as is plainly illustrated in the following example:

**Text 4.2** (Toriumi *et al.* 2002: 144)

Suzuki-naikaku wa Tennoo no saidan to iu irei na katachi o totte, gunbu no ichibu ni atta sensookeizoku-ron o osae, 1945- (Shoowa 20-) nen 8-gatsu juuyokka, Potsudamu-sengen no judaku o saishuu-teki ni kettei-shite, kore o Rengookoku-gawa ni tsuukoku-shita. Yoku 8-gatsu 15-nichi, Shoowa Tennoo jishin no rajio-hoosoo o tsuujite, kokumin ni kore o akiraka ni shita.

Kooshite, 6-nen ni mo watatte, zensekai ni kuuzen no sangai o motorashita Dainiji-sekaitaisen wa, Kujikujin'ei no haiboku ni yotte owari o tsugeta.

Translation: The Suzuki cabinet took the unprecedented step of the Emperor's decision, and suppressed the view of continuing the war which existed within some sections of the armed forces, and on 14 August 1945 (Shoowa 20) finally decided on acceptance of the Potsdam Declaration, and informed the Allied side of this. The next day, on 15 August, the Shoowa Emperor himself [Hirohito, CB] made this clear to the people by a radio broadcast.

Thus, the conclusion of the Second World War, which had lasted for all of six years and brought unprecedented carnage to the world, was signalled with the defeat of the Axis Powers.

What happens in many textbooks, as shown by Text 4.2 above, is that once there is a nominalization, this means that the noun phrase itself can be manipulated by the grammar in a variety of ways. The argument is again the same as previously made: when what would be the process in the congruent realization gets encapsulated in a noun phrase, then what would be the process slot in the congruent realization becomes empty, and can then be filled by a large number of processes. I previously discussed the process slot being filled with innocuous or semantically rather empty verbs, as in examples like 'the Nanking Massacre occurred'. In Text 4.2 above, and in many of the textbooks, we see the *opposite* happening; the process slot is filled with semantically 'heavy' verbs, and ones that suggest determination and freedom of choice, such as 'consider/decide on/announce/inform the Allies of/convey to the Japanese people acceptance of the Potsdam Declaration'.

What happens in these cases is that by nominalizing 'Potsdam Declaration' it can be grammatically controlled and manipulated. And then, being able to manipulate it in this way becomes indistinguishable

*The surrenders of Germany and Japan* 137

from being able to control and manipulate the historical events themselves. The Japanese state thus, according to the textbooks, is very much in control of the development of historical events. Again, there is little threat to its negative face, and its positive face is actually being respected.

Thinking of this in terms of clause primacy, another effect of this nominalization of 'Potsdam Declaration' is that what should surely be the main point of the narrative (namely, the fact that 'Japan *accepted* the Potsdam Declaration', present in an alpha clause) does not occur in the text, but, rather, the main point of the narrative is encoded in other acts that respect the positive face of the state by showing that it was acting responsibly and of its own volition – in the example above, 'informed the Allied side of this'. The argument here is the same as the argument concerning clause primacy with reference to the German and Japanese attacks.

As I have said above, the surrender very frequently never *takes place* in the pages of the textbooks because it gets into the story by the backdoor, in the form of a piece of paper that various representatives sign. The ceremonial nature of the surrender is thus emphasized. In the above example, we can read between the lines, and assume that Japan was made to sign the document, or had no other choice but to sign the document. In other words, Japan was coerced in some way, and its negative face was thereby threatened. However, in some textbooks the signing ceremony is between the Allies and Japan on an equal basis. The following purposefully selected example shows this:

**Text 4.3** (Esaka, Takeuchi *et al.* 2002: 320)

Gunbu wa hondoo kessen o sakende, nao sensoo o keizoku-shiyoo to shita ga, seifu wa kokutai no goji (tennoo-sei no iji) o jooken ni, 8-gatsu juuyokka, Tennoo no saidan ni yori, tsui ni Potsudamu-sengen o judaku-suru koto o kime, yokujitsu, Shoowa Tennoo wa rajio o tsuujite, mizukara kore o kokumin ni tsugeta. Soshite 9-gatsu futsuka, Tookyoowan-joo no Amerika gunkan Mizuuri-goo de, Rengookoku-daihyoo to Nihon-daihyoo to no aida ni, koofuku-bunsho no chooin-shiki ga okonawareta.

Translation: The military clamoured for a decisive battle on the home islands [the four main islands of Japan, CB], and made as if to continue the war, but the government with the preservation of the national polity (maintenance of the imperial system) as a condition, on 14 August, by means of the Emperor's decision, finally decided on accepting the Potsdam Declaration, and the next day the Shoowa Emperor himself over the radio informed the people of this. And then on 2 September on the American warship, *Missouri*, in Tokyo Bay, the signing ceremony of the surrender document was held between the Allied countries' representatives and the Japanese representatives.

Actually, looking at the last sentence more closely, it is noticeable that the participatory roles of the Allied representatives and the Japanese representatives are attenuated by the grammar. The various representatives do not sign the document, nor is the document even signed by them (according to a strict reading of the text), but the representatives are a kind of location ('the ceremony was held between the Allied countries' representatives and the Japanese representatives') in which the signing ceremony takes place.

The highly face-threatening act of being made to sign the document of surrender on an American battleship in Tokyo Bay, crowded with the Allied warships, in front of representatives of all the Allied nations and thousands of soldiers and sailors, with American warplanes flying overhead in their hundreds, is very far from being a kind of ceremony held between various representatives on an equal basis.

Also, in Text 4.3 the Allies do not figure in the narrative until they become part of a location for the signing ceremony. They only exist insofar that it may be assumed that they are, in some sense, behind the Potsdam Declaration. The history is one centred on Japan, with no reference made to outside force and threats.

In Text 4.3, also note the words that denote control and decision-making power on the part of the Japanese leaders (i.e. 'the Emperor's decision', 'decided on accepting', 'informed the people'). The impression created here is very similar to that discussed in Text 4.1 (and actually also in Text 4.2).

### *Talking across vs talking down*

The textbooks also protect the negative face of the Japanese state and Hirohito by portraying the state as 'talking across' to the Allies as equals, almost always by using the word 'informed' (*tsuukoku-suru*). There is nothing in this word that suggests unequal power relations. But then the Japanese people are 'talked down' to, usually by Hirohito. For the sake of ease of reference part of Text 4.2 is repeated here:

## The surrenders of Germany and Japan  139

**Text 4.4** (repetition of part of 4.2)

... Potsudamu-sengen no judaku o saishuu-teki ni kettei-shite, kore o Rengookoku-gawa ni tsuukoku-shita. Yoku 8-gatsu 15-nichi, Shoowa Tennoo jishin no rajio-hoosoo o tsuujite, kokumin ni kore o akiraka ni shita.

Translation: ... finally decided on acceptance of the Potsdam Declaration, and informed the Allied side of this. The next day, on 15 August, the Shoowa Emperor himself made this clear to the people by a radio broadcast.

What stands out in this text is the way the Japanese leadership preserve their power, but the people are put in their places, as they were in Hirohito's actual surrender broadcast (paragraph 12: 'Our good and loyal subjects'; paragraph 15: 'so that you may enhance the innate glory of the Imperial State'). It is made rather clear to pupils studying these textbooks what the writers of the textbooks regard as the normal relationship between the Japanese government and the Emperor, on the one hand, and the mass of Japanese people, on the other hand. Even if this position of subservience to the Emperor and government was the norm before 1945, one would at least hope that in modern history textbooks the authors themselves might seek to challenge it. However, this is certainly not what we see.

In functional grammar terms what we have is a transitivity configuration of Speaker + Verbiage (the matter that is spoken or communicated) + Receiver (the party who receives the speech or communication) + Verbal process (the act of saying or communicating). We can label these as follows:

1   *Suzuki-naikaku wa*
    Speaker
    **The Suzuki cabinet**

    *kore o (viz. Potsudamu-sengen no judaku o kettei-suru koto)*
    Verbiage
    **this** (viz. decision to accept the Potsdam Declaration)

    *Rengookoku-gawa ni*
    Receiver
    **to the Allied side**

*tsuukoku-shita*
Verbal process
**informed**

*Shoowa Tennoo jishin*
Speaker
**the Shoowa Emperor himself**

*kokumin ni*
Receiver
**to the people**

*kore o (viz. Potsudamu-sengen no judaku o kettei-suru koto)*
Verbiage
**this** (viz. decision to accept the Potsdam Declaration)

*akiraka ni shita*
Verbal process
**made clear** (i.e. made clear in words)

**The Suzuki cabinet informed the Allied side of this. The Shoowa Emperor himself made this clear to the people**

In fact, the Japanese people at the surrender are almost always given passive roles or ignored. They are acted on by their government and their leaders.

I am not advocating a people's history. School textbooks in most countries centre on the actions of the government and view the country and the people living in that country as being equal to the government or the army or large interest groups. Nevertheless, the following purposefully selected text, shows that ordinary people can be included as responsible thinking, feeling, human beings, rather than just recipients of knowledge which is conveyed to them by their superiors:

**Text 4.5** (Ienaga *et al.* 2002: 290)

Koko ni itari, Nihon-seifu mo tsui ni koofuku-sezaru o enaku nari, 8-gatsu juuyokka Rengookoku ni sono mune o tsuuchi-shita. Kokumin wa yoku 15-nichi no Tennoo no rajio-hoosoo ni yotte koofuku o shitta.

Translation: Things having come to this [the Soviet declaration of war against Japan, etc., CB] the Japanese government, finally having no choice but to surrender, notified the Allied countries to this effect on 14 August. On the next day, the 15th, the people knew about the surrender by means of the Emperor's radio broadcast.

It is a history in which ordinary people are given active roles in the narrative. The transitivity configuration of the relevant part of this can be shown as follows:

2  *Kokumin wa*
   Senser
   **The people**

   *Tennoo no rajio-hoosoo ni yotte*
   Circumstance of means
   **by means of the Emperor's radio broadcast**

   *koofuku o*
   Phenomenon
   **surrender**

   *shitta.*
   Mental process
   **knew about**

As this shows, the people, as a Senser of a Mental process, can become a focus of the historical narrative; history does not have to be a story of ordinary peoples' betters telling them what is happening or, as is usually the case in the textbooks, what *has already happened*. Such a way of writing history, perhaps, goes some small way towards encouraging pupils to ask such questions as, 'How did my grandfather feel about what happened on 15 August 1945?'

## *Time-slips*

One very common characteristic of the textbooks is the existence of time-slips. This term is used when the text does not clearly record an event as taking place, although the context as well as the assumed background knowledge of readers might, to a greater or lesser extent, lead to the interpretation that the event actually did occur. There are frequent time-slips with reference to the Japanese surrender; in some sense the surrender is in the text because we can assume from a common-sense reading that the surrender took place, but it is nevertheless time-slipped by the grammar. (Whether children, who probably come to these textbooks with little background knowledge and reading, can do the same thing is, of course, another matter.)

In both Text 4.1 and Text 4.2 above there are examples of time-slips. In Text 4.1 the reader is told that 'the government and military leadership decided on acceptance of the Potsdam Declaration in accordance with the decision of the Shoowa Emperor, and on the 14th the government informed the Allied side of this'. With a casual reading of this text, in both the original Japanese and the English translation, the interpretation would probably be that 'the government informed the Allied side that the government accepted the Potsdam Declaration'. However, a more careful reading and interpretation is that 'the government informed the Allied side that the government had decided to accept the Potsdam Declaration', with the 'this' (*kore*) referring back, not to 'accepted the Potsdam Declaration' (*Potsudamu-sengen o judaku-shita*), but to 'decided to accept the Potsdam Declaration' (*Potsudamu-sengen no judaku o kettei-shi*). According to this strict interpretation of the text, the acceptance of the Potsdam Declaration is not unequivocally recorded as having taken place, since to decide to accept something does not necessarily mean that one actually finally accepts it. By this use of a time-slip, the face-threatening act of accepting the Potsdam Declaration (more realistically, of having no choice but to accept the Potsdam Declaration) only occurs in the text by intimation, and the even more face-threatening act of surrendering (more accurately, of having no choice but to surrender) enters the historical narrative by the back-door – by means of being a document that is signed by various Japanese representatives.

In Text 4.2, no actual surrender of Japan takes place and the Japanese defeat is not even individually mentioned, but is wrapped up with the defeats of all the other Axis Powers and evaluated in generalized and all-encompassing terms, while at the same time it is present in the text as a sort of retrospective summary, and by virtue of this is outside the main narrative of events. The Japanese defeat is, with all the defeats, presented as one of the reasons or means by which the Second World War ended, and thus is, again, not given an independent existence in this textbook. This is another example of a time-slip.

Admittedly, there is room to argue against my interpretations of the above texts. Thus, what I have called the careful interpretation of Text 4.1 could be disputed, with the view being put forward that an interpretation based on a more casual reading is the more natural and likely one. In Text 4.2, the lack of mention of the Japanese surrender, and then wrapping up the Japanese defeat in the defeats of the other Axis Powers might have been necessary to save space. However, although such explanations might be persuasive in individual cases, they do not explain the overwhelming pattern in the textbooks of the disappearance of the surrender from the historical narrative.

Even if the above two texts (Text 4.1 and Text 4.2) are examples of excusable, minor time-slips, surely the following is not:

**Text 4.6** (Fukuda *et al.* 2002: 194)

> Shikashi, 8-gatsu juuyokka no gozenkaigi de wa, Tennoo no saidan ni yotte, Potsudamu-sengen no judaku ga kettei-sareta. Yokujitsu ni wa, rajio-hoosoo ni yotte sensoo-shuuketsu no shoosho ga happyoo-sare, kokumin ni haisen ga shirasareta.

> Translation: However, at the imperial conference on 14 August the acceptance of the Potsdam Declaration was decided on by means of the Emperor's decision. On the next day, by means of a radio broadcast, the imperial rescript ending the war was announced, and the people were informed of the defeat in the war.

In this example, the Allies, the party that was coercing Japan and threatening its negative face, have disappeared from the story (although they are present in the paragraph following the one above as part of the location in which the surrender ceremony takes place, as in Text 4.1 above), and the surrender of Japan has become a domestic affair, with a considerable amount of decision-making power being assigned to Hirohito ('acceptance of the Potsdam Declaration was decided on by means of the Emperor's decision'; 'the imperial rescript ending the war was announced'), with his position of authority over the Japanese people made clear ('the people were informed of the defeat').

It is the time-slip in the narrative that makes this possible; readers are simply not told what happened between the decision to accept the Potsdam Declaration and the issuing of the imperial rescript. Even the defeat itself has been time-slipped by the grammar of the text, in that it does not occur in its proper place in the temporal unfolding of events but by the time the people were informed of it, it *had already* taken place. The people are removed as witnesses to history and sufferers from the hardships of war, who every day must have been worrying how the war was going to be brought to an end and how this would affect their lives. According to this text, the people are simply given information by their superiors. It is difficult not to draw the conclusion that the authors of this textbook and the examiners who allowed it to pass the authorization process either hold the Japanese people of the time in great contempt, or are incapable of reproducing anything but the ideology of the imperial state that goes back to the pre-war and wartime periods, in which the Japanese were not citizens of a country, but subjects of the Emperor.

The jumping over of the face-threatening act of surrender by the textbooks, could be explained away if we just had a few examples of it. But the pattern is a very common one in the corpus. In Text 4.7 below, 'surrender' exists in this text as a noun, functioning as a Circumstance of means, which the text assumes to have *already taken place*. The logical connection, or cause and effect relationship, between 'accepted the Potsdam Declaration' (*Potsudamu-sengen o judaku-shita*) and 'by Japan's surrender' (*Nihon no koofuku de*) is very weak, especially when one considers that one of the major aims of pedagogic materials is to make things clear to pupils:

**Text 4.7** (Takahashi *et al.* 2002 :154)

8-gatsu juuyokka, Nihon wa tsui ni Potsudamu-sengen o judaku-shita. Nihon no koofuku de, Dainiji-sekaitaisen wa kanzen ni shuuketsu-shita ga, dooji ni Manshuu-jihen irai, 15-nen ni oyonda Nitchuukan no sensoo ni mo shuushifu ga utareta.

Translation: On 14 August, Japan finally accepted the Potsdam Declaration. By Japan's surrender, the Second World War was competely concluded, and at the same time a close was brought to the war between Japan and China, which had lasted fifteen years from the time of the Manchurian Incident.

By this use of 'Japan's surrender' functioning as a Circumstance of means, the text succeeds in presenting new information as if it were already commonly known information. 'Surrender' is, in some sense, assumed to be 'inside' 'accepted the Potsdam Declaration' and readers of the text are assumed to be cognizant of this. The surrender is then explicitly revealed in the following sentence, not as a central part of the narrative (since it can, for example, be deleted and it has no status at the level of the clause), but as a piece of information explaining the means by which the war ended. To express this differently, the surrender does not stand independently in the sentence in its own right, with the authors validating its existence and allowing readers to negotiate its meanings and question its implications. The point being made here is similar to the one previously made regarding giving a name to the Nanking Massacre at the same time that it occurs. The surrender is presented as a sort of fait accompli which has been taken care of by the omniscient author and about which the readers of the textbooks do not need to concern themselves, or question in any way.

It is difficult to believe that this is a normal writing of history. Either the authors consciously desire to protect the negative face of the Japanese state at the time of the surrender, or they are uncritically recycling the face-saving ideology present in, for example, Hirohito's broadcast.

Interpreting 'time-slip' in rather wide terms (for example, to cover those cases in which 'surrender' only enters the narrative through 'surrender document', and cases such as Text 4.7 above, in which 'surrender' is recorded in the text, but only insofar as it is *assumed to have already taken place*, and therefore outside the normal chronological sequence of the narrative), an examination of all the textbooks reveals that there are 34 instances of time-slips with reference to the Japanese surrender. The corresponding figure for Germany is two.

The Japanese surrender in 1945 was certainly one of the most important events in Japanese history. The present geographical extent of Japan, its constitution, laws, social structure, educational system, economic system, the language itself, and so on, can all be traced back, in one form or another, to the events of August and September 1945. Bearing this in mind, it is very difficult to believe that the history textbooks are writing about these events in a normal manner. What we see in the textbooks is the continuing reproduction of a naturalized ideology.

## *A comment on inaccuracies*

In this book I have kept away from the question of historical 'truth' in the textbooks (which is primarily a question of content), both because I believe a linguistic analysis can be more revealing about ideology in the textbooks and also because the question of 'truth' in a history textbook can be difficult to resolve, with everyone having his or her version of what truth is. In looking at the ABCD line, it was necessary to locate the discussion in terms of what would constitute reasonable historical interpretations of the encirclement of Japan, so to that extent I was dealing with 'truth'.

But the inaccuracies in the textbooks regarding the Japanese surrender, particularly Hirohito's broadcast, are so common and so glaring that it seems necessary to deal with them briefly here. As a simple fact, Hirohito did not even mention the word 'Potsdam' in his broadcast, as asserted by a large number of textbooks (e.g. Text 4.2: '... finally decided on acceptance of the Potsdam Declaration ... The next day, on

15 August, the Shoowa Emperor himself made this clear to the people by a radio broadcast.'). The Japanese government certainly did not want ordinary citizens to know how it had been groping towards surrender, while exhorting the people to greater sacrifices – allowing both military personnel and civilians to die for the glory of the Emperor. To mention the word 'Potsdam' would have made this groping process too clear by anchoring it firmly in time and space – by giving it a name and an identity. Hence, the use of the vaguer term, 'joint declaration'. Neither did Hirohito make clear the fact that Japan had surrendered and was defeated, as many textbooks assert (e.g. Text 4.5: 'On the next day, the 15th, the people knew about the surrender by means of the Emperor's radio broadcast.'; Text 4.6: '... the imperial rescript ending the war was announced, and the people were informed of the defeat in the war.').

The whole point of the broadcast was to bring the war to a close *without* mentioning such words as 'defeat' or 'surrender' to the Japanese people. To do so would of course have meant admitting to the Japanese people that both the negative face (infringement on territory of the other party) and the positive face (rejection of values held by the other party) of the imperial state were being very seriously threatened by the Allies. One major aim of the broadcast was to *avoid* making clear to the Japanese people that Japan had been defeated, but yet intimate this in as face-saving and euphemistic a manner as possible.

So why should the textbooks overwhelmingly write of the Emperor/ government informing/making clear the acceptance of the Potsdam Declaration to the Japanese people? This is so far from what was the actual state of affairs of the time that one has to conclude that the writers and the Ministry of Education consciously deem it very important to protect the face of the wartime imperial state and the Emperor. The way that the textbooks write about Hirohito's broadcast validates the ideology present in this broadcast. Or, another interpretation for this type of historical writing, and the one that I believe is the more likely, is that the people concerned with the production of these textbooks have been so naturalized to the ideology of face-protection clearly shown in Hirohito's broadcast that they are actually incapable of producing textbooks that do not reproduce this ideology uncritically; they are in thrall to a naturalized ideology.

As a matter of fact, by the time of Hirohito's broadcast, a large proportion of the Japanese population had already been receiving more accurate information from the newsheets dropped by the millions by the American air force, than they had from their own government.

The *Rakkasan Nyuusu* ('Parachute News' newsheets dropped on Japan) of 4 August (2000: 51), gave a translation of the text of the Potsdam Declaration, 11 days before Hirohito's broadcast. The source of knowledge was certainly not solely the Emperor, and the knowledge he gave was not as clear as that supplied by the American air force. Bix (2000: 495) states that seven million leaflets were dropped revealing the terms of the Potsdam Declaration.

According to a post-war American air force survey in 33 cities in which these newsheets were dropped, half the respondents had read these sheets or been told about information in them from someone else. Among these, 32 per cent believed them, 24 per cent believed them with reservations, and 33 per cent did not believe them at all (*Rakkasan Nyuusu* 2000: 8).

For the textbooks to write about this would be a serious threat to the negative face of the Japanese state of 1945. First, it would make it clear that the leaders of the state had been lying to the Japanese people about the progress of the war. Second, it would make it clear that the state was, at that time, no longer in control of the dissemination of information within its national territory. Third, it would destroy the semi-sacred nature of this broadcast, which derives this status in part from the fact that the Emperor humiliated himself, that is to say unselfishly allowed his negative face to be greatly threatened (paragraph 11: 'by enduring the unendurable and suffering what is insufferable'), not only for the good of Japan, but the whole world, including future as yet unborn generations (paragraph 3: 'To strive for the common prosperity and the happiness of all nations as well as the security and well-being of our subjects ...'; paragraph 11: 'We have resolved to pave the way for a grand peace for all generations to come ...'). Related to this is, fourth, it would jeopardize the special nature of the broadcast as the founding document of the post-war ideological realignment of Japan, and one of the sources for the revisionist views regarding the war Japan fought as being a war of national self-preservation and not territorial expansion, and of Asian liberation, in which the ten years of war against China which preceded the Pacific War get lumped together with the war against the Western Allies (paragraph 5: 'But now the war has lasted for nearly four years').

## Clause primacy

The discussion on clause primacy will be a brief one since the argument is the same as that in the previous chapter.

148   *The surrenders of Germany and Japan*

The face-threatening act that is the most important part of the narrative is clearly 'surrender'. According to the argument in Chapter 3, we would expect 'surrender' to occur as the main verb of the sentence (i.e. the verb in the alpha clause) rather frequently. In none of the examples above is 'surrender' present in the sentence as a verb – and in only one of them is there any mention of surrender, in which case it is a noun functioning as a Circumstance of means by which the war ends. (I am here excluding 'surrender' entering the texts by the 'back-door', namely, being part of the noun 'surrender document', which is signed by Japan.)

But in order not to give a wrong impression, 'surrender' does occur in some textbooks, as in the following example, in which it is a verb – if not the verb in the alpha clause:

**Text 4.8** (Saitoo *et al.* 2002: 156, 157)

Nihon-seifu wa 8-gatsu juuyokka, kokutai no goji (tennoo-sei no iji) o jooken ni, Potsudamu-sengen o judaku-shite mujookenkoofuku-shi, yoku 15-nichi, Tennoo ga rajio o tsuujite kore o kokumin ni tsugeta. Kooshite nagai sensoo no jidai ga owatta.

Translation: On 14 August the Japanese government, with the preservation of the national polity (the maintenance of the imperial system) as a condition accepted the Potsdam Declaration and surrendered unconditionally, and on the next day the Emperor conveyed this to the people over the radio. Thus the period of long war finished.

Again, it goes without saying that exactly what the Emperor did not convey to the people was that Japan had surrendered, let alone surrendered unconditionally, and he did not mention '*Potsdam* Declaration'.

The data for 'surrender' and clause primacy will be presented in the statistical analysis.

*The surrender: by whom and of what nature?*

This example of 'the Japanese government ... surrendered unconditionally' in Text 4.8 above brings us back to my earlier points regarding what kind of surrender it was that took place in Tokyo Bay, and exactly which party surrendered. There are, as I have pointed out, a variety of opinions regarding this. But laying aside for the moment

*Table 4.1* Scenarios showing threats to negative face

|  | Unconditional surrender | Surrender |
|---|---|---|
| Country surrenders | + + | + – |
| Armed forces surrender | – + | – – |

Note: + indicates a strong threat to negative face; – indicates a weak threat to negative face.

the differences in historical interpretations and confining ourselves to the language of the textbooks and face theory, it seems reasonable to argue as follows:

a) When the state surrenders, this involves a serious threat to the negative face of the state (to which I will give the symbol '+').
b) When the armed forces surrender, this involves a weaker threat to the negative face of the state, since it is only an organ of the state that surrenders (to which I will give the symbol '–').
c) When the surrender is unconditional, this involves a strong threat to the negative face of the state ('+').
d) When the surrender is not unconditional, but simply 'surrender', this involves a weak threat to the negative face of the state ('–').

From the point of view of the 'worst and best case scenarios' regarding the threat to negative face, the above can be set out in a matrix (Table 4.1).

This is a useful way of thinking of the negative face-threat to the state. The worst case scenario, from the point of view of face theory, would be when there is an unconditional surrender of the country (+ +); the best case scenario would be when the armed forces surrendered (– –). This best case scenario is the one that is closest to the views, mentioned at the beginning of this chapter, of those who maintain that Japan agreed to the surrender of its armed forces based on certain conditions. The other two scenarios are midway between the best case and worst case ones, and are marked with either '– +' or '+ –' in Table 4.1.

## Statistical analysis

In this section I will make a comparison between the German and Japanese surrenders in terms of the degree to which the textbooks record the negative face of the states as being threatened, and in order to clarify

Table 4.2 Language forms in the German and Japanese surrenders

| Language form (and negative face-threat) | Germany | Japan | Totals |
|---|---|---|---|
| Country surrenders unconditionally (+ +) | 40 | 7 | 47 |
| Other than country surrenders unconditionally (− +) | 3 | 4 | 7 |
| Country surrenders (+ −) | 10 | 10 | 20 |
| Other than country surrenders (− −) | 0 | 3 | 3 |
| Surrender verb in alpha clause | 29 | 5 | 34 |
| Totals | 82 | 29 | 111 |

Note: $p = 0.0001$ (chi-square = 23.2482; $df = 4$).

whether, in the Japanese case, the country vs armed forces/unconditional vs conditional controversy finds its way into the textbooks, and, more importantly, to see if the differences in the language used to describe the surrenders of Germany and Japan are examples of the ideology of face-protection. The data are presented in Table 4.2.

There is a significant statistical difference ($p = 0.0001$) in the language used to describe the German surrender and the Japanese surrender. To summarize this table:

a) In the case of the German surrender, the most common pattern is for the country itself to surrender unconditionally (i.e. the worst case scenario of + +), with 40 occurrences, 72.7 per cent.
b) In the case of the Japanese surrender, the most common pattern is for the country to surrender (i.e. an intermediate scenario), with 10 occurrences, 18.2 per cent.
c) In the case of the Japanese surrender, the country very rarely surrenders unconditionally (7 occurrences, 12.7 per cent).
d) In the case of surrender being recorded in the main verb, this happens frequently in the case of Germany (29 occurrences, 52.7 per cent) but very rarely in the case of Japan (5 occurrences 9.1 per cent).

In terms of negative face, we can conclude from this that the textbooks protect the face of the Japanese state, compared with the German state. However, regarding the first four language forms, what the data might represent is a playing out in the textbooks of a genuine historical controversy regarding what kind of surrender it was that was imposed on Japan in 1945. Therefore, we should be careful not to overinterpret this. However, it is difficult to see what historical (or stylistic or educational or editorial) decision would cause Japan's surrender to be reported by a verb in the alpha clause in only five of the 55 textbooks.

In the previous chapter, I showed that the aggressive act of attacking Pearl Harbor was regularly not encoded in an alpha clause. In this chapter, the surrender of Japan is also rarely encoded in an alpha clause. The fact that in *both* these cases the grammar downgrades the most ideologically sensitive part of the historical narrative (in the first case, the ideology of irresponsibility; in the second case, the ideology of face-protection) lends support to the view that the textbooks seek to minimize what I have called the 'weight of meaning' of these ideologically sensitive parts of the textbooks by downgrading them in the grammar.

## Summary and conclusion

As well as the statistical analysis, and conclusions drawn from it, the patterns that are not easily analysed statistically suggest that the textbooks, as a whole, are indeed protecting the negative face of the Japanese state, together with the Emperor and imperial system. Some of these patterns are:

a) the use of verbs showing freedom of action and responsible behaviour on the part of the Japanese state;
b) 'Potsdam Declaration', rather than 'surrender', becoming the main focus of the narrative;
c) the intimation that 'rejection of the Potsdam Declaration' existed as a realistic alternative;
d) the stressing of the ceremonial nature of the surrender;
e) the disappearance of the Allies from parts of the narrative in which they could be present as coercers of Japan;
f) the inaccuracies regarding the nature and content of Hirohito's broadcast;
g) the uncritical acceptance of the normality of the leaders of Japan talking down to the ordinary Japanese people, with this being mentioned in close proximity to the Japanese government talking across to the Allies as equals;
h) the presence of time-slips, which mean that the surrender disappears from the narrative, or at least its occurrence is downplayed.

I have argued above that the use of language we see in the textbooks protects the negative face of the Japanese state of 1945, and also, to a lesser extent, respects its positive face. I have also connected this language use to Hirohito's broadcast. In the discussion of the Japanese attack, it was suggested that we see a recycling of wartime language in the textbooks. Similarly, the way the textbooks write about the acceptance of the Potsdam Declaration is, I would claim, itself a reworking of Hirohito's words in his broadcast, which are given below followed by my close translation (and therefore different from the translation previously given):

Chin wa Teikoku-seifu o shite Bei, Ei, Shi, Ro yonkoku ni taishi sono kyoodoo-sengen o judaku-suru mune tsuukoku-seshimetari

Translation: We have had the Imperial Government communicate to America, Britain, China, and the Soviet Union to the effect that we accept their joint declaration.

Firm control, room to manoeuvre, presence of choice, (Potsdam) Declaration standing for surrender, the potentially face-threatening act of accepting the Declaration not being a main verb – this is exactly what we see in the textbooks. The very words are the same: 'declaration' (*sengen*), 'accept' (*judaku-suru*), 'communicate' (*tsuukoku (-seshimetari*)). These words are 'insects in amber' (Dower 1999: 36), as shown by their repetition in history textbooks used in Japan today.

The history of Japan's surrender could look very different. It could picture the great hardships of the ordinary Japanese people (who had far less to eat and far less adequate bomb shelters – if they had any at all – than their leaders), the spreading criticism of the war among the common people, about which the leadership class was becoming increasingly worried. The increasing vigilance of the thought police (*Tokkoo*). The wasting of precious time while soldiers and civilians were dying, the confusion of the people, the dropping of millions of propaganda and information leaflets by the American air force and thereby the gradual losing of control by the government of the flow of information, and the number of lives that were lost by every minute the war was prolonged. It could certainly picture a people who had been led into a rash expansionist war while they were being continually fooled and hoodwinked. But this is not what we see in the textbooks.

# 5 Conclusion

## Locating the findings in a wider context

In this book the history textbook problem in modern Japan has been discussed in some detail, and many examples of the actual language used by the textbooks in writing about the Rape of Nanking, the attacks that started the Second World War and the Pacific War, and the Japanese and German surrenders in 1945 have been critically analysed using functional grammar as a tool. The conclusion drawn from this analysis is that the textbooks encode an ideology of irresponsibility and face-protection. The approach has been to move beyond a content-type approach to the language of the textbooks which, by its nature, tends to revolve around views of what should and should not be in the textbooks. But all such views may to a greater of lesser extent be reasonable, or at least it can be argued that they are reasonable. Thus, content-type analyses of the textbooks do not address the issue deeply enough. It is only by looking carefully at the language of all the textbooks with suitable linguistic tools, that we can truly elucidate the ideology within the texts. Whether the issue of the sex slaves should be included or not in the textbooks, either because it has not been historically verified, or because (in the case of junior high school pupils), pupils are too immature to understand it – both of which views have been put forward by those reluctant to include such information, are certainly important issues. But these are surface issues. What is more relevant, and more important, is the pervasive naturalized ideology in the textbooks.

At this stage it is convenient and useful to summarize the major findings of this study:

(1) The language of the textbooks blocks critical questioning of the Rape of Nanking by, for example, including Japanese soldiers in the historical narrative in indirect and attenuated ways, and by assigning knowledge of Nanking to people or organizations who may be assumed

to be anti-Japanese. Related to the attenuated presence of Japanese soldiers at Nanking is the lack of criticism of these same soldiers, since the criticism is mainly directed to the atrocity itself or the acts that constitute the atrocity. One of the results of this way of writing about Nanking is that the historical thread of evidence linking modern Japan to the Nanking of 1937/1938 is cut. Also, the fact that the Japanese military and governmental authorities covered up, or tried to cover up, the atrocities at Nanking may be assumed from a careful reading of some of the texts, but this is nowhere stated. The manner in which the Rape of Nanking comes into being in the pages of the textbooks was also considered. The argument was made that giving an event a name at the same time as it occurs leaves little room to question that event since the event is presented to the reader as a sort of fait accompli. It was also argued that encapsulating the participants and processes that constitute the event in a noun phrase can obfuscate the nature of the event itself. Despite giving information about the type of atrocities committed and presenting a range of reasonable opinions concerning casualty figures at Nanking during the time of the Rape, the language of the textbooks displays a degree of caution or ambivalence when writing about the Nanking atrocities. In general, the language of the textbooks leaves ample ideological space in which those who deny the historical reality of Nanking can manoeuvre.

(2) The formation of the ABCD line serves as an important justification for the start of the Pacific War. But an examination of the language used to refer to the ABCD line (in terms of attribution, averral, and hedging) shows that the textbooks are ambivalent regarding the historical and historiographical status of this line of encirclement. When it comes to the Japanese attacks that started the Pacific War phase of the Asia-Pacific War, there is the remarkable fact that there is not a single example in the textbooks of Japan attacking another country in 1941. A careful examination of the textbooks reveals that there are significantly different ways of writing about the German attack and the Japanese attack, and in the Japanese case the aggressive nature of the attack is downplayed. This was shown in some detail in the discussion of grammatical metaphor and clause primacy. It was also suggested that wartime language was being recycled in the textbooks, both in the use of 'plunged into war' and in the use of the wartime term '*Shinjuwan*', which in modern Japanese usage would be '*Paaruhaabaa*' (Pearl Harbor). A strong case could not be made for this recycling of language, but what lends persuasiveness to this suggestion is the very obvious

recycling of wartime language (i.e. 'ABCD line' and parts of Hirohito's broadcast) in other parts of the textbooks.

(3) It was argued that the language used to write about Japan's surrender in 1945 strongly protects the negative face of the Japanese state (by minimizing the coercion and imposition that were exerted on the state at that time), and also to a lesser extent respects its positive face (by valuing what the state at the time of the surrender valued). In Hirohito's broadcast, also, there is a use of language that protects his negative face and the negative face of the state, and obfuscates the issue of the responsibility and the nature of the war that Japan fought from 1931 to 1945. I argued that this is what we see in the textbooks, even to the extent of the textbooks frequently echoing Hirohito's language. And furthermore, the language of this broadcast itself echoes through the various resolutions passed by assemblies in Japan, and the various announcements by important politicians, academics, and the like. By carrying out a comparative analysis, this time with respect to the German and Japanese surrenders, I both strengthened the other analyses in this book and showed that the genre objection was not tenable: the types of language use prevalent in the textbooks cannot be explained away simply in terms of 'this is how history is written'.

(4) When one considers the recycling of wartime language in the textbooks, the views expressed in modern Japan today (but having roots in the Japan prior to the surrender) by a vocal minority, for many of whom the war was a war of national self-preservation and colonial liberation, the degree to which the language of the textbooks subtly accords with these views, or at least makes no consistent, committed attempts to deny them, and the very repetitive nature of the language used in the textbooks as a whole, then it seems that there are very strong grounds for claiming that the language of the textbooks encodes a naturalized ideology.

(5) Looking at this ideology more closely, two strands can be identified, to which the names 'ideology of irresponsibility' and 'ideology of face-protection' have been given.

(6) At several points in this book, it has been argued that what contributes to the encoding of this ideology is a set of *copatterning* resources of the grammar, such as in the system of transitivity, the system of taxis and clause primacy, the presence and structure of noun

phrases, the uses of averral and attribution, the presence of time-slips, and so on. Whereas it might be possible to dismiss the conclusions by, for example, arguing that my interpretation of the effect of noun phrases when they encapsulate the important parts of the historical narrative is not tenable, when it comes to considering a wide range of the grammatical resources and the meanings they create, then the arguments and interpretations advanced seem to be rather secure. It is, therefore, very unlikely that what we see in these textbooks can be explained away in terms such as 'this is how history is written' – in other words, in terms of the genre objection. Far from this being the case, the meaning potential of language has been utilized in a variety of ways to produce a naturalized ideological discourse with reference to three important events in modern Japanese history.

In order to get some sort of subjective feel for the language of the textbooks, we can ask ourselves the curious question: If Hirohito and his top advisers had been given the job of writing Japanese history textbooks immediately after the war, what would the textbooks have looked like? The Allied occupiers would have been looking over their shoulders, so there would have been some constraint on what could have been written. But I think their finished products would have been rather similar to the ones we see now being used in modern Japan. Knowledge of the Rape of Nanking would have been minimized, the aggressiveness of Japanese actions would have been downplayed, the claim would have been made that Japan had to go to war against the Western Allies for reasons of self-preservation, the role of Hirohito in ending the war would have been stressed, while the question of whether he played a positive role in starting the war would not have been pursued, and mention of the destruction of the ideological and educational foundations on which the imperial state rested, together with the mythohistorical nature of these foundations, would have been as far as possible avoided. This is what we see in the textbooks.

The events chosen for the analyses in this book show the ideological components identified precisely because of their sensitive ideological nature in modern Japan. The Rape of Nanking, in terms of numbers killed and the level of brutality, towers over all the many other atrocities committed by the Japanese during the period from 1931 to 1945. It certainly proves that Japan was not fighting for Asian liberation (as revisionists would argue), nor, as Hirohito claimed in his broadcast for 'the stabilization of East Asia'. The Japanese attacks that started the

Pacific War are open to the charge that they were perfidious and in violation of international law. These attacks were also highly irrational in character; or even if at the time they were seen as rational behaviour, in hindsight, they must almost certainly be judged to be irrational. These attacks also ultimately brought death to millions of Japanese and terrible destruction to Japan. Thus, the people who were responsible for this have some explaining to do. The surrender was also ideologically sensitive since it clearly showed that, whatever the Japanese people had been taught (both in schools and by the media, etc.) about their racial and spiritual superiority, there was no way that Japan could stand up to the overwhelming might of the Allies – a might that was the product of social and political systems that, within Japan, had been held up to contempt, or at least compared unfavourably with those of Japan. By the time of the surrender it had become rather plain to very many Japanese that they had, over the years, been lied to about the superiority of the Japanese system in order to serve the expansionist aims and the elitist structure of the imperial state. As van Wolferen writes (1989: 263), 'For the first time in history, foreign conquerors arrived to disprove the notion of superior valour based on ethnic unity and an unbroken line of Emperors'.

It is important to emphasize that the ideologies present in the textbooks are there for reasons connected with the events themselves, the nature of present-day Japanese society, and the structure of power within the modern Japanese state. When writing about these events the textbooks exhibit an ideology of irresponsibility and face-protection precisely because of the debates within Japanese society concerning the nature of the war, the question of war responsibility, and the culpability, or, alternatively, justification, for aggressive actions undertaken by Japan.

Textbooks themselves reflect history and society – they are not products of an ahistorical and asocial vacuum. Hirohito's broadcast of 15 August, his acknowledgement of a four-year war, but not of a 15-year war in this broadcast, the disinclination, until very recently, of Japanese prime ministers to make an apology for Japan's actions in the war, the resolutions passed by local assemblies, the accidental involvement theory of Asian suffering caused by Japan (see pages 3 and 4) are all examples of the ideology of irresponsibility or of face-protection. It would be surprising if we did not find the same thing in the governmentally and bureaucratically controlled textbooks.

The control of the curriculum, including the system of textbook authorization, by the Ministry of Education is a prime example of the way in which the modern Japanese state protects its face. If anyone could write a textbook and, by putting it on the market, make it available to schools, this would infringe on the jealously guarded preserve of the Ministry of Education. As I pointed out in my discussion of face theory, this, since it would involve a threat to territory, would thereby constitute a threat to negative face. The ministry has thus ensured that its own face is protected, and the tenacious way it has fought the many challenges to its power over the years shows that it regards the responsibility for education in Japan as being vested in itself, and not in the people. Given this way of thinking, it is not surprising that the ministry sees nothing anachronistic about uncritically accepting a type of historical writing that puts the Japanese people in a position of inferiority to the governmental authorities at the time of the surrender. Platzer (1988: xiii) in his editor's introduction to Horio (1988) traces this present-day bureaucratic attitude back to the pre-war years:

> ...those bureaucrats in the Ministry of Education who today attempt to rule Japanese educational life from their offices in Tokyo are the inheritors of the attitude of contempt for the human rights of the Japanese people which was perfected by their predecessors in the prewar Imperial State apparatus.

## Reasons for the ideologies

In Chapter 1, I discussed the background to the history problem and the history textbook problem in modern Japan, and that discussion touched on some of the possible reasons for the existence of the ideologies of irresponsibility and face-protection. As part of this concluding chapter, it is worthwhile to pull these reasons together and address them in a more direct way. These reasons are developed below, but are here listed: unresolved questions from the war, the continuity of the state, the imperial taboo, the supposed moral purity of Japan, the non-civil nature of Japanese society, the Ministry of Education's reticence regarding its own wartime role, intimidation by the Ministry of Education, reproduction in historiography and the invisibility of ideology, the authority of textbooks, and Japanese education as banking education.

### *Unresolved questions from the war*

The question of war reparations has still not been finally and satisfactorily settled. And even if it can be argued that this question has been settled, or is in the process of being settled, there has still not been closure to the moral aspects of the war. If the present negotiations on the normalization of diplomatic relations with North Korea proceed, one of the issues on the table will be apologies from Japan, and reparations for the years of Japanese colonial rule.

But the matter is wider than reparations to North Korea. At the beginning of this book I mentioned the demands for proper apologies and significant monetary compensation from both the Japanese government and major Japanese companies who profited, for example, from indentured- or slave-labour during the war. The standard answer, and indeed for many years the satisfactory answer, that issues of compensation had been settled in the San Francisco Peace Treaty of 1951 between Japan and the Allies, and subsequent bilateral treaties between Japan and other countries, is increasingly being held up to legal challenge under new interpretations of international law (McCormack 1996: 273, 274). This matter is brought into sharp relief when one considers the very small compensation Japan paid out compared with the compensation that Germany has paid and continues to pay (see McCormack 1996: 245 for actual figures). Added to this is the increasingly urgent and vocal means by which aggrieved parties, many of whom have kept silent for many decades (often from feelings of shame and resignation) and who are now elderly, are pressing their claims (McCormack 1996: 244–277).

The textbooks have frequently fought a rearguard action regarding admitting clear culpability for Japanese actions. The long series of lawsuits by Ienaga, particularly with reference to the Rape of Nanking have clearly shown this.

## *The continuity of the state*

Although the question of the continuity between the wartime state and the modern state was taken up in Chapter 1, it will be developed further here. Many writers claim that the bureaucratic and political system has not essentially changed since the pre-war and war years, and that by the time the occupation came to an end, many of the bureaucrats and politicians from the pre-war and war years were back in positions of authority and influence (Dower 1995: 11; Johnson 1995: 124, 125; van Wolferen 1989: 359, 360). Buruma (1994: 61, 62) writes that, 'Very few wartime bureaucrats had been purged. Most ministries remained intact. Instead it was the Communists, who had welcomed the Americans as liberators, who were purged after 1949, the year China was "lost"'.

Following the many threads linking the bureaucratic and political personnel from the pre-war years, to the wartime period, right up to the

Japan of today is complex. There are marriage alliances, many cases of Diet seats passing down from father to son through several generations, bureaucrats moving into politics, and so on. Samuels (2001) traces the present governmental system in Japan from the war years to the present and discusses the continuity of government. As pointed out by Samuels, Kishi Nobusuke (1896–1987), one of Japan's most important and influential post-war politicians, who became prime minister in 1957, was charged and imprisoned as a Class A war criminal by the occupation authorities, but, being fortunate enough to escape trial due to the change in American policy (which needed the support of the Japanese elite in the fight against Communism), was released in 1948. As Minister of Commerce during the war, he would have been thoroughly familiar with, and almost certainly intimately involved in, Japan's programmes of forced- and slave-labour of Chinese and Koreans, and Allied prisoners-of-war.

Japan certainly did not experience a wrenching dislocation from its past. One result of this was that there was little deep moral reflection on Japanese actions during the war years. It was, in short, very much a matter of back to business. The post-war Japanese state has very deep roots in the pre-war and wartime state, and particularly the more unsavoury elements of that state, as mentioned by McCormack (1996: 232):

> It is symptomatic of the confused moral climate of postwar Japan that confinement to Sugamo Prison should have come to be regarded as a matter of pride rather than shame, and that the network of contacts developed among Class A war criminals [presumably this should be 'suspected criminals', since they were released before being brought to trial, CB] held there should have become central to the evolution of the postwar state.

This continuity extended to the Ministry of Education which, far from just having the innocent task of educating children, was at the forefront of 'reversing the "excesses" of occupation policy on education' (van Wolferen 1989: 77), including taming the Japanese Teachers' Union. Van Wolferen (1989: 76–78, 359) gives examples of bureaucratic and government heavyweights from the pre-war and wartime periods moving into the ministry in order to accomplish these aims. To give just one example, he mentions (1989: 77) that Odachi Shigeo, mayor of Singapore during the notorious Japanese occupation, was appointed minister of education in 1953. It was people of this type who returned to important and influential positions after the end of the occupation.

## The imperial taboo

What, perhaps more than anything else, maintained the continuity of the state was the fact that Hirohito was neither deposed nor tried as a war criminal, nor was he called to give evidence at the Tokyo trials. How could anyone object to a member of the wartime cabinet becoming prime minister of Japan when the Emperor himself had successfully avoided giving any accounting of his wartime role?

But the issue of Japanese aggression during the war years, and responsibility for this, brings up the role of Hirohito. In fact, the question of war responsibility cannot be discussed without examining the responsibility of Hirohito (Bergamini 1971; Bix 2000; Dower 1999), in whose name the war was started and fought. Certainly, while Hirohito was alive this subject was taboo (McCormack 1996: 176, 235); but even after more than a decade since his death, this taboo remains strong. Bix (2000: 17) links the question of Hirohito's evasion of responsibility with the general lack of a critical examination of the war within modern Japan:

> Eventually Hirohito became the prime symbol of his people's repression of their wartime past. For as long as they did not pursue his central role in the war, they did not have to question their own.

Free discussion of war responsibility is, even today, a sensitive subject in Japan. The danger of discussion of responsibility getting out of hand and leading to Hirohito's door was, and still is, a real one. In January 1990, Motoshima Hitoshi, mayor of Nagasaki, was shot in the back and almost killed for having previously stated that Hirohito bore some responsibility for the war.

Thus, this 'imperial taboo' is but one part of a wider taboo concerning free discussion of war responsibility in Japan. For example, in modern Japan, citizens' groups are not infrequently prevented from holding conferences and seminars in facilities generally available to the public and paid for by taxpayers if these events deal with such matters as war responsibility, military comfort women, and so on. In one case (*Asahi Shimbun*, 1 Oct. 2000) the organizers of a conference in a public facility in Yokohama were allowed to hold the conference provided they changed the words '*sensoo sekinin*' (war responsibility) in the title of a speech and the publicity brochures, and they distributed flyers only to the actual participants.

## The supposed moral purity of Japan

The view that Japan is a pure and morally unsullied land, set apart from the other countries of the world, is a not uncommon one in modern Japan, and such a way of thinking has deep roots in Japanese history. Indeed, to question such views is seen to strike at the heart of much of what 'being Japanese' involves. This is certainly behind the *Tsukuru-kai*'s desire for a 'Japanese history for the Japanese people'.

One of the most recent and startling revelations of how a leader of Japan can still be stuck in the past and hold antiquated, reactionary views on the nature of the Japanese state concerned a pronouncement on 15 May 2000 by the then prime minister, Mori Yoshiroo, when he said in a speech (*Asahi Shimbun*, 16 May 2000), 'I would like all Japanese to fully understand the fact that the country of Japan is certainly a divine country centring on the Emperor'. (*Nihon no kuni wa masa ni tennoo o chuushin to suru kami no kuni de aru to iu koto o kokumin no mina-san ni shikkari to shoochi-shite itadaku.*) The Japanese constitution states that sovereignty is vested in the people. The idea of Japan being a country centring on the Emperor is nothing more than a recycling of pre-surrender rhetoric.

This view of Japan as a sacred land also goes back far in Japanese history, and was one of the central tenets of wartime school education and propaganda. When one considers the active promotion of the imperial cult up to the time of Japan's surrender (Bix 2000: 30–32, 283; Brownlee 1997; McCormack 1996: 176) and the suffering and hardship that this caused the Japanese people, that a Japanese prime minister could make such a statement is truly remarkable.

Mori then made the comment (*Asahi Shimbun*, 4 June 2000) that if the Communist Party were to be part of a government, the national polity (*kokutai*) of Japan would not be able to be preserved. This word *kokutai* is a complex one, and one that was especially popular during the war. It implies the special nature of Japan as a homogeneously racial imperial state, composed of one family, with the Emperor as head – ideas that were either directly mentioned or indirectly alluded to in the Emperor's broadcast of 15 August 1945.

It is difficult to believe that anyone with some knowledge of what happened in the war, the causes of the war, the present Japanese constitution, the meaning of freedom of conscience and freedom of religion, and the nature of citizenship in a modern democratic state could ever make comments such as those made by Mori – especially one who is reputed to be a specialist in education, as Mori was.

Mori's comments show to what extent views that Japan is a divine country centring on the Emperor and possessor of a special national polity are not outside the mainstream of conservative thought in Japan. The purity of Japanese motives in its past behaviour is a theme constantly mentioned (McCormack 1996: 171). Those who argue that Japan's war was justified, by arguing that Japan was unselfishly fighting to liberate fellow Asians from white colonialism, place themselves squarely in this camp, as did the Emperor in his surrender broadcast. To impugn the unsullied nature of these motives is to challenge much that lies at the heart of Japanese identity, as seen by traditionalists and conservatives within Japan.

## The non-civil nature of Japanese society

A number of authors argue (e.g. van Wolferen 1989) that Japanese society is one in which the space in which citizens, as citizens with responsibility for creating and changing their own civil society, can move is rather limited. McVeigh (1998: 85) writes that, 'Rather than a "citizens' sector" composed of privately administered, non-profit public interest organizations that monitor, scrutinize, and criticize government policies, "para-state organizations" occupy much of the social space between the individual and the authorities'.

The case of the conference on war responsibility mentioned above is a very typical example of how administrative and governmental organs constrain citizens' behaviour in Japan. The reason given by the Yokohama authorities (*Asahi Shimbun*, 1 Oct. 2000) for imposing restrictions on the conference was that, 'Since it is a public facility, we judged that it was not a suitable place to deal with a subject regarding which opinions among citizens are divided'. In other words, it is the job of the authorities to judge what people can say and think! Actually, probably a more important reason why the authorities put restrictions on the conference was that they were worried about right-wing protests and violence, directed both against themselves and the conference participants, and also did not want to take on the trouble and expense of protecting the conference participants and policing the surrounding area. What is truly revealing about the reason given for imposing the restrictions is that it is, in a supposedly democratic society, itself regarded as being a reasonable justification for limiting the freedom of speech of citizens who are attempting, in their own small way, to change Japanese society.

Van Wolferen (1989: 368) sees the control of citizens and citizenship as not necessarily being malicious in character:

Japan's administrators, of course, do not see themselves as hatching questionable schemes, out of questionable motives, to increase their hold over the ordinary citizen. The Japanese bureaucratic tradition has conditioned them to believe that society will be undermined if they relax their guard; the idea of citizens who have the political right to decide for themselves remains alien to them.

Such a way of bureaucratic thinking has its roots in the Japanese bureaucratic tradition going back to the Meiji period (see Johnson 1995: 124, 125).

## *The Ministry of Education's reticence regarding its own wartime role*

I cannot state with one hundred per cent confidence that in some corner of some textbook there is no mention of the role the pre-war and wartime Ministry of Education itself played in the cynical manipulation of the Japanese people up to the time of Japan's defeat. However, neither I nor my research assistant have been able to find one such reference. One would have thought that if Japanese pupils studying history in modern Japan are to have any idea of what kind of war it was that Japan fought from 1931 to 1945, and seek to understand the behaviour of the Japanese people, including Japanese troops, during this war, the role of the ministry in this should be made very clear. There are references to the media exaggerating the threat posed by the ABCD line and encouraging xenophobic sentiments at the time of the Manchurian Incident. The role that the ministry itself played in ideological manipulation and propagandization is surely of greater importance. This reluctance of the Ministry of Education to give a frank accounting of the role played by its lineal predecessor up to the time of the defeat in the war seems to me to be an attempt to absolve the wartime ministry from any responsibility for deceiving the Japanese people.

I doubt that there is any publisher brave enough to submit a textbook for official authorization that dealt with this matter in a straightforward manner – in other words, dealt with the role that the ministry played in leading the Japanese people to death and destruction. Ienaga (1978: 31, 32) forcefully makes the point that education was one of the means by which the Japanese people were manipulated:

> The prewar state kept the populace in a powerful vise: on one side were the internal security laws with their restrictions on freedom of

speech and thought; on the other side was the conformist education that blocked the growth of a free consciousness and purposive activity for political ends. The vise was tightened whenever any individual or popular resistance challenged reckless military action. The laws and public education, used as instruments of coercion and manipulation, were the decisive factors that made it impossible for the Japanese people to stop their country from launching the Pacific War.

The role that the pre-surrender ministry played in promoting and inculcating values and false beliefs which themselves were largely responsible for leading the Japanese nation to destruction is not something that should be hidden from pupils studying books that are in those pupils' hands only because they have been through the compulsory authorization process of the direct lineal successor of this ministry.

## *Intimidation by the Ministry of Education*

Over the years, writers and publishers have certainly learnt what the unspoken and unwritten rules are regarding textbook authorization, as mentioned on pages 13 and 14. Having one's textbook fail the authorization procedures and therefore not getting on the market, or having the textbook undergo revision, is not an expense that publishers wish to bear.

The ministry has made it clear that it will tenaciously protect its authority over textbook authorization. Since the ministry can pursue any lawsuit at taxpayers' expense, this means its funds are more or less unlimited. Also, as mentioned on pages 14 and 15, the Japanese bureaucracy is, in many cases, unaccountable, a point also made by McVeigh (1998: 84, 85), and therefore it is very difficult for citizens to bring legal, or other, pressures to bear against it.

## *Reproduction in historiography and the invisibility of ideology*

The naturalized ideology that we see expressed in the textbooks is easily reproduced precisely because it is more or less invisible – and, therefore, more or less unchallengable. No one textbook can be said to express a particular ideology since in its own right, and when considered in isolation, it is written in a perfectly acceptable way. When examining a textbook, one could certainly quibble about and object to certain parts, but, on the whole, the textbook would most likely seem rather reasonable. However, when the totality of textbooks is examined, the picture that emerges is a very different one, as I have shown in this book.

To notice, in one textbook, that 'the Japanese army caused the Nanking Massacre Incident' or that Japan did not attack another country in 1941, because it attacked places and geographical expressions, is not surprising, or even worthy of comment. What is surprising and is worthy of comment is the fact that such uses of language extend across the whole corpus. But we can only ascertain this is so if we look at all the data. Naturally, this is not a task that too many people are willing to undertake.

This means that the view of history that is being taught, and thereby reproduced, in Japan is a very restricted and circumscribed one, from which it is almost impossible to break away. Some of the children in Japanese schools will grow up to become history teachers, history textbook writers, and academic historians. Having being raised on this naturalized ideology, it is likely to be difficult for them to think about history in any original or different way.

Any native speaker of Japanese with moderate editorial skills could lay half-a-dozen or a dozen of these history textbooks down on a table, and then using a scissors-and-glue approach could produce his or her own 'original' textbook. The textbooks are so alike, that it would be impossible for anyone to accuse this person of plagiarism. The great similarity among the textbooks means that by a rather natural logical fallacy one is likely to believe that they are all writing about history in a way that is free from unreasonable or excessive ideological baggage: If they are all saying the same thing does not this mean that they are all right? The alternative is to believe that the great majority of all the 55 history textbooks, produced by 11 different publishers and written by hundreds of different authors are presenting a history that contains a particular ideology. But of course my aim in this book has been to show that this is exactly the case – to show how naturalized ideologies can be present in a corpus in the form of the accepted common sense.

Since the history textbooks are so similar, this means that the responsibility for writing history in a particular way, or not writing it in a particular way, is dissipated among all the various publishers and authors by a sort of safety-in-numbers process. No publisher has to take responsibility for a particular use of language in a textbook, since a large number of other textbooks are using the same language. In order to clarify some use of language in the textbooks, I have at times phoned publishers. On several occasions, I received the answer that there can be no problem with such-and-such a use of language since it is common throughout the textbooks, and anyway, since the textbook has been approved by the Ministry of Education, this means that there is no problem with the use of language. In other words: everyone is doing it, and the people in charge say it's okay, so there can't be any problem.

Since the type of history writing currently used in history textbooks in Japan is widely and uncritically accepted, this means that any writer of any textbook, as long as he or she stays within a certain, rather narrowly delimited area, has to use very few critical or authorial skills. The motto seems to be 'just do what everyone else does'.

## *The authority of textbooks*

It is very difficult for pupils, and probably even teachers, to challenge the facts, assumptions, explanations, and methods of presentation of material in textbooks. Textbooks, by their very nature are thought of as being well-researched, carefully checked, free of any possible bias, and selected by teachers or boards of education who are knowledgeable in the particular field, and educational theory in general. Thus, it is very difficult to identify, let alone attack, the basic assumptions and implicit ideologies that may lie, probably hidden, in textbooks. The textbook, by the very fact of being a textbook, is surrounded by an aura of veracity and authority. When we consider the ideological nature of Japanese textbooks, this is a rather depressing thought.

In questioning my own students about the meaning or interpretation of a particular section of a textbook, several times they have replied that since such-and-such is in the textbook, or is written in such a way, it must be correct.

## *Japanese education as banking education*

That Japanese education promotes rote memorization, rather than analytical or critical approaches to learning, is a point frequently made. In Freire's terms (1993: 53), Japanese education is a good example of banking education, in which students are seen as receptacles to be filled by teachers and 'knowledge is a gift bestowed by those who consider themselves knowledgeable upon those whom they consider to know nothing'. Freire (1993: 54) points out that the banking concept leads to 'good' students being less than fulfilled social beings since they have been deprived of initiative and the ability to think for themselves:

It is not surprising that the banking concept of education regards men as adaptable, manageable beings. The more students work at storing the deposits entrusted to them, the less they develop the critical consciousness which would result from their intervention in the world as transformers of that world. The more completely they accept the passive role imposed on them, the more they tend simply to adapt to the world as it is and to the fragmented view of reality deposited on them.

One of the reasons for studying the textbooks is obviously to successfully finish one's high school education and receive one's diploma. Another important reason is to memorize enough facts to pass university entrance examinations. These entrance exams require almost no critical thinking whatsoever; as long as examinees can regurgitate a large number of disconnected facts on demand, they can pass the entrance exam. Pupils are not required to think deeply about the causes for the Pacific War, or the connection between the Japanese education system in the 1930s and the behaviour of Japanese soldiers at Nanking. They are deemed to 'know' history as long as they can remember 'ABCD line' or the date of the Nanking Massacre Incident.

## Conclusion

These reasons, discussed above, for the existence of a naturalized ideology in the textbooks are perhaps better seen, not as direct causative reasons, but rather as factors that allow or encourage the ideology – enabling factors as it were. The textbooks are written as they are because of the existence of a certain climate of opinion or pervasive values within Japanese society, and these influence writers and producers of textbooks. I am quite sure that the bureaucrats who authorize textbooks are not consciously aware that they are inheritors of traditions from the pre-war and wartime state, and thus behave in conformity with these traditions. Rather, such traditions are woven into the fabric of the bureaucratic system and the wider Japanese society. Mori's comments are themselves examples of how pre-surrender traditions continue in the modern Japanese state. If a prime minister believes that his country is a sacred land centring on an Emperor, it is not surprising that the officially authorized textbooks used in that country's schools are reluctant to write frankly about the terrible aggressiveness of a war which that country waged. It is difficult to actually prove that the Ministry of Education intimidates authors and publishers. However, I myself, from my own experience of being involved in the production of high school English-language textbooks in Japan, know that the reaction of the ministry to content and presentation is almost always in the minds of both authors and publishers. I am quite sure that a more critical study of Hirohito's role in the war would not be allowed, and that any publisher who attempted to deal with the true nature of the imperial state and the role of the Ministry of Education in perverting education in the period up to the time of the surrender would not have the textbook passed – and I am sure that all publishers know this. I also know from my own experience that when a new textbook is being planned, the first thing that the committee of publishers and authors does is to lay all the other relevant textbooks from other publishers down on a table and look at them carefully. They know that what is in these textbooks is deemed to be both necessary and acceptable by the authorization committee in the Ministry of Education. So, almost unavoidably, they end up writing the same kind of history, and a history that unavoidably reproduces this invisible and naturalized ideology. There is no incentive to write in any other way, since one of the main aims of the textbook is to teach the pupils the 'facts' so that they can pass university entrance examinations. It is common practice for university entrance exam committees to examine high school textbooks when setting the exams. Therefore, there is no advantage to any publisher who wants to produce a textbook that deals with anything other than the same events in the same way; the incentive for writing a different history is certainly not great – probably almost non-existent.

In the following quote, Buruma (1994: 296) sums up much of the above argument: the continuation of the bureaucratic system, the removal of power from the hands of the citizenry, the lack of debate regarding the Second World War, and an ideology of irresponsibility and face-protection ('legitimize their grip on power by justifying or at least ignoring the past'):

> The state was run by virtually the same bureaucracy that ran the Japanese empire, and the electoral system was rigged to help the same corrupt conservative party to stay in power for almost forty years. This arrangement suited the United States, as well as Japanese bureaucrats, LDP [Liberal Democratic Party, CB] politicians, and the large industrial combines, for it ensured that Japan remained a rich and stable ally against Communism. But it also helped to stifle public debate and stopped the Japanese from growing up politically. As far as the history of World War II was concerned, the debate

got stuck in the late 1940s, around the beginning of the Cold War: bureaucrats and conservative politicians continued to legitimize their grip on power by justifying or at least ignoring the past.

I believe that one of the reasons for the extreme care placed on the face-protection of the state in the textbooks is that the ministry has not moved away from a Meiji-period way of regarding Japanese citizens, and is unwilling to reveal to citizens that the state or organs of the state were coerced in 1945. To admit this would be to weaken the power and authority of the governmental and bureaucratic organs in the people's eyes, and suggest to the people that even they themselves might have the power to coerce the authorities of the state, such as by, for example, making them change the way textbooks are authorized, or insisting that they have the right to produce their own textbooks. It is, therefore, not surprising that the signing of the instrument of surrender is so often portrayed as a ceremony taking place, on a voluntary basis, between equals or near equals.

The Japanese attack on Pearl Harbor is open to the charge that it was perfidious and in violation of international law; this attack is burnt into the folk memory of people in many countries. This attack was also highly irrational in character; or even if at the time it was seen as rational behaviour, with hindsight, it must almost certainly be judged to be irrational. The attack also ultimately brought death to millions of Japanese and terrible destruction to Japan – laying aside the far greater suffering and death outside Japan. Thus, the people who were responsible for this have some explaining to do. But to do this would raise the whole question of accountability and responsibility.

Quite a while ago I carried out a web search to see what Japanese reactions were to an earlier, very different, Japanese version of this present book (Barnard 1998b). One of the people who posted an opinion agreed generally with the points I had made, and said, for example, sentences like 'Japan plunged into war' or 'a signing ceremony was held on the *Missouri*' had always appeared to him perfectly normal, but based on my arguments and data he certainly had to concede that there was something very wrong or strange about this way of writing history. This illustrates the hold that a naturalized ideology can have over us. The person in question went on to say that I could write the book precisely because I was a foreigner, and was thus not ruled by this naturalized ideology, but could see the language of the textbooks and the events in a different light from Japanese people. This again illustrates the powerful hold of naturalized ideology.

But if this is the case, it is certainly troubling and cause for concern. I do not expect any practising history teacher in Japan to go through all the history textbooks and try to deconstruct their ideologies using some linguistic model of grammar and meaning. I would, however, like to think that there are teachers, and even pupils, in Japan who in their everyday reading and studying of these textbooks notice that there is something 'funny' going on as far as these textbooks are concerned.

It is unlikely that any teacher of history in a Japanese high school will ever read this present book. Nevertheless, it has been one of my aims to show that readers actively questioning texts can restore people, actions, and causes to history. Any perceptive reader should be able to dig into a text and find out what it is really saying. Anyone who takes the time can notice certain participants missing from a narrative. Time-slips are not that difficult to identify. And, as I have shown, sometimes we find that so much grammatical effort has been put into certain parts of the text that these parts just jump out and hit us in the face.

In present-day Japan, where the content and language of history textbooks is closely controlled by the Ministry of Education, with textbooks teaching the same things in the same order in the same repetitive language, and with authors and publishers knowing very well what the unwritten rules of the textbook authorization system are, there is very little chance that any pupils will ever become 'transformers of the world', as mentioned by Freire. What we will see is subsequent generations of pupils growing up without any critical skills that would help them to question their textbooks.

In Japan, today, at any given moment, there is likely to be some government-sponsored committee examining education. These committees frequently make recommendations or proposals regarding how to foster individuality and critical, original thinking in pupils. The point is made that Japan will find it increasingly difficult to keep up with other countries in the present age of information technology unless its citizens learn to think in more individualistic, original, creative, critical ways. The case of the history textbooks shows that however admirable such aims may be they are doomed to failure since what is being valued more than anything else is uncritical conformity, certainly in the case of history education, but I believe throughout all education – the history textbooks are only a case in point.

There are certainly numbers of teachers who attempt to develop more interesting and critical approaches to history education by, for example, introducing supplementary materials in the classroom. But given the pressures of covering the curriculum in the assigned time, and the need

## Conclusion

to prepare for entrance examinations, this is not an easy task. Unfortunately, the history textbooks will continue to have a baleful effect on Japanese education. If young Japanese are to grow up with a more open-minded view of the modern history of their own country, this is something they will have to do by themselves, since they are unlikely to learn it at school.

# Works cited

Anyon, J. (1979) 'Ideology and United States history textbooks', *Harvard Educational Review*, 49, 3: 361–386.
Apple, M. (1982) *Education and Power*, Boston, MA: Routledge & Kegan Paul.
*Asahi Shimbun* (1 Oct. 1994, morning edition: 35) '*Sensoo de Ajia dokuritsu*' [Asian independence due to the war].
—— (supplement) *15-nen sensoo* [The fifteen-year war] (1 Jan. 1995: 2) '*Kakuryoo gonin no "shinryaku" gimonshi hatsugen*' [Statements by five cabinet ministers doubting the 'invasions'].
—— (17 March 1995, morning edition: 2) '*Watashitachi ga tatakatta no wa Beiei de, Ajia de wa nai*' [It was America and Britain that we fought, not Asia].
—— (8 Dec. 1996a, morning edition: 3) '*Beijin shoogen uwamawaru kachi*' [Value above that of the Americans' testimony].
—— (8 Dec. 1996b, morning edition: 3) '*Daigyakusatsu no sonzai urazuke*' [Support for the occurrence of a great massacre].
—— (16 May 2000, morning edition: 1) '*Shushoo "Nihon wa kami no kuni"*' [The Prime Minister: 'Japan is a sacred country'].
—— (4 June 2000, morning edition: 1) '*Kyoosan-seiken de "kokutai" mamoreru no ka*' [Can the 'national polity' be preserved under a Communist government?'].
—— (1 Oct. 2000, morning edition: 39) ' *"Juugun-ianfu" endai dame*' [Speech dealing with 'military comfort women' turned down].
—— (5 Dec. 2000, evening edition: 14) '*Nihon ni yuiitsu genzon no aarudeko kenchiku*' [The only surviving art deco building in Japan].
—— (8 May 2001) '*Kankoku, 35-ka-sho saishuusei yookyuu*' [Korea: request for further corrections in 35 places]. Online. Available http://www.asahi.com/special/newtext/010508a.html (accessed 10 August 2002).
—— (18 May 2001) '*Rekishi-kyookasho e no Chuugoku shuusei yookyuu*' [Chinese requests for corrections in history textbooks]. Online. Available www.asahi.com/special/newtext/010518b.html (accessed 10 August 2002).
—— (16 Aug. 2001, morning edition: 1) ' *"Tsukuru-kai" hen 1% miman*' [*Tsukuru-kai*'s edition: less than 1 per cent].
—— (30 May 2002a, morning edition: 38) '*Genkoku-gawa ga zenmen haiso*' [Complete defeat for plaintiff].
—— (30 May 2002b, morning edition: 38) ' *"Misshitsu kentei": hihan ima mo*' [Still criticism of 'closed-door authorization'].

—— (28 Aug. 2002, morning edition: 1) '*Saikin-sen no sonzai nintei*' [Recognition of the existence of germ warfare].
—— (26 Sept. 2002, evening edition: 1) '*Moto Beihei horyoo meguri koochookai*' [Public hearings on former US prisoners-of-war].
—— (28 Oct. 2002, evening edition: 18) '*Choosenjin gunjin gunzoku miharai chingin*' [Unpaid wages of Korean military personnel].
Askew, D. (2002) 'Review of *"Nankin Jiken" no tankyuu – sono jitsuzoo o motomete*' [An enquiry into the 'Nanjing Incident': the search for the true picture], *Japanese Studies*, 22, 1: 77–82.
Barnard, C. (1998a) 'Ideology in Japanese high school history textbooks: a functional grammar approach', unpublished doctoral dissertation, Temple University, Philadelphia.
—— (1998b) *Nankin-gyakusatsu wa 'okotta' no ka: Kookoorekishi-kyookasho e no gengogaku-teki hihan* [Did the Nanking Massacre 'occur'? A linguistic criticism of high school history textbooks] trans. E. Kaji, Tokyo: Chikuma.
—— (2000a) 'Protecting the face of the State: Japanese high school history textbooks and 1945', *Functions of Language*, 7, 1: 1–35.
—— (2000b) 'The Rape of Nanking in Japanese high school textbooks: history texts as closed texts', *Revista Canaria de Estudios Ingleses*, 40: 155–169.
—— (2000c) 'The Tokaimura nuclear accident in Japanese Newsweek: translation or censorship?', *Japanese Studies*, 20, 3: 281–294.
—— (2001) 'Isolating knowledge of the unpleasant: the Rape of Nanking in Japanese high-school history textbooks', *British Journal of Sociology of Education*, 22, 4: 519–530.
—— (2002) 'Through the ideological filter: Japanese translations of a Western news source', in R. Donahue (ed.) *Japanese Enactments of Culture and Consciousness*, Stamford, CT: Ablex.
—— (forthcoming) 'Pearl Harbor in Japanese high school history textbooks: the grammar and semantics of responsibility', in P. Chilton and R. Wodak (eds) *Discourse Approaches to Politics, Society and Culture*, Amsterdam: Benjamins.
Beauchamp, E. R. and Vardaman, J. M., Jr. (eds) (1994) *Japanese Education Since 1945: A Documentary Study*, Armonk, NY: M. E. Sharpe.
Behr, E. (1990) *Hirohito: behind the myth*, New York: Vintage.
Bergamini, D. (1971) *Japan's Imperial Conspiracy*, London: Heinemann.
Bix, H. P. (2000) *Hirohito and the Making of Modern Japan*, New York: HarperCollins.
Bloor, T. and Bloor, M. (1995) *The Functional Analysis of English: a Hallidayan Approach*. London: Edward Arnold.
Brown, P. and Levinson, S. C. (1978, reissued 1987) *Politeness: Some Universals in Language Usage*, Cambridge: Cambridge University Press.
Brownlee, J. S. (1997) *Japanese Historians and the National Myths: the Age of the Gods and Emperor Jinmu*, Vancouver: University of British Columbia Press.
Buruma, I. (1994) *The Wages of Guilt: Memories of War in Germany and Japan*, New York: Farrar Straus Giroux.
Calvocoressi, P., Wint, G., and Pritchard, J. (1995) *Total War: The Causes and Courses of the Second World War*, 2nd rev. edn, London: Penguin.

Campbell, A. E. (1995) 'Unconditional surrender', in I. C. B. Dear and M. R. D. Foot (eds) *The Oxford Companion to the Second World War* (pp. 1174–1176), Oxford: Oxford University Press.
Chang, I. (1997) *The Rape of Nanking: The Forgotten Holocaust of World War II*, New York: Basic Books.
Chilton, P. (ed.) (1985) *Language and the Nuclear Arms Debate: Nukespeak Today*, London: Pinter.
Clark, K. (1992) 'The linguistics of blame: representations of women in *The Sun*'s reporting of crimes of sexual violence', in M. Toolan (ed.) *Language, Text and Context: Essays in Stylistics* (pp. 208–224), London: Routledge.
Coffin, C. (1997) 'Constructing and giving value to the past: an investigation into secondary school history', in F. Christie and J. R. Martin (eds) *Genres and Institutions: Social Processes in the Workplace and School* (pp. 196–230), London: Cassell.
Conrad, S. and Biber, D. (2000) 'Adverbial marking of stance in speech and writing', in S. Hunston and G. Thompson (eds) *Evaluation in Text: Authorial Stance and the Construction of Discourse* (pp. 56–73), Oxford: Oxford University Press.
Cook, G. (1992) *The Discourse of Advertising*, London: Routledge.
*Daily Yomiuri, The* (20 July 1994: 2) 'Publishers follow ministry "suggestions"'.
Daws, G. (1994) *Prisoners of the Japanese: POWs of World War II in the Pacific*, New York: William Morrow.
de Castell, S., Luke, A., and Luke, C. (eds) (1989) *Language, Authority and Criticism: Readings on the School Textbook*, London: Falmer Press.
Dear, I. C. B. and Foot, M. R. D. (eds) (1995) *The Oxford Companion to the Second World War*, Oxford: Oxford University Press.
Dower, J. H. (1995) 'The useful war', in J. H. Dower, *Japan in War and Peace: Essays on History, Culture, and Race*, London: HarperCollins. (First published in *Daedalus*, summer 1990, special issue.)
—— (1999) *Embracing Defeat: Japan in the Wake of World War II*, Norton: New York.
Eco, U. (1979) *The Role of the Reader: Explorations in the Semiotics of Texts*, Bloomington, IN: Indiana University Press.
*Economist, The* (Sept. 2000: 79) 'A god dethroned'.
Eggins, S. (1994) *An Introduction to Systemic Functional Linguistics*, London: Pinter.
——, Wignell, P., and Martin, J. R. (1993) 'The discourse of history: distancing the recoverable past', in M. Ghadessy (ed.) *Register Analysis: Theory and Practice* (pp. 75–109), London: Pinter.
Fairclough, N. L. (1989) *Language and Power*, London: Longman.
—— (1992) 'Introduction', in N. Fairclough (ed.) *Critical Language Awareness* (pp. 1–29), London: Longman.
FitzGerald, F. (1980) *America Revised: History Schoolbooks in the Twentieth Century*, New York: Vintage Books.
Fogel, J. A. (2000) 'Introduction: The Nanjing Massacre in history', in J. A. Fogel (ed.) *The Nanjing Massacre in History and Historiography* (pp. 1–9), Berkeley: University of California Press.
Fowler, R., Hodge, R. I. V., Kress, G., and Trew, T. (1979) *Language and Control*, London: Routledge & Kegan Paul.

Freire, P. (1993) *Pedagogy of the Oppressed* (New rev. edn), trans. M. R. Ramos, New York: Continuum.

Fujiwara, A. (1999) '*Rekishi-shuuseishugi no Nankin-daigyakusatsu hiteiron wa uyoku no iibun sono mono da*' [The revisionist argument for the denial of the Great Nanking Massacre is nothing but a right-wing claim], in *Nankin-jiken Choosa Kenkyuukai* [Research Group on the Nanking Incident] (eds) *Nankin-daigyakusatsu hiteiron 13 no uso* [The 13 lies of the argument for the denial of the Great Nanking Massacre], Tokyo: Kashiwa Shoboo.

Gerow, A. (2000) 'Consuming Asia, consuming Japan: the neonationalistic revisionism in Japan', in L. Hein and M. Selden (eds) *Censoring History: Citizenship and Memory in Japan, Germany, and the United States* (pp. 74–95), Armonk, NY: M. E. Sharpe.

Goldhagen, D. J. (1996) *Hitler's Willing Executioners: Ordinary Germans and the Holocaust*, London: Little, Brown.

Guillain, R. (1981) *I Saw Tokyo Burning: an Eyewitness Narrative from Pearl Harbor to Hiroshima*, trans. W. Byron, Garden City, NY: Doubleday.

Halliday, M. A. K. (1994) *An Introduction to Functional Grammar*, 2nd edn, London: Edward Arnold.

—— and Matthiessen, C. M. I. M. (1999) *Construing Experience Through Meaning: a Language-based Approach to Cognition*, London: Cassell.

Hata, I. (1983) 'From Mukden to Pearl Harbor', in H. Wray and H. Conroy (eds) *Japan Examined: Perspectives on Modern Japanese History*, Honolulu: University of Hawaii Press.

Hein, L. and Selden, P. (2000) 'The lessons of war, global power, and social change', in L. Hein and M. Selden (eds) *Censoring History: Citizenship and Memory in Japan, Germany, and the United States* (pp. 3–50), Armonk, NY: M. E. Sharpe.

Hicks, G. (1994) *The Comfort Women: Japan's Brutal Regime of Enforced Prostitution in the Second World War*, New York: W. W. Norton.

Hodge, R. and Kress, G. (1993) *Language as Ideology*, 2nd edn, London: Routledge.

Horio, T. (1988) *Educational Thought and Ideology in Modern Japan: State Authority and Intellectual Freedom*, trans. and ed. S. Platzer, Tokyo: University of Tokyo Press.

Hunston, S. (2000) 'Evaluation and the planes of discourse: status and value in persuasive texts', in S. Hunston and G. Thompson (eds) *Evaluation in Text: Authorial Stance and the Construction of discourse* (pp. 176–207), Oxford: Oxford University Press.

Hyland, K. (1998) *Hedging in Scientific Research Articles*, Amsterdam: Benjamins.

Ienaga, S. (1964) *Shin Nihonshi*, Tokyo: Sanseidoo.

—— (1978) *The Pacific War, 1931–1945: a Critical Perspective on Japan's Role in World War II*, trans. F. Baldwin, New York: Pantheon Books. (Original work published in Japanese in 1968.)

——, Ihara, K., Oobinata, S., *et al.* (2002) *Shin Nihonshi B*, Tokyo: Sanseidoo.

Iokibe, M. (1995) '*Shinchuu-gun*' [The stationed army], in Y. Satoo (ed.) *Sensoo to shomin, 1940–1949: Dai 4 kan. Shinchuu-gun to furooji* [The war and the people: vol. 4. The stationed army and the homeless children], p. 31, Tokyo: *Asahi Shimbun*.

*Japan Times, The* (27 April 2002: 1) 'Forced laborers win suit: Mitsui Mining ordered to pay ¥165 million'.
Johnson, C. (1995) *Japan: Who governs? The Rise of the Developmental State*, New York: Norton.
Kanji, N., Kobayashi, Y., Takamori, A., *et al.* (2001) *Atarashii rekishi-kyookasho (Shihan-bon)* [New History Textbook (version for public sale)], Tokyo: Fusoosha.
Knowles, M. and Malmkjær, K. (1995) *Language and Control in Children's Literature*, London: Routledge.
Kobayashi, Y. (ed.) (1998) *Atarashii rekishi-kyookasho o 'Tsukuru Kai' to iu undoo ga aru* [There is a movement called the 'Committee to Make' new history textbooks], Tokyo: Fusoosha.
*Kokushi daijiten (dai-ni maku)* [Encyclopaedia of Japanese History (volume 2)], (1980) Edited by *Kokushi Daijiten henshuu iinkai* [editorial committee of the Encyclopaedia of Japanese History], Tokyo: Yoshikawa Koo Bunkan.
Kress, G. (1989) *Linguistic Processes in Sociocultural Practice*, 2nd edn, Oxford: Oxford University Press.
Kunii, I. M., Tashiro, H., and Na, S. (*Time*, 17 June 1996: 50–51) 'Victims of history'.
Loewen, J. W. (1995) *Lies My Teacher Told Me: Everything Your American History Textbook got Wrong*, New York: Touchstone.
Luke, A. (1989) 'Open and closed texts: the ideological/semantic analysis of textbook narratives', *Journal of Pragmatics*, 13: 53–80.
McCormack, G. (1996) *The Emptiness of Japanese Affluence*, Armonk, NY: M.E. Sharpe.
—— (2000) 'The Japanese movement to "correct" history', in L. Hein and M. Selden (eds) *Censoring History: Citizenship and Memory in Japan, Germany, and the United States* (pp. 53–73), Armonk, NY: M. E. Sharpe.
McVeigh, B. J. (1998) *The Nature of the Japanese State: Rationality and Rituality*, London: Routledge.
—— (2002) *Japanese Higher Education as Myth*, Armonk, NY: M. E. Sharpe.
Martin, J. R. (1993) 'Life as a Noun: arresting the universe in science and humanities', in M. A. K. Halliday and J. R. Martin (eds) *Writing Science: Literacy and Discursive Power*, London: Falmer Press.
—— (2000a) 'Close reading: functional linguistics as a tool for critical discourse analysis', in L. Unsworth (ed.) *Researching Language in Schools and Communities: Functional Linguistic Perspectives* (pp. 275–302), London: Cassell.
—— (2000b) 'Beyond APPRAISAL systems in English', in S. Hunston and G. Thompson (eds) *Evaluation in Text: Authorial Stance and the Construction of Discourse* (pp. 142–175), Oxford: Oxford University Press.
—— and Veel, R. (1998) *Reading Science: Critical and Functional Perspective on Discourses of Science*, London: Routledge.
Martin, S. (1975) *A Reference Grammar of Japanese*, New Haven, MA: Yale University Press.
Matsumura, T. (1998) *'Nankin-gyakusatsu' e no daigimon* [Grave doubts regarding the 'Nanking Massacre', Tokyo: Tendensha.

Matthiessen, C. M. I. M. and Bateman, J. A. (1991) *Text Generation and Systemic-Functional Linguistics: Experiences from English and Japanese*, London: Pinter.
Miller, R. A. (1982) *Japan's Modern Myth: the Language and Beyond*, New York: Weatherhill.
Mills, S. (1995) *Feminist Stylistics*, London: Routledge.
Minear, R. H. (1972) *Victors' Justice: The Tokyo War Crimes Trial*, Tokyo: Tuttle.
Miura, N. (1995) '*17-ken gikai no senbotsusha tsuitoo ketsugi ni gimon*' [Doubts about memorial resolutions by seventeen prefectural assemblies for those who fell in the war]. *Asahi Shimbun*, 23 March, morning edition: 4.
Morris-Suzuki, T. (2000) 'The view through the skylight: Nishio Kanji, textbook reform and the history of the world', in *Japanese Studies*, 20, 2: 133–139.
Nakamura, A. (1990) *Daitooa-sensoo e no michi* [The road to the Great East Asia War], Tokyo: Tendensha.
Nozaki, Y. and Inokuchi, H. (2000) 'Japanese education, nationalism, and Ienaga Saburoo's lawsuits', in L. Hein and M. Selden (eds) *Censoring History: Citizenship and Memory in Japan, Germany, and the United States* (pp. 96–126), Armonk, NY: M. E. Sharpe.
Okano, K. and Tsuchiya, M. (1999) *Education in Contemporary Japan: Inequality and Diversity*, Cambridge: Cambridge University Press.
*Oosaka Mainichi Shimbun* (9 Dec. 1941a, second evening edition: 1) '*Beiei-gun to kaisen-su*' [Commencing hostilities with American and British forces].
—— (9 Dec. 1941b, second evening edition: 2) '*Iza "Kooa no teki gekimetsu" da!*' [Now is the moment of 'attacking and destroying the enemy of Asian advancement'!].
Platzer, S. (1988) 'Editor's introduction', in T. Horio (author) *Educational Thought and Ideology in Modern Japan: State Authority and Intellectual Freedom*, Tokyo: University of Tokyo Press.
Rabe, J. (1998) *The Good Man of Nanking: the Diaries of John Rabe*, E. Wickert trans. and J. E. Woods (ed.), New York: Alfred A. Knopf.
*Rakkasan Nyuusu, Beigun Manira shireibu hakkoo (fukkokuban)* [Parachute News Published by American Forces Manila Headquarters (reproduction)] (2000) Osaka: Shinpuu Shoboo.
Rose, D. (1996) 'Pitjantjatjara processes: an Australian experiential grammar', in R. Hasan, C. Cloran, and D. G. Butt (eds) *Functional Descriptions: Theory in Practice* (pp. 287–323), Amsterdam: Benjamins.
Samuels, R. J. (2001) 'Kishi and corruption: an anatomy of the 1955 system', *Japan Policy Research Institute Working Paper no. 83*, December 2001. Online. Available www.jpri.org/wpapers/wp83.html (accessed 20 August 2002).
Seddon, T. (1987) 'Politics and curriculum: a case study of the Japanese history textbook dispute 1982', *British Journal of Sociology of Education*, 8, 2: 213–225.
Simpson, P. (1993) *Language, Ideology and Point of View*, London: Routledge.
Stephens, J. (1992) *Language and Ideology in Children's Fiction*, London: Longman.
Teruya, K. (forthcoming) 'Metafunctional profile of the grammar of Japanese', in A. Cafferel, J. R. Martin, and C. M. I. M. Matthiessen (eds) *Language Typology: a Functional Perspective*, Amsterdam: Benjamins.

Thompson, G. (1996) *Introducing Functional Grammar*, London: Arnold.
Thompson, J. B. (1990) *Ideology and Modern Culture: Critical Social Theory in the Era of Mass Communication*, Stanford: Stanford University Press.
Thomson, E. (2001) 'Exploring the textual metafunction in Japanese: a case study of selected written texts', unpublished doctoral thesis, University of Wollongong.
*Tookyoo Asahi Shimbun* (18 Dec. 1937, second evening edition: 1) *Banzai no arashi/kyoo Nankin-nyuujooshiki no sookan* [A storm of banzais: today's magnificent spectacle of the ceremonial entry into Nanking].
van Wolferen, K. (1989) *The Enigma of Japanese Power: People and Politics in a Stateless Nation*, London: Macmillan.
Veel, R. (1997) 'Learning how to mean – scientifically speaking: apprenticeship into scientific discourse in the secondary school', in F. Christie and J. R. Martin (eds) *Genres and Institutions: Social Processes in the Workplace and School*, London: Cassell.
Villa, B. L. (1976) 'The US Army, unconditional surrender, and the Potsdam Proclamation', *Journal of American History*, 63, 1: 66–92.
Weintraub, S. (1996) *The Last Great Victory: the End of World War II, July/ August 1945*, New York: Truman Talley Books/Plume.
Whitty, G. (1985) *Sociology and School Knowledge: Curriculum Theory, Research and Politics*, London: Methuen.
Wray, H. (1983) 'The lesson of the textbooks', in H. Wray and H. Conroy (eds), *Japan Examined: Perspectives on Modern Japanese History* (pp. 282–290), Honolulu: University of Hawaii Press.
Yamazumi, M. (1989) 'State control and the evolution of ultranationalistic textbooks', in J. J. Shields, Jr (ed.) *Japanese Schooling: Patterns of Socialization, Equality, and Political Control* (pp. 234–242), University Park, PA: Pennsylvania State University Press.
Yoshida, T. (2000) 'A battle over history: the Nanjing Massacre in Japan', in J. A. Fogel (ed.) *The Nanjing Massacre in History and Historiography* (pp. 70–132), Berkeley: University of California Press.
Yoshida, Y. (1999) *Hontoo ni dare mo ga Nankin-jiken no koto o shiranakatta no daroo ka* [Is it really so that no one at all knew about the Nanking Incident?] in *Nankin-daigyakusatsu hiteiron 13 no uso* [The 13 lies of the argument for the denial of the Great Nanking Massacre], *Nankin-jiken Choosa Kenkyuukai* [Research Group on the Nanking Incident] (eds), Tokyo: Kashiwa Shoboo.

The history textbooks quoted in this study are listed below. Numbers in square brackets refer to the text number within the body of this book.

Aoki, M., Fukaya, K., Juubishi, S., *et al.* (1996) *Shookai Nihonshi*, Tokyo: Sanseidoo. [1.2]
Bitoo, M., Masuda, T., Yoshida, T., *et al.* (2002) *Shinsen Nihonshi B*, Tokyo: Tookyoo Shoseki. [2.4]
——, Fujimura, M., Masuda, T., *et al.* (2002). *Nihonshi B*, Tokyo: Tookyoo Shoseki. [3.4]

# Works cited

Egami, N., Yamamoto, T., Hayashi, K., *et al.* (2002) *Yoosetsu Sekaishi*, Tokyo: Yamakawa Shuppan. [3.10]

Esaka, T., Takeuchi, R., Seno S., *et al.* (2002) *Shin Nihonshi B*, Tokyo: Kirihara Shoten. [3.8; 4.3]

Fukuda, T., Iwasaki, H., Iokibe, M., *et al.* (2002) *Seisen Nihonshi B*, Hiroshima: Daiichi Gakushuusha. [4.6]

Ienaga, S., Ihara, K., Oobinata, S., *et al.* (2000) *Shin Nihonshi B*, Tokyo: Sanseidoo. [2.2; 4.5]

Ikeda, O., Ichikawa, K., Ueda, M., *et al.* (2002) *Yookai Sekaishi B*, Tokyo: Shimizu Shoin. [2.5]

Ishii S., Itoo T., Kasahara, K., *et al.* (2002) *Shin Nihonshi*, Tokyo: Yamakawa Shuppan. [4.1]

Kanda N., Kitani, T., Shibata, M., *et al.* (2002) *Sekai no Rekishi*, Tokyo: Yamakawa Shuppan. [3.6]

Kodama, K., Gomi, F., Toriumi, Y., *et al.* (2002) *Nihon no Rekishi*, Tokyo: Yamakawa Shuppan. [1.3]

Mayuzumi, H., Oohashi, S., Hoshino, R., *et al.* (2002) *Shookai Nihonshi B*, Tokyo: Shimizu Shoin. [3.2]

Miyaji, M., Fujiki, M., Esaka, T., *et al.* (2002) *Shin Nihonshi A*, Tokyo: Kirihara Shoten. [3.5]

Nitani, S., Kasahara, T., Yui, D., *et al.* (2002) *Sekaishi A*, Tokyo: Hitotsubashi Shuppan. [2.1]

Nunome, C., Noguchi, Y., Kawakita, M., *et al.* (1995) *Zusetsu Sekaishi B*, Tokyo: Teikoku Shoin. [2.8; 2.9]

Saitoo, T., Kamo, Y., Oota, K., *et al.* (2002) *Shin Sekaishi A*, Tokyo: Kirihara Shoten. [4.8]

Sakamoto, S., Iokibe, M., Iwasaki, H., *et al.* (2002) *Shin Nihonshi B*, Hiroshima: Daiichi Gakushuusha. [3.3]

Takahashi, S., Shiba, K., Ueda, M., *et al.* (2002) *Shin Sekaishi A*, Tokyo: Shimizu Shoin. [4.7]

Tanaka, A., Kinbara, S., Katoo A., *et al.* (2002) *Nihonshi A – Gendai kara no rekishi*, Tokyo: Tookyoo Shoseki. [2.6]

Tanigawa, M., Satoo, I., Imanaga, S., *et al.* (2002) *Sekaishi B*, Hiroshima: Daiichi Gakushuusha. [3.7]

Toriumi, Y., Noro, T., Mitani, H., *et al.* (2002) *Gendai no Nihonshi*, Tokyo: Yamakawa Shuppan. [1.1; 3.1; 3.9; 4.2]

Tsurumi, N., Chizuka, T., Kojima, Y., *et al.* (2002) *Sekaishi B*, Tokyo: Jikkyoo Shuppan. [2.3]

# Index

*Note*: Entries for the major historical events dealt with in the main body of the book (viz. the ABCD line, the German and Japanese atttacks, the German and Japanese surrenders and the Rape of Nanking) are indexed under two separate sections: a history and background section, followed by an analysis and discussion section. The actual texts quoted from the textbooks, as well as the locators of these sections, are shown in **bold** print.

ABCD line (American, British, Chinese, Dutch): history and background 50, 81, 145, 164: asset freezing and oil embargo 90, 91, 94; historical background 84–5; Japanese media reporting 85, 87, 89–91; justification for inclusion of China 85, 93–4; as justification for war 88, 154; as propaganda and naturalized ideology 93; *see also* self-preservation/defence argument

ABCD line: textbook analysis and discussion 117: **Text 3.1 84–5**, 91; **Text 3.2 85–8**, 89, 91; **Text 3.3 89**, 91; **Text 3.4 89–91**; **Text 3.5 91–5**; attribution/averral/hedging 87–8, 89, 92, 95; grammatical patterning/copatterning 88–9, 90, 117–18; language/voice ambiguity 86–7;

advertising, linguistic analysis of 20

Amritsar Massacre (1919) 75–6

Anyon, J. 18, 21

Aoki, M. 39

Apple, M. 18

*Asahi Shimbun* 3, 6, 8, 14, 15, 17, 66, 76, 77, 80, 161, 162, 163

Asaka, Prince 63, 76–7, 80

Asia-Pacific War 1, 2, 3, 37, 82, 94; selection of major events dealt with 46–7; *see also* Pacific War (1941–45)

Askew, D. 56

*Atarashii Rekishi-kyookasho o Tsukuru Kai* (Japanese Institute for New History Education) *see Tsukuru-kai*

atomic bombs on Hiroshima and Nagasaki 16, 131, 134

atrocities: in China 16, 129; Japanese denial and lack of remorse 4–6, 55; in Japanese textbooks 55, 58; lawsuits against Japanese government and companies 7–8; motivation 62; Nanking Massacre 14, 56, 58, 63–70, 78–80, 154, 158; perpetrators 19, 50, 58, 61–2, 78; victims 7, 50, 58, 62 averral and attribution concepts 8, 87–8, 89, 90, 156; hedged averral 88, 89

Barnard, C. 20, 22, 35, 48, 170
Bateman, J.A. 52
Beauchamp, E.R. 10, 12
Behavioural processes 29, 31, 32, 36
Behr, E. 123, 127
Bergamini, D. 7, 56, 65, 77, 123, 161
Bitoo, M. 67, 89
Bix, H.P. 1, 7, 63, 82, 94, 123, 126, 127, 147, 161, 162
Bloor, T. and M. 22–3
Brown, P. 21, 121, 126, 128, 130, 135, 162
Brownlee, J.S. 21, 126, 162
Burma–Thailand Railway 4
Buruma, I. 2, 6, 53, 56, 159, 169

Calvocoressi, P. 56–7, 82
Campbell, A.E. 123
Chang, I. 52, 56
Chilton, P. 20
China 159; Japanese aggression 1, 82, 85, 147; Japanese atrocities 16, 129; protests at textbook portrayal of Japanese actions in China 17; *see also* Rape of Nanking
Chomsky, Noam 23
Circumstance(s) 29, 98; of duration 29; of location 30, 32, 38, 40, 59, 103, 113; of manner 29; of means 45, 104, 105, 106, 141, 144, 148; of motion towards 40
Clark, K. 20
clauses: downgrading/upgrading 44–5; embedded/modifying 35, 44, 45; finite/non-finite 44–5; hypotactic 33–4, 44, 108–9; levels (alpha, beta, etc.) 108–12; linking of 33–5; paratactic 33–4, 44; primacy 95, 108–14, 147–8, 154, 155; tactic relations 33–4, 35, 36, 43–5
closed texts, nature of 72–3

Coffin, C. 22, 81, 96
colonial/Asian liberation argument 2, 4, 50, 117, 129, 147, 155–6, 163
comfort women 7, 161; *see also* sex slaves issue
Communist Party/Communism 159, 160, 162, 169
compensation claims against Japanese government and companies 8, 159
Conrad, S. 81
Cook, G. 20
critical discourse analysis 22, 53, 60; and ideology 20–1, 37, 49; *see also* functional grammar

Daws, G. 4
Dear, I.C.B. 4
Dower, J.H. 4, 121, 126, 135, 159, 161, 192

Eco, U. 73
*Economist, The* 8–9
education *see* Japanese education
Egami, N. 112
Eggins, S. 22, 25
embedding/embedded clauses 28, 35, 44, 45; *see also* modification
Esaka, T. 106, 137
Existential processes 30, 31, 60

'Fabrication of the "Nanking Massacre", The' (Tanaka Masaaki) 64
face theory 128–30, 158; application to Japanese surrender 131–49; negative/positive face definitions 130, 158; and organizations 132; respect to positive face 130, 135, 137, 152; threat to (negative) face 49, 121, 126, 128, 130–5, 137, 138, 142–4, 146–5, 152, 158; *see also* face-protection ideology; threat to positive face 130

## Index    183

face-protection ideology 49, 131–49, 153, 155, 158, 169
Fairclough, N.L. 20, 21, 60, 72, 86
Fifteen Years War (1931–45) 1
FitzGerald, F. 18, 21
Fogel, J.A. 47
Foot, M.R.D. 4
Fowler, R. 20
Freire, P. 167, 171
French Indochina 2; *see also* Vietnam
Fujiwara, A. 2, 64
Fukuda, T. 143
functional grammar: appraisal and evaluation 81; as grammar of choice 106–7, 134; and Japanese language 35–7; and lexicogrammar 24–5; preliminary analysis 37–46; as a social/sociological view of language 22–36; theory of 54; as tool for critical discourse analysis 22, 35, 37, 49; transitivity configurations 98, 104, 105, 113, 115, 139–40; variations between languages 35–6
functional participants: Actor 38, 39, 42, 58, 69, 71, 96; Attribute 30; Behaver 29; Carrier 30; Existent 38; Goal 29, 32, 38, 40, 41, 42, 58, 59, 69, 70, 71, 96, 98, 100, 101, 102, 103, 105, 113; Phenomenon 30; Sayer 30, 38, 63, 140; Senser 29, 38; Verbiage 30, 138
Fundamental Law of Education (1947) 10

genre objection/argument 51, 52, 74, 95, 118, 155, 156
German/Japanese attacks: history and background 81–119: comparisons 95–114, 154; historical background 82–95; invasion of Poland 51, 82, 95; and war responsibility 1–2; accidental involvement theory 3–4; and aggressor role 50, 51; causal explanations/justifications 47, 50; on Malay peninsula 46; motives for 94–5, 118, 156–7; on Pearl Harbor 1, 46, 82–3, 95; *see also* self-preservation defence argument
German/Japanese attacks: textbook analysis and discussion: **Text 3.6 99–102**, 109; **Text 3.7 102–6**; **Text 3.8 106–9**; **Text 3.9 109–12**; **Text 3.10 112–14**; attribution 134–5; clause primacy 95, 108–14; congruency 101, 102, 105, 106, 107, 108; downgrading concept 105–6, 111; encapsulation 136; genre objection 95; grammatical metaphor 96, 105, 107, 154; hypotactic clauses/labelling 100–1, 108–12; language comparisons 47, 51, 81, 95–117, 154; language slippage patterns 95–6; linguistic encoding 105, 114–15, 117, 118; nominalization 104, 115; noun phrase/verb encapsulation/modification 100, 103, 104, 106, 107; participants and processes 96–108; process elements 98, 103; statistical analysis 108, 114–17; summary and conclusion 117–19; transitivity configurations 98, 104, 105, 115; use of wartime language 112–14, 117, 154–5
German/Japanese surrenders: history and background 84, 121–52: Allied occupation 122, 128; American newsheets 146–7, 152; and defeat of Axis powers 142; as face-saving/threatening act 142, 151; government indecisiveness 134–5, 136, 146; Hirohito's surrender broadcast *see* surrender broadcast; historical background/debate 122–6, 131, 145; Japanese armed forces 149; Japanese humiliation 126–8; Japanese imperialism 121; Japanese people 121, 138–9, 143–4, 152;

Japanese propaganda and foundation myths 126–8; Japanese surrender 123–4, 148–9; signing ceremony 137–8, 170; *see also* face theory; Hirohito, Emperor; Potsdam Declaration

German/Japanese surrenders: textbook analysis and discussion: **Text 4.1** 133–5, 138, 141, 143; **Text 4.2** 136–7, 138, 141, 142, 143; **Text 4.3** 137–8; **Text 4.4** 139–40; **Text 4.5** 140–3; **Text 4.6** 143–4; **Text 4.7** 144–5; **Text 4.8 148–9**; as Circumstance of means 144; clause encoding 151; clause primacy 137, 147–8; congruent realization 136; and face theory 131–49; face threats 126–8; German surrender 150; grammatical control and manipulation 136–7; grammatical downgrading 151; grammatical metaphors 135; indirect ('back door') reference 50, 134, 138, 142, 148; comparison of languages used in 122; language patterns 151–2; nominal/verbal exchange patterns 134–5, 144; nominalization 135–7; noun phrases 135, 136; process elements 137; protection of negative face 131, 132, 134–5, 138, 143, 145, 146, 147, 149–50, 151–2, 155; statistical analysis/comparisons 149–51; talking across vs. talking down 138–41; textual inaccuracies 145–7; time-slips 141–5, 151; transitivity configurations 139–41; transitivity labelling 139–40, 141; use of euphemisms 128; use of wartime language 121, 152, 154–5; verbs denoting decisiveness/control 134, 135, 138; weight of meaning 151; *see also* surrender broadcast

Gerow, A. 12, 17, 55
Goldhagen, D.J. 19–20, 39

grammar: copatterning resources 88–9, 90, 117–18, 155; levels of 51; as meaning-making resource 26–8, 34; as a system of choice 107–8; *see also* functional grammar

grammatical metaphor concept 82, 96–108, 135, 154; and congruency 96, 102, 106; encoding 51, 96, 151; ideological uses of 100–1; nominalization 70–2, 98, 104, 115, 118–19, 135–7

Guillain, R. (French journalist) 83, 126

Gulf War 15

Hague Convention (1907) 83
Halliday, M.A.K. 22, 23, 28, 35, 36, 53, 54
Hashimoto Ryuutaroo 3
Hata Ikuhiko, Professor 66
Hawaii 83
Hein, L. 8
*Hinomaru* (Japanese Rising Sun flag) 11–12
Hirohito, Emperor 6, 7, 63, 94, 127, 156, 169; decision-making power 143; evasion of responsibility 161; imperial rescript 143, 146; and Japanese people 138–9, 143–4; as a war criminal 122, 123, 128, 161; *see also* surrender broadcast
Hiroshima 12, 131, 134
historiography 4, 18, 158, 165–7; and linguistic usage 19, 39, 79
history education 9; aims of 18–19; textbook content/interpretations 14–15, 27–8, 171; and young people 16
Hodge, R. 20
Holocaust 19
Hong Kong 16
Horio, T. 13, 14, 158
Hunston, S. 81. 87
hypotactic clause relations 33–4, 44, 108–9; in Japanese 36–7

ideational metafunction 26–8; experiential and logical components 27
ideology: in American textbooks 18–19; anti-woman 20; in closed texts 72–4; and critical discourse analyses 20–1, 49; definition of 20, 21; dominant 21; encoding in language 51, 114–15, 155; of face-protection 49, 121–52, 153, 155, 158, 169; invisibility of 165–7; of irresponsibility 49, 81–119, 151, 153, 155, 157, 158, 169; Japanese emperor 127–8, 143–4; linguistic analysis of 20–2, 25; naturalized 28, 55, 74, 79, 82, 114, 117, 155, 165–6, 168, 170; of progress 18–19; reasons for 158–68; summaries of 78–9 (on Rape of Nanking), 116–18 (on attacks), 150–2 (on surrenders), 153–6 (overall)
Ienaga Saburoo 56, 57, 94; dispute with Ministry of Education 14, 55, 58, 61; on Japanese educational system 118, 164–5; on Japanese surrender 127, 134; on Pearl Harbor attack 83
Ikeda, O. 68
imperialism 6, 121; cult of 157, 161, 162; taboo 161
Inokuchi, H. 14
international law 8; violations 157, 170
International Military Tribunal for the Far East 2, 56, 65; *see also* Tokyo war crimes trials
internationalization concept 12; and nationalism 17
interpersonal metafunction 26–8
irresponsibility, ideology of 49, 81–119, 151, 153, 155, 157, 158, 169
Ishii, S. 133
Ishiwara Kanji 40
Itagaki Seishiroo 40

Japan: and Allied economic sanctions 2, 50, 82; defeat 132–3; economic system 145; history problem/mytho-history 1–9, 17, 21–2, 145–7; identity 163; imperial cult 157, 161, 162; issue of responsibility 8, 45–6, 76–7, 79, 155; language 35–7; postwar Allied occupation 10; propagandization 87, 126–8; sacredness and moral purity of 162–3; *see also* ABCD line; German/Japanese surrenders
Japanese army 1, 7, 57, 153; and atrocities 14, 61–8; biological warfare unit 8; germ warfare experiments 17; Kwantung army 38–46; and sex slaves 7, 20
Japanese atrocities: climate of deniability 55; international criticism 79; lawsuits 7–8; perpetrators 50, 58, 62–3, 69, 73, 75; resolutions of remorse 4–6; victims 7, 8, 50, 58, 62
Japanese education: as banking education 158, 167–8; cultivation of patriotism 11–12; democratization 10; as a form of social control 10–11; and mytho-history 21–2; and naturalized ideology 166–7; post-war 10–19; post-war/modern 10–19, 171–2; and school curriculum 17–18, 157; and society 17–18; subordination to economic policy 11; system 78, 118, 145
Japanese Maritime Self-Defense Force (navy) 15
Japanese Ministry of Education: censorship/control 55, 92–3, 146, 169, 171; Ienaga dispute 14, 55, 58, 61; intimidation by 165, 168–9; in post-war period 10, 160; textbook screening process 14, 47, 51, 157–8; wartime role 164–5

Japanese society: and bureaucracy 168–9; and education 17–18; non-civil nature of 163–4
Japanese state: continuity of 6–7, 159–60; controls 161, 163–4; and democracy 163; *see also* imperialism
Japanese surrender 47; textbook accounts 50–1; *see also* German/Japanese surrenders
Japanese Teachers' Union 160
Japanese textbook authorization system 1, 10–19, 53; inclusion of 'significant historic persons' 13–14; language and ideology 78–9; screening procedures 47; *see also* Japanese Ministry of Education
Japanese textbooks: authority of 167; authors and publishers 13–14, 15–16, 18, 47–9, 132, 165–9; content-type analysis 153; design and layout 47–8; history problem 8–9, 166–7; linguistic encoding of naturalized ideology 155; preliminary analysis of 37–46; and students' views 16, 167; use of language 132–3; *see also* studies of Japanese textbooks
Johnson, C. 159, 164

Kanda. N. 99, 100
Kanji, N. 17, 39, 40
Kasahara Tokushi, Professor 66
*Kimigayo* (Japanese national anthem) 11–12
Kishi Nobusuke 160
Knowles, M. 20
Kodama, K. 43
Korea, Japanese invasion of 14
Kress, G. 20
Kunii, I.M. 8
Kwantung 1
Kwantung army 38, 39, 40, 42

language: analysis of 23; bureaucratic 98; meaning-making potential of 24–5; metafunctions 25–8; paradigmatic (vertical) axis 23, 24, 134; patterning/copatterning 64, 67, 78, 88–9, 90, 95–6, 117–18, 155; patterns 64, 67, 78, 151–2; recycling of wartime terms 112–13, 117, 121, 152, 154–5; as a semiotic system 23–4, 52, 106; social/sociological view of 22–36; syntagmatic (horizontal) axis 24; theory of 25, 35; weight of meaning 37, 111, 151
lawsuits: against Japanese government and companies 7–8; textbook screening 14–16
Levinson, S.C. 130, 135
lexicogrammar: and functional grammar 24–5; *see also* grammar
linguistic analyses 28–35, 121; children's literature 20; and fragmentation 32; pragmatics 121; and taxis system 33–5, 44; and transitivity system 28–32
Liutiaohu Incident 40
Loewen, J.W. 9, 18, 21
Luke, A. 73

MacArthur, General Douglas 7
McCormack, G. 2, 3, 6, 7, 8, 56, 159, 160, 161, 162, 163
McVeigh, B.J. 10, 11, 163
Malaya, Japanese attack (1941) 1, 46, 82, 95
Malmkjaer, K. 20
Manchuria 84, 85; Japanese defeat in 133
Manchurian Incident 1, 53, 144, 164; Japanese version of events 17; Text 1.1 analysis 37–9; Text 1.2 analysis 39–43; Text 1.3 analysis 43–5; Text 1.4 analysis 45–6
Martin, J.R. 22, 81
Martin, S. 109

Material processes 28–9, 36, 38, 58, 60, 69, 71, 96, 113
Matsui Iwane, General 75–6, 77
Matsumura, T. 56
Matthiessen, C.M.I.M. 52
Mayuzumi, H. 85
meaning-making, language as meaning making behaviour/resource 23, 24, 25–8, 52
Meiji period 128, 164, 170
Mental processes 29–30, 31, 32
metafunctional hypothesis 25–8; and transitivity 28–32; *see also* ideational metafunction
metaphor, grammatical 82, 83, 96–108, 135, 154
Miller, R.A. 123–4
Mills, S. 20–1, 32
Minear, R.H. 65, 77
Miura, N. 5
Miyaji, M. 91
modification 44, 70, 95, 96, 104, 108
Mori Yoshiroo 3, 162, 168
Morris-Suzuki, T. 17
Motoshima Hitoshi 161
Mukden Incident (1931) 1, 37–9; *see also* Manchurian Incident
mytho-history, Japanese 21–2

Nagano Shigeto 3
Nagasaki 131, 134
Nakamura, A. 56
Nanking Massacre *see* Rape of Nanking; Rape of Nanking: textbook analysis and discussion
nationalism: and internationalization concept 17; Japanese 11–12
naturalized discourse/ideology 21, 22, 28, 49, 55, 56, 73, 74, 79, 82, 93, 114, 117, 122, 145, 146, 153, 155, 156, 165, 166, 168, 169, 170
Nitani, S. 57
nominalization/nouning process 70–2, 98, 104, 115, 118–19, 135–7

North Korea 159
noun phrases 69, 70–2, 73, 95, 156; encapsulation (of heinous acts/of processes and participants) 69, 70, 73, 98, 99, 154, 156; unpacking of noun phrases, and congruency 98–9, 105–6;
Nozaki, Y. 14
nuclear arms debate: linguistic analysis of 20
Nunome, C. 75

Odachi Shigeo 160
Okano, K. 11
Okinawa, battle of 14
Okuno Seisuke 2–3
Oosaka Mainichi Shimbun 113, 126
Organization for Economic Cooperation and Development (OECD), Report on Japanese Education (1970) 12–13, 14
overwording 60–1

Pacific War (1941–5) 1, 4, 95, 114, 153, 157, 165; casualty figures 3; historical background 82–95; Japanese justifications for 81, 93–4, 154
paradigmatic (vertical) linguistic relations 23–4
paratactic clause relations 33–4, 37, 44
Pearl Harbor attack (1941) 1, 46, 95; historical background 82–3
personalized/depersonalized acts 61
Pitjantjatjara 36
Platzer, S. 158
Poland, German invasion of 51, 82, 95
political economy, and American textbooks 18–19
post-war education, and textbook authorization 10–19
Potsdam Declaration 47, 122, 123, 131, 148; American newsheets (*Rakkasan Nyuusu*) 146–7; 'joint declaration' standing for

surrender/Potsdam declaration 134, 145, 146, 152; as a nominalization 135–8; Potsdam declaration standing for surrender 127, 134, 144, 151, 152; and time-slips 141–4
process types in functional grammar *see* Behavioural processes, Existential processes, Material processes, Mental processes, Relational processes, Verbal processes
progress: and American history 18, 21; ideology of 18–19

Rabe, John 66–7
rape 14, 56, 59, 61, 62, 70
Rape of Nanking: history and background 3, 46, 85: atrocities 14, 68–70; death toll 56, 92, 154; denial/ignorance of events within Japan 55–6, 67, 79–80; as example of naturalized ideology 55, 56; historical background 56–7, 154; knowledge of events within Japan 62–7; ongoing controversy and debate 2, 56; reports/witnesses 65–7; and responsibility 76–7, 79; Tokyo war crimes trials 2, 64
Rape of Nanking: textbook analysis and discussion 46, 117, 153–4: **Text 2.1 57–8**, 64; **Text 2.2 59–64**; **Text 2.3 64–7**; **Text 2.4 67–8**; **Text 2.5 68–71**; **Text 2.6 71–2**; **Text 2.7 72–4**; **Text 2.8 75**; **Text 2.9 75–6**; circumspect use of language 55, 78; Circumstance of location 59; closed texts 72–4; functional grammar usage 58, 60, 63, 69–72; functional processes 55–80, 56; insertion of authorial voice 72; language analyses 47, 62–3, 78–80; language patterns 64, 67, 78; location of knowledge 64–72; motivation 62; naming the atrocity 68–70; objections/criticisms 67–8, 74–6; participants 55–80, 56; perpetrators 58, 58–62, 59; transitivity (processes, participants, Circumstances) 58–74, 78–80; verbal use and tenses 62, 70, 71–2; voice switching 72
*Rape of Nanking, The* (Chang, Iris) 55
Relational processes 30, 36
Report on Japanese Education (OECD, 1970) 12–13, 14
responsibility issues 2, 8, 45–6, 76–7, 79, 155; ideology of irresponsibility 49, 81–119, 151, 153, 155, 157, 158, 169; and Japanese denials/evasion 6–8, 161
revisionists (Japanese) 2, 9, 93; *see also* self-preservation/defence argument
Rose, D. 36

Saitoo, T. 148
Sakamoto, S. 89
Samuels, R.J. 160
San Francisco Peace Treaty (1951) 159
Second World War (1939–45) 1, 142, 153; historical background 82–95; lack of debate in Japan 169; *see also* German attacks; German/Japanese surrenders; Japanese attacks; Pacific War (1941–5)
Seddon, T. 10–11
self-preservation/defence argument 2, 5, 50, 84–5, 93, 95, 124, 147, 155
sex slaves issue 7, 17, 92–3, 153
Shidehara (Japanese foreign minister) 38–9
*Shin Nihonshi* (Ienaga) 58
Shinto religion 22
Simpson, P. 21, 51, 55
Singapore 16, 160
Sino-Japanese War (1894–5) 14
slave-labour 159, 160

South-East Asia 2
South Korea 17
South Manchurian Railway 1, 39
Soviet Union 85, 110, 112, 124, 131, 132–3, 152
Stephens, J. 20
studies of Japanese textbooks: data and selection procedures 46–9; and grammatical metaphor 83; ideological encoding in grammar 51; language comparisons of German/Japanese attacks 51, 81; language as a meaning-making resource 53; language system and use 54; potential objections to studies 51–2; roles of participants and processes 82, 100; in terms of transitivity and taxis 82; *see also* textbook analysis and discussion entries for: ABCD line; German/Japanese attacks; German/Japanese surrenders; Rape of Nanking
surrender broadcast 84, 93, 95, 121–2, 124–5 (quoted in full), 126, 129, 131, 133–4, 139, 145–7, 151, 152, 155–7, 162–3
surrender document (standing for surrender) 134, 145, 148
Suzuki Teiichi 94
syntagmatic (horizontal) axis of language 24
systemic-functional grammar/linguistics: language choice/variation 52–3; *see also* functional grammar

Takahashi, S. 144
Takashima Nobuyoshi, Professor 15
talking across vs. talking down 138–41
Tanaka Masaaki 64
Tanigawa, M. 102
taxis system in linguistic analysis 33–5, 44, 82, 95; clause primacy 108–14, 155; and linking clauses 33; and modification 95, 108
Teruya, K. 36, 60, 103, 113
textbooks: linguistic analysis of 20–35; US publishing 18; writer–reader relationship 27–8; *see also* Japanese textbooks
texts: and ideologies 72; open/closed 72–4; and readers' engagement 72–3
textual metafunction 26–8
Thailand 4; Japanese attack on 82, 117
Thompson, G. 23, 28, 70, 96
Thompson, J.B. 20, 25
Thomson, E. 36
time-slips 141–5, 151, 156, 171
Tokyo war crimes trials 2, 6, 16, 64, 65, 161
Tomonaga Shin'ichiroo 14
*Tookyoo Asahi Shimbun* 77
Toriumi, Y. 37, 84, 109, 110, 136
transitivity system 28–32, 70, 98, 113, 155; and linguistic analyses 32, 82
truth: historical 52, 87, 145; and inaccuracies 145–7; truth-value 87–8, 90
*Tsukuru-kai* (Japanese Institute for New History Education) 16–17
Tsurumi, N. 64

United States (US): and Communism 169; dropping of newsheets on Japan 146–7; freezing of Japanese assets 90; and Japanese sanctions 2; and textbook publishing 18–19

van Wolferen, K. 6, 157, 159, 160, 163–4
Veel, R. 22
Verbal processes 30, 31, 36, 38
verbs: semantically heavy 136; semantically neutral 58, 71–2; usage and tenses 62, 70, 71–2

Vietnam 2, 82
Villa, B.L. 122

Wakatsuki cabinet 40, 41, 42
war 9, 61; reparations 158–9; responsibility issues 2, 8, 45–6, 76–7, 79, 155; unresolved questions 158–9
war crimes/criminals: executions 77; and Hirohito 122, 123, 128; Kishi Nobusuke 160; Sugamo Prison 160; Tokyo trials 127, 128, 161
Weintraub, S. 84, 123, 124, 127
Whitty, G. 18
Wray, H. 21, 126

Yamazumi, M. 10
Yoshida, T. 2, 9, 63, 64, 67
Yoshida, Y. 63, 64, 67